GIFTS OF THE SPIRIT

Gifts of the Spirit

Duane S. Crowther

ISBN: 0-88290-210-5
Library of Congress Catalog Card No.: 65-29176
Horizon Publishers Catalog & Order No.: 1071
Thirteenth Printing, February 1986

Printed and distributed
in the United States of America by

Horizon
Publishers
& Distributors, Incorporated
50 South 500 West   P.O. Box 490
Bountiful, Utah 84010-0490

This book is affectionately dedicated to

Don, Scott, Laura, Lisa, David, William, Sharon and Bethany.

May they join their father in the belief that

"by the power of the Holy Ghost

ye may know the truth of all things."

Moroni 10:5

Author's Testimony

I could not properly end this book without telling of the manner in which this study has increased my testimony of the gospel of Jesus Christ. One does not receive aid from the Spirit in researching and writing a book such as this without knowing that God exists and guides man through His Spirit. Nor does one learn of the numerous instances of Divine guidance which have shaped this Church without knowing that it is God's Church — that it was brought into existence by Him and is functioning under His direction today. One does not test the manifestations of the Spirit of our present Prophet without knowing without doubt that he is a Prophet, a spokesman and a companion of God. One does not study the great gifts promised to man without knowing of God's love for His children and His desire that they might grow and progress. One does not learn of the mighty faith and deeds of the chosen servants of God without being compelled to humbly recognize his own insignificance and lack of faith. And one does not learn of the joys of serving God without having a strong and unyielding desire to serve His Lord and Master. To all these things I bear witness, in the name of Jesus Christ.

Duane S. Crowther

INTRODUCTION

Purposes of This Book

Gifts of The Spirit has been written to accomplish three purposes:

1. *To show that spiritual gifts exist; and to bear witness to their divine origin.* The gifts of the Spirit are a major theme of the scriptures, for a multitude of passages from the Standard Works speak of them. A careful study of these passages leaves one standing in awe of the power and love for God which are shown through them. Surely there can be no doubt that God grants special powers and blessings to man through the Holy Ghost.

2. *To explain the nature of the various spiritual gifts.* It is sometimes difficult to distinguish between the gifts of the Spirit. They often overlap, and frequently an experience partakes of the nature of several spiritual gifts at one time. This book attempts to define the various gifts, to explain them, and to show both their differences and their similarities.

3. *To show how man can gain the influence of the Holy Ghost and the gifts of the Spirit to enrich his own life.* To know of the existence and reality of the various spiritual gifts is of little value unless one can tap this source of spiritual power to aid him as he labors in the Lord's vineyard. Man's "spiritual temperature" varies. At some periods in his life he is in tune with the Infinite and able to enjoy the blessings of close and continuing contact with the Divine. At other times he finds himself out of harmony and unable to communicate meaningfully with God. Many people have never had even one experience where they have known without doubt that they had come in contact with Deity. They have never sought with diligence the gifts and guidance of the Holy Ghost which others enjoy. It is hoped that this book, by showing the message of the scriptures and by analyzing the experiences of others, can aid those who honestly seek to draw nearer to God.

Classifications of Spiritual Gifts

In the largest sense, all blessings, guidance, and answers to prayer given by God may be considered as being spiritual gifts. *Gifts of The Spirit*, however, confines itself almost exclusively to the gifts listed in the three major scriptural discussions of spiritual gifts found in Doctrine and Covenants 46:8-30, Moroni 10:4-18, and I Corinthians 12:4-11.

Various classifications can be made of the gifts of the Spirit. In this book they are grouped as gifts of knowledge, gifts of faith, gifts of communication, gifts of church administration, and gifts of salvation and exaltation; these groupings being the most advantageous for the purposes of the book.

A major problem in categorizing the gifts and segregating them for study is that often in practice more than one gift is manifest at a time. In this book therefore instances of the manifestation of one gift are sometimes mentioned while another gift is being examined, because the two are inseparable.

This book is a pioneer in its chosen area of L.D.S. doctrine. No other book has attempted to examine the gifts of the Spirit in such detail. Of necessity the author has had to make interpretations in some cases, but while he bears full responsibility for such interpretations, he has done his best to insure that they are always consistent with Church doctrine.

Are the Experiences Reported in This Book True?

The cautious student may well inquire as to the veracity of the seemingly miraculous experiences which are reported within these covers. Are they true? Are they actual contacts with the Divine, or are they merely imagined events and hallucinations? In reporting such events one cannot by logic prove their actuality. Most spiritual experiences are individual in nature. They happen to only one person, and usually take place when he is alone. The recording of such events are subject to the limitations of that individual's memory, his ability to record his feelings and sensations accurately, and his natural veracity. It is rarely possible to prove that a person actually had a dream, or saw a vision, or had his life in some other way molded and shaped by the Holy Spirit, unless the reader is willing to accept his testimony of the occurrence. The gifts of the Spirit are not for scoffers. They are granted to those who will place their faith in the things of the Divine and will humbly seek to be participants in the eternal workings of God. In reality, the only way in which a person may know if another has truly received a manifestation of the Holy Spirit is for the questioning individual to also partake of that Spirit. Only then may he apply the test of the Spirit which Moroni described:

> And when ye shall receive these things, *I would exhort you that ye would ask God, the Eternal Father, in the name of Christ, if these things are not true;* and if ye shall ask with a sincere heart, with real intent, having faith in Christ, *he will manifest the truth of it unto you, by the power of the Holy Ghost.*
>
> *And by the power of the Holy Ghost ye may know the truth of all things.*
>
> And whatsoever thing is good is just and true; wherefore, nothing that is good denieth the Christ, but acknowledgeth that he is.
>
> *And ye may know that he is, by the power of the Holy Ghost; wherefore I would exhort you that ye deny not the power of God; for he worketh by power, according to the faith of the children of men, the same today and tomorrow, and forever.*
>
> And again, I exhort you, my brethren, that ye *deny not the gifts of God, for they are many;* and they come from the same God. And *there are different ways that these gifts are administered;* but it is the same God who worketh all in all; and *they are given by the manifestation of the Spirit of God unto men, to profit them.*[1]

It is worthwhile observing that those who recorded the experiences would have had nothing to gain by falsehood and deception.

For his part, the author has sought the aid of the Spirit in selecting and preparing the material for this study, his efforts to insure doctrinal and historical accuracy in this work having taken various forms, such as the following:

------

1. Moro. 10:4-8.

1. *Establishing a pattern of scripture which serves to define and explain each gift of the Spirit.* The reader will soon observe that the manifestations of spiritual blessings cited herein conform to the scriptural patterns. (For convenience, please note that the scriptural passages cited herein are tabulated in the back of the book for those who wish to examine them more carefully.)

2. *Determining that the experiences themselves fit into a harmonic pattern.* The fact that they have many common characteristics and take place in much the same manner helps to substantiate them. They follow both the pattern of the scripture and their own pattern.

3. *Examining many hundreds of spiritual experiences in preparing this manuscript.* The reader should note, however, that (with few exceptions) the experiences cited herein are chosen from long published, well-accepted sources which have withstood the tests of time and careful inspection.

Acknowledgements

The completing of a study such as *Gifts of The Spirit* is a process which requires many hundreds of hours of time, combined with much effort and patience. Others besides the author have labored to achieve the publication of this book. Their assistance is greatly appreciated. Mrs. Bonnie Bird rendered valuable service by typing the original manuscript. Mrs. Jo Ann Thomas provided invaluable assistance by reading it for technical corrections. Their services are greatly appreciated. They both deserve commendation for their willingness to labor under the heavy time pressures to which they were submitted.

Appreciation is also expressed to others who have lent assistance — to Jim Adams, principal of the Smithfield L.D.S. Seminary, for the loan of several rare volumes; to Mrs. Bertha Purser, librarian at the Logan L.D.S. Institute, for her extending of special library privileges which made the task of collecting and typing of many items easier; and to numerous clerks and librarians in the major university, public and Church libraries of Logan, Salt Lake City, and Provo. Without exception they rendered prompt and courteous assistance whenever called upon to do so. My thanks, also, to Bookcraft Publishers, and Publishers

Press for their assistance and graphic implementation of this project.

Surely the greatest load was carried by my wife, Jean, who read and reread the manuscript, typed much of it, offered many valuable suggestions and much needed encouragement, and kept order in our home during the many times when I was away researching and writing. My love and gratitude to her are eternal. May she be truly blessed for her goodness.

The Author.

EXPLANATION OF FOOTNOTE AND
REFERENCE PROCEDURES

Ibid., — (for the Latin *ibidem,* "in the same place") means that the quotation is taken from the same source as the reference which precedes it.

Op. Cit., — (For the Latin *opere citato,* "in the work cited") means that the quotation is taken from the same book which has previously been quoted by that author.

Jenson, I, p. 253. — means Andrew Jenson, *L.D.S. Biographical Encyclopedia,* volume one, page 253.

HC, V, p. 265. — means Joseph Smith, *History of the Church of Jesus Christ of Latter-day Saints,* volume five, page 265.

Mt. 18:24. — means St. Matthew, chapter eighteen, verse twenty-four.

2 Ne. 33:1. — means Second Book of Nephi, chapter thirty-three, verse one.

Moses — The Book of Moses

Abra. — The Book of Abraham

JS — Writings of Joseph Smith

A. of F. — The Articles of Faith

Cf — means compare

Standard abbreviations are used for scriptural references.

CONTENTS

PART IV
GIFTS OF COMMUNICATION

PART V
GIFTS OF CHURCH ADMINISTRATION

PART VI
GIFTS OF SALVATION AND EXALTATION

Part I

THE QUEST

CHAPTER I

Seeking The Gifts of The Spirit

An Approach to the Doctrine of Spiritual Gifts

One of the most vital doctrines of the Gospel is that the power and influence of God are available to man through the functioning of the Holy Ghost. Hundreds of scriptural passages make reference to this divine Being and His labors among mankind. The Holy Ghost plays a vital role in preparing man for salvation and exaltation. Indeed, man cannot attain those goals without gaining a knowledge of Him and without His divine assistance. This book is written to assist those who possess a true desire to know more about the gifts of the Holy Spirit and to experience them in their lives.

Gifts of The Spirit may be considered a "how-to" book, a book designed to help the reader follow an outlined path to accomplish a definite goal. It will help every man who will give it prayerful consideration to make contact with the Holy Ghost and to partake of the rich gifts which are available to him.

The Purpose of Spiritual Gifts

Ye are commanded in all things to ask of God, who giveth liberally; and that which the Spirit testifies unto you even so I would that ye should do in all holiness of heart, walking uprightly before me, considering the end of your salvation, doing all things with prayer and thanksgiving, that ye may not be seduced by evil spirits, or doctrines of devils, or the commandments of men; for some are of men, and others of devils.

Wherefore, beware lest ye are deceived; and *that ye may not be deceived seek ye earnestly the best gifts, always remembering for what they are given;*

For verily I say unto you, *they are given for the benefit of those who love me and keep all my commandments, and him that seeketh so to do;* that all may be benefited that seek or that ask of me, that ask and not for a sign that they may consume it upon their lusts.

2   GIFTS OF THE SPIRIT

> And again, verily I say unto you, *I would that ye should always remember and always retain in your minds what those gifts are, that are given unto the church.*[1]

With this admonition the Lord introduced the most extensive listing of the gifts of the Spirit which is found in the scriptures. These gifts are far-reaching in their scope. As enumerated in the passage, the gifts of the Spirit are given to serve several purposes:

1. to benefit those who love God.[2]
2. to prevent man from being deceived by false doctrine.[3]
3. to bless the entire membership of Christ's Church.[4]
4. to cause man to walk uprightly before God.[5]
5. to cause man to commune with God.[6]
6. to cause man to consider the end of his salvation,[7] and
7. to characterize those who are true believers.[8]

Signs to Follow Believers

In every dispensation of the gospel, the gifts of the Spirit have served as signs which have characterized the Church. The significance of these signs was the final message of the Savior to His apostles before His ascension into heaven.

> *These signs shall follow them that believe;* In my name shall they cast out devils; they shall speak with new tongues;
>
> They shall take up serpents; and if they drink any deadly thing, it shall not hurt them; they shall lay hands on the sick, and they shall recover.[9]

The Lord repeated and amplified His message in a revelation found in the Doctrine and Covenants.

> *These signs shall follow them that believe —*
> In my name they shall do many wonderful works;
> In my name they shall cast out devils;
> In my name they shall heal the sick;

---

1. D & C 46:7-10.
2. D & C 46:9.
3. D & C 46:7-8.
4. D & C 46:29.
5. D & C 46:7.
6. *Ibid.*
7. *Ibid.*
8. D & C 84:65-73.
9. Mk. 16:17-18. See also Morm. 9:24; Eth. 4:18.

In my name they shall open the eyes of the blind, and unstop the ears of the deaf;

And the tongue of the dumb shall speak;

And if any man shall administer poison unto them it shall not hurt them;

And the poison of a serpent shall not have power to harm them.[10]

These signs are not characteristic only of the Church as a collective body. They may also be promised as a representation of the deeds of a specific individual. For instance, a promise of this nature was made to William Law, an early member of the Church.

Let my servant William Law also receive the keys by which he may ask and receive blessings; let him be humble before me, and be without guile, and *he shall receive of my Spirit, even the Comforter, which shall manifest unto him the truth of all things,* and shall give him, in the very hour, what he shall say.

And these signs shall follow him — he shall heal the sick, cast out devils, and shall be delivered from those who would administer unto him deadly poison;

And he shall be led in paths where the poisonous serpent cannot lay hold upon his heel, and he shall mount up in the imagination of his thoughts as upon eagle's wings.

And what if I will that he should raise the dead, let him not withhold his voice.[11]

These signs and wonders are available to any Church member who shall ask in faith, for the Lord has revealed His promise that "Whoso shall ask it in my name in faith, they shall cast out devils; they shall heal the sick; they shall cause the blind to receive their sight, and the deaf to hear, and the dumb to speak, and the lame to walk."[12]

Signs Not to Satisfy Personal Ambitions or Lusts

The Savior's message has continually been that signs are given to those who already believe and have exercised their faith. They are not given to those who are novelty seekers or those striving to use them for personal gain. When the Scribes and

---

10. D & C 84:65-72.
11. D & C 124:97-100.
12. D & C 35:9.

Pharisees of His day asked, "Master, we would see a sign of thee," His reply was that "An evil and adulterous generation seeketh after a sign; and there shall be no sign given to it . . ."[13] He taught also that those who sought signs unworthily would be granted such signs, but unto their condemnation.

> *He that seeketh signs shall see signs, but not unto salvation.*
>
> Verily, I say unto you, there are those among you who seek signs, and there have been such even from the beginning;
>
> But, behold, *faith cometh not by signs, but signs follow those that believe.*
>
> *Yea, signs come by faith, not by the will of men, nor as they please, but by the will of God.*
>
> *Yea, signs come by faith, unto mighty works, for without faith no man pleaseth God; and with whom God is angry he is not well pleased; wherefore, unto such he showeth no signs, only in wrath unto their condemnation.*
>
> Wherefore, I, the Lord, am not pleased with those among you who have sought after signs and wonders for faith, and not for the good of men unto my glory.[14]

By the same token, the righteous to whom signs are granted are commanded not to boast of them nor to flaunt them before the world. The Lord has said, "A commandment I give unto them, that they shall not boast themselves of these things, neither speak them before the world; for these things are given unto you for your profit and for salvation."[15]

Gifts, Not Signs, to be Sought

Though it may seem paradoxical to some, man is commanded not to seek outward signs of divine power, but he is commanded to seek the gift to use divine power himself. Perhaps this is because the seeking of a sign or a religious manifestation (such as witnessing someone heal the sick) requires little or no personal preparation. On the other hand, the acquisition of a gift or gifts

---

13. Mt. 12:39. He continued by saying that He would give them only one sign—his entombment: "There shall no sign be given to it, but the sign of the prophet Jonas: For as Jonas was three days and three nights in the whale's belly; so shall the Son of man be three days and three nights in the heart of the earth." Mt. 12:40).
14. D & C 63:7-12.
15. D & C 84:73.

of the Spirit requires increased personal discipline, self-control, and spiritual growth. The Lord commanded the Church to "Seek ye earnestly the best gifts."[16] Moroni's final admonition bore a similar command for he said he would ". . . Exhort you that ye would come unto Christ, and *lay hold upon every good gift*, and touch not the evil gift, nor the unclean thing."[17] Paul's advice was to "Covet earnestly the best gifts."[18]

There can be no doubt, then, that the will of God is that man seek to obtain one or more of the gifts of the Holy Spirit. It is not to be done in a disorganized, unenergetic manner. Man is to "covet earnestly" these blessings and "deny not the gifts of God."[19] Every member of the Church is promised that he may obtain at least one gift:

> For all have not every gift given unto them; for there are many gifts, and to every man is given a gift by the Spirit of God.
>
> To some is given one, and to some is given another, that all may be profited thereby.[20]

A faithful member may obtain more than one gift of the Spirit, and it is he himself who controls the number available to him: ". . . All these gifts come by the Spirit of Christ; and they come unto every man severally, according as he will."[21] It is apparent that the desire of the individual is that which controls, to a great extent, the magnitude of his reception.

It should be noted, also, that the admonition to seek the 'best gifts" implies a difference in the quality or usefulness of these gifts to an individual. It would be difficult to say that one gift is better than another in the absolute sense, but surely particular gifts can be of greater use to an individual at a certain time, in connection with his callings in the Church and his life's work.

Where Much is Given, Much is Required

The obtaining of one or more gifts of the Spirit places a responsibility upon an individual, *"For unto whomsoever much is*

16. D & C 46:8.
17. Moro. 10:30.
18. I Cor. 12:31.
19. Moro. 10:8.
20. D & C 46:11-12.
21. Moro. 10:17.

given, of him shall be much required: and to whom men have committed much, of him they will ask more."[22] Man would do well to remember the parable of the talents. In this story, a rich man went traveling and left his goods in the hands of three servants. Unto one he gave five talents, to the second two, and to the last servant one, "to every man according to his several ability."[23] While the master was away, the servants with the five and the two talents increased them and doubled their value. The third servant buried his talent and increased it not at all. When the master returned he dealt with each servant. The manner of his dealing conveys three morals which are meaningful to every seeker after the gifts of the Spirit.

First, the third servant, who was given a talent but buried it, was regarded as unprofitable and the command was given, "Cast ye the unprofitable servant into outer darkness: there shall be weeping and gnashing of teeth."[24] To receive a talent or gift and then not increase it brings condemnation to an individual which he would not have received if he had not first received the gift. Acceptance of any blessing or responsibility in the Lord's kingdom creates the expectation for further growth and productivity.

Second, the two servants who increased their talents were rewarded with the words, "Well done, good and faithful servant; thou hast been faithful over a few things, I will make thee ruler over many things: enter thou into the joy of thy Lord."[25] It is the magnifying and increasing of man's talents and gifts which bring him eternal reward.

Third, the talent which had been given to the unprofitable servant was taken from him and given to the servant who had ten, "For unto every one that hath shall be given, and he shall have abundance: but from him that hath not shall be taken away even that which he hath."[26] The individual who receives talents and gifts to the full extent of his ability and does his very best to increase them is granted additional talents and gifts even beyond his developed ability.

---

22. Lk. 12:48.
23. Mt. 25:15.
24. Mt. 25:30.
25. Mt. 25:23.
26. Mt. 25:29.

How to Seek the Gifts of the Spirit

Many words of instruction as to how to seek the guidance of the Holy Ghost have been given by inspired men. A choice dissertation on this subject was set forth by President Wilford Woodruff in his volume, *Leaves From My Journal:*

> In order to obtain revelation from God, and in order to know, when we do obtain a revelation, whether it is from God or not, we must follow the teachings of the revelations of God unto us. St. James says: 'If any man lack wisdom, let him ask of God, that giveth to all men liberally, and upbraideth not; and it shall be given him.' Again, it is said, 'Ask, and it shall be given you; seek, and ye shall find; knock, and it shall be opened unto you.'

> It was upon this promise that Joseph Smith went before the Lord and prayed in the name of Jesus Christ, and asked for knowledge, wisdom and understanding, in order to know what to do to be saved; and he proved the promise of St. James before the Lord, and the heavens were opened to his view, and the Father and Son were revealed unto him, and the voice of the great Eloheim unto him was: 'This is my beloved Son, hear ye [sic] Him.'

> This was the first revelation of God to him. He did hearken to the voice of Jesus Christ all his life afterwards, and received a code of revelations and the word of the Lord unto him as long as he dwelt in the flesh.

> Joseph Smith left as strong a testimony as was ever given to the human family, and sealed that testament with his own life and blood.

> *We all have to pursue the same course in order to obtain revelations from God.* But I wish to impress this truth upon the rising generation and all who read this testimony, that *the Lord does not give revelations or send angels to men or work miracles to accommodate the notions of any man who is seeking for a sign.*

> *When we have the principles of the gospel revealed to us through the mouth of the Savior, or by inspired prophets or apostles, we have no need to ask the Lord to reveal that unto us again.* While the priesthood is restored to the earth, and the revelations of God are revealed to us through the mouths of prophets and apostles concerning the fullness of the gospel — doctrine, ordinances and principles, we should study them, and

treasure up knowledge by faith. *We should study out of the best books, and the Holy Ghost will bring to our remembrance those things which we stand in need of, in the self-same hour that we are called to teach the people.*

But when any priest, elder, prophet, apostle or messenger is sent of God to preach the gospel, gather the Saints, work in temples, or perform any work for the Lord, and that man is faithful and humble before the Lord, in his prayers and duty, and there is any snare or evil in his path, or the righteous to be sought out, or danger to the emigration of the Saints either by sea or land, or knowledge needed in a temple, *then the Lord will reveal to him all that is necessary to meet the emergency.*

The teachings of the Prophet Joseph Smith to President John Taylor and the rest of us was to *obtain the Holy Spirit, get acquainted with it and its operations, and listen to the whisperings of that Spirit and obey its voice, and it soon would become a principle of revelation unto us.*

We have found this true in our experience, and in order to prove whether a revelation is from God or not *we follow out the principles revealed to us, and if we find that which was manifested to us proved true, we know it was from God;* for truth is one of His attributes, and the Holy Ghost deceiveth no man. *When a man becomes acquainted with the whisperings of the Holy Ghost, which is revelation, he should be very careful to obey it, for his life may depend upon it.*[27]

Another individual who well knew the value of continual guidance of the Spirit was Elder Oliver B. Huntington, an early convert. He left this advice.

The inspiration of the Holy Ghost which is given to all who obey the gospel by baptism and the laying on of hands of Elders, was promised by the Lord to every one that earnestly and sincerely repents of his sins and obeys the gospel, and 'it shall guide him into all truth.'

I will tell you, my young friends, how that Holy Ghost will guide you. If, when you are made clean from sin by baptism, you do not willingly enter again into sin, pray often, keep the Sabbath day holy, always try as earnestly as you can to be a peacemaker, help every institution of Zion, cheerfully obey every call of the Lord through those who have the authority from

27. Wilford Woodruff, *Leaves From My Journal* (Salt Lake City: Juvenile Instructor Office, 1881), pp. 86-7.

God to call, and live lives of purity in every way, that *Holy Ghost will be in you all the time and influence you in all your thoughts and words and actions, bring to your mind things forgotten when you need them, and suggest to your mind principle and doctrine, when really necessary, that has never been taught you in this life, but which you knew before you came to this world.*[28]

But these instructions involve so many things! How can one who has never known the guidance of the Holy Ghost begin to seek it? Where is the starting point, and how should one proceed? Here outlined is a step-by-step program which one may endeavor to follow in seeking and gaining the gifts of the Spirit.

1. **Have the desire.** A true desire to attain these choice blessings is the first ingredient which is necessary. It cannot be simply an intellectual resolve or a "wouldn't-it-be-nice-if" attitude. It must be an actual quality of which the Master spoke when He taught that "Blessed are all they who do hunger and thirst after righteousness, for *they shall be filled with the Holy Ghost.*"[29]

2. **Choose goals by the Spirit.** If a person is to seek the "best gift" or the gifts which would be most vital to his progress at a particular time, he must choose that gift which he needs most and direct his effort towards obtaining it. In making his choice he must seek advice from God; he must ask that He will grant the understanding necessary to make a proper choice. The Savior's instruction was, "Draw near unto me and I will draw near unto you; *seek me diligently and ye shall find me; ask, and ye shall receive;* knock, and it shall be opened unto you."[30]

God must be approached in prayer and an answer must be received. To know which gift God wants him to seek, and individual must approach Deity with the Spirit so that he may receive an answer by the same medium, for *"He that asketh in Spirit shall receive in Spirit."*[31] For one who is just beginning to seek spiritual gifts, this is an extremely challenging undertaking. He may never have had an actual spiritual experience, one in

28. *Eventful Narratives* (Salt Lake City: Juvenile Instructor Office, 1887), p. 84.
29. 3 Ne. 12:6.
30. D & C 88:63.
31. D & C 46:28.

which has has been granted a direct answer to his prayers. He may never have experienced spiritual promptings to the degree that he knew without doubt that the Holy Ghost was being manifested. Choosing a goal by the Spirit, then, creates for him a real dilemma: he must first have the Spirit to receive guidance in selecting the gift for which he should seek. How should one start? A few basic suggestions may be of value to the reader to help him begin this vital undertaking.

A. *Choose a time to begin.* To make one's first real effort to come in contact with God ·one must commit himself to a firm beginning. He must choose it in advance so that he will have time to prepare himself. He might choose a Sunday and actually resolve that he will devote the entire day to seeking and obtaining his answer.

B. *Eliminate routine distractions.* One should be sure that household chores are done and that he has a private place where he will be free from interruptions. One should avoid the influences that would keep him from enjoying the Spirit of the Lord. Watching a horror movie on T.V., for example, will not aid him in attaining his goal.

C. *Prepare by praying in advance.* Even if one does not feel that his prayers are being heard or answered, he should ask for guidance in making his choice. He should pray especially that the Spirit will be with him to guide him on the special day he has chosen.

D. *Avoid actions which exclude the Spirit.* If one has habits which he knows are not right, he must make a definite decision to stop them and then hold fast to the resolution. He should make a planned program which he can follow to keep him from returning to his habits. This should be done before the special day so he can tell the Lord of his resolves and attest that he is keeping them.

E. *Know about the gifts of the Spirit in advance.* One should review them mentally and know what the scriptures say of each of them. Then he will be able to pray more effectively.

F. *Seek the Spirit by fasting.* Fasting is designed to diminish the influence of the flesh and increase the power of the Spirit. It is without value, however, if one refrains from eating and drinking and then spends his time thinking about how hungry he is. He should devote his time to prayer, meditation, and the study of the scriptures, and banish thoughts of his physical needs and desires.

G. *Resist evil thoughts.* Those times when one tries to come closest to God are often the times when Satan tries to exercise his greatest influence over him. He should be prepared to combat evil thoughts and desires that may come into his mind at this time. It is helpful for one to decide in advance of something he will think about to force evil thoughts from his mind. He may recite a poem or a scripture, sing a hymn, etc. Whatever he decides to do, he should be prepared to withstand Satan's influences by substituting pre-determined good thoughts for evil ones.

H. *Seek inspiration at Church.* If the day one has chosen to seek special guidance is a Sunday, one should be sure to participate in the activities of the Church. He should be ready in plenty of time, travel in a leisurely manner, arrive early, sit quietly and enjoy the devotional prelude. If it is a Fast Sunday, he could bear his testimony. He should seek the Spirit and inspiration of the meetings, and should not allow himself to be distracted by others. He should pray during the prayers and during the sacramental service. It should be done inconspicuously, not "to be seen of men." These are the times when the influence of the Spirit should be the strongest.

The Lord has commanded that "Ye shall call upon me while I am near."[2] Certainly during Church services is such a time, for the Savior has said that "Where two or three are gathered together in my name, as touching one thing, behold, *there will I be in the midst of them —* even so am I in the midst of you."[3]

I. *Try to talk with God.* One should devote much of the remainder of his special day to prayer. He should try

2. **D & C** 88:62.
3. **D & C** 6:32.

to communicate with God. He should ask Him to help in making his decision and as he seeks to cultivate his gift of the Spirit. One could outline his life plans to God, and tell Him how he feels about the Lord's work and His Church. One may ask Him specific questions and pray that he will be given an answer and that he may know that the answer comes from God.

J. *Ask close relatives for help.* One may wish to enlist the aid of his family or close friends. He might tell them he has a special matter about which he wishes to receive guidance from God, and then ask them to pray for him that he might have the Spirit to prompt him. It is unfortunate that in the Church there are a few who misunderstand such a request. Not having tasted the guidance of the Spirit themselves, they scoff and treat the request lightly. One's search for the gifts of the Spirit is a private matter and should not become a topic to be discussed by others except with the individual who is seeking. Care should be taken in choosing those whose aid one might wish to solicit. There are those, however, whose faith and insight into the things of the Spirit can be of great aid to the person seeking divine guidance. It would be well to enlist their assistance.

K. *Learn the methods by which the Holy Ghost communicates.* One should learn to recognize the promptings of the Holy Ghost so that he will be able to recognize his answer. This can be done by careful study of many of the instances of divine guidance collected in this book and by study of other such instances collected in various histories and biographies of past and present Church leaders.

It is possible that one may seek guidance from God and yet not receive an answer. He should then examine his actions and attitudes. Did he prepare himself properly? Was there a fault or sin which was obstructing his progress? Did he pray earnestly and sincerely? Did he truly strive to communicate with God? He would do well to find his error, choose another time, and renew his effort. He must know God's will in the matter before he can go further.

3. **Seek spiritual gifts to serve God.** The gifts of the Spirit must be used to serve God. The blessings of the Spirit are intended for those who are receptive to the Holy Ghost. They are designed as aids for furthering the Lord's work. The man who seeks these gifts must sincerely intend to use them to function in his Church obligations or they will likely not be granted to him. This was a key element in the formula for obtaining such gifts which was expounded by Moroni:

> O then despise not, and wonder not, but hearken unto the words of the Lord, and *ask the Father in the name of Jesus for what things soever ye shall stand in need.* Doubt not, but be believing, and begin as in times of old, and come unto the Lord with all your heart, and *work out your own salvation with fear and trembling before Him.*
>
> Be wise in the days of your probation; strip yourselves of all uncleanness; *ask not, that ye may consume it on your lusts, but ask with a firmness unshaken, that ye will yield to no temptation, but that ye will serve the true and living God.*[34]

Paul also made service the prime reason for the obtaining of the gifts of the Spirit. He counseled that "Forasmuch as ye are zealous of spiritual gifts, *seek that ye may excel to the edifying of the church.*"[35] Is not the desire to serve Him the basic element in remembering Christ, which man covenants to do each time he partakes of the Sacrament? It is this element that prompted the Savior's teaching that "If ye do always remember me ye shall have my Spirit to be with you."[36]

4. **Strive for the blessings of the Spirit with humility.** An important lesson can be learned from the story of Martin Harris, who desired to be one of the three witnesses to the Book of Mormon. In response to his desire, the Lord granted the following revelation:

> Behold, I say unto him, *he exalts himself and does not humble himself sufficiently before me;* but if he will bow down before me, and humble himself in mighty prayer and faith, in the sincerity of his heart, *then will I grant unto him a view of the things which he desires to see.*

---

34. Morm. 9:27-8.
35. I Cor. 14:12.
36. 3 Ne. 18:7.

And now, except he humble himself and acknowledge unto me the things that he has done which are wrong and covenant with me that he will keep my commandments, and exercise faith in me, behold, I say unto him, he shall have no such views, for I will grant unto him no views of the things of which I have spoken.[37]

The prophet Alma also gave a formula for seeking the Spirit which stressed the need for humility.

And now, my brethren, I wish from the inmost part of my heart, yea, with great anxiety even unto pain, that ye would hearken unto my words, and cast off your sins, and not procrastinate the day of your repentance;

But that ye would humble yourselves before the Lord, and call on his holy name, and watch and pray continually, that ye may not be tempted above that which ye can bear, and thus be led by the Holy Spirit, becoming humble, meek, submissive, patient, full of love and all long-suffering;

Having faith on the Lord; having a hope that ye shall receive eternal life; having the love of God always in your hearts, that ye may be lifted up at the last day and enter into his rest.[38]

5. **Be free from sin.** Alma stated a basic principle when he told what the effects of sin are on man's ability to possess that which is holy:

And now behold, I tell you by the spirit of prophecy, that if ye transgress the commandments of God, behold, these things which are sacred shall be taken away from you by the power of God, and ye shall be delivered up unto Satan, that he may sift you as chaff before the wind.

But if ye keep the commandments of God, and do with these things which are sacred according to that which the Lord doth command you, (for you must appeal unto the Lord for all things whatsoever ye must do with them) behold, no power of earth or hell can take them from you, for God is powerful to the fulfilling of all his words.

For he will fulfil all his promises which he shall make unto you, for he has fulfilled his promises which he has made unto our fathers.[39]

---

37. D & C 5:24, 28.
38. Al. 13:27-9.
39. Al. 37:15-17. Although in this instance Alma was talking about the possession of the Nephite records and other sacred relics, the same principle would reasonably apply to the possession of the gifts of the Spirit.

A modern revelation also warns that sin will cause man to forfeit his right to the Spirit of the Lord:

> . . . when we undertake to cover our sins, or to gratify our pride, our vain ambition, or to exercise control or dominion or compulsion upon the souls of the children of men, in any degree of unrighteousness, behold, *the heavens withdraw themselves; the Spirit of the Lord is grieved;* and when it is withdrawn, Amen to the priesthood or the authority of that man.[40]

6. **Ask in prayer for help.** A fundamental principle of growth which God has required of His children is that they recognize their dependance upon Him as the bestower of blessings and guidance. If man desires assistance or help from Deity, he must ask for it and actively seek it. The promise is repeatedly given in the scriptures that God will give heed to man's righteous requests and grant an appropriate reply. Consider the words of Jesus in His Sermon on the Mount:

> *Ask, and it shall be given you; seek, and ye shall find; knock, and it shall be opened unto you:*
>
> *For every one that asketh receiveth; and he that seeketh findeth; and to him that knocketh it shall be opened.*
>
> Or what man is there of you, whom if his son ask bread, will he give him a stone?
>
> Or if he ask a fish, will he give him a serpent?
>
> If ye then, being evil, know how to give good gifts unto your children, how much more shall your Father which is in heaven give good things to them that ask him?[41]

The Savior emphasized that God will answer man's prayers because He recognizes the many needs which His children experience. To demonstrate this principle He related this parable:

> Which of you shall have a friend, and shall go unto him at midnight, and say unto him, Friend, lend me three loaves;
>
> For a friend of mine in his journey is come to me, and I have nothing to set before him?
>
> And he from within shall answer and say, Trouble me not: the door is now shut, and my children are with me in bed; I cannot rise and give thee.

---

40. D & C 121:37.
41. Mt. 7:7-11. See 3 Ne. 14:7-11.

> I say unto you, *Though he will not rise and give him, because he is his friend, yet because of his importunity he will rise and give him as many as he needeth.*
>
> *And I say unto you, Ask, and it shall be given you; seek, and ye shall find; knock, and it shall be opened unto you.*[42]

The principle that man must call upon God is basic to his spiritual growth and is required by our Father in Heaven, for the Brother of Jared testified that

> We know that thou [the Lord] art holy and dwellest in the heavens, and that we are unworthy before thee; because of the fall our natures have become evil continually; nevertheless, O Lord, *thou hast given us a commandment that we must call upon thee, that from thee we may receive according to our desires.*[43]

Certainly, if God will grant unto His children according to their desires, and if He has commanded man to seek the gifts of the Spirit, man may expect that his prayers to this end will be accounted as righteousness and will be answered. The scriptures, however, place certain restrictions on the manner in which man must pray. These are that man must

A. *ask in faith.*

B. *believe he will receive an answer.*

C. *keep the commandments.* Nephi combined these three prerequisites when he asked, "Do ye not remember the things the Lord hath said? — If ye will not harden your hearts, and ask me in faith, believing that ye shall receive, with diligence in keeping my commandments, surely these things shall be made known unto you."[44]

D. *pray for what is right.* The Savior said, "Whatsoever ye shall ask the Father in my name, *which is right*, believing that ye shall receive, behold it shall be given unto you."[45]

E. *pray for what is necessary.* Man must gain the ability to analyze his own needs and to determine those goals which are really necessary. To pray for that which is superfluous is to

---

42. Lk. 11:5-9.
43. Eth. 3:2.
44. 1 Ne. 15:11.
45. 3 Ne. 18:20.

bring condemnation upon the individual. The message of the Master is that "Whatsoever ye ask the Father in my name it shall be given you, that is expedient for you; *And if ye ask anything that is not expedient for you, it shall turn unto your condemnation.*"[46]

Certainly man should pray for assistance in performing his duties in the Church and for the gifts of the Spirit to aid him,

> For if ye would hearken unto the Spirit which teacheth a man to pray ye would know that ye must pray; for the evil spirit teacheth not a man to pray, but teacheth him that he must not pray.
>
> But behold, I say unto you that ye must pray always, and not faint; that *ye must not perform any thing unto the Lord save in the first place ye shall pray unto the Father in the name of Christ, that he will consecrate thy performance unto thee, that thy performance may be for the welfare of thy soul.*[47]

F. *pray with real intent.* When one's prayer is void of sincerity his prayer becomes a detriment, rather than a help, to his progress. Such was the message of Mormon, who said that "Likewise also is it counted evil unto a man, if he shall pray and not with real intent of heart; yea, and it profiteth him nothing, for God receiveth none such."[48]

G. *give thanks.* God requires that man demonstrate gratitude for the blessings which are granted to him. This attitude must be a characteristic of one's manner of praying. As Paul admonished, "Be careful for nothing, but in every thing by prayer and supplication with thanksgiving let your requests be made known unto God."[49] Alma also taught that in his prayers man must be found "Asking for whatsoever ye stand in need, both spiritual and temporal; always returning thanks unto God for whatsoever things ye do receive."[50]

H. *pray in "mighty prayer."* The prayer which brings results is offered when the individual is "praying in the Holy Ghost,"[51] and when a continued effort, involving one's complete

46. D & C 88:64-5.
47. 2 Ne. 32:8-9.
48. Moro. 7:9.
49. Phil. 4:6.
50. Al. 7:23.
51. Jude 20.

energy, is exerted. This was the manner of Alma's prayer, for he "labored much in the spirit, wrestling with God in mighty prayer, that he would pour out his Spirit. . . ."[52] The same quality characterized the supplication of Enos, who testified that "My soul hungered; and I kneeled down before my Maker, and I cried unto him in mighty prayer and supplication for mine own soul; and all the day long did I cry unto him; yea, and when the night came I did still raise my voice high that it reached the heaven."[53] It would seem that this was the manner of prayer which Jesus used when he "continued all night in prayer to God,"[54] before choosing his apostles.

Outlined above is a six-point program which man may follow to seek the gifts of the Spirit. Embodied in them are the elements which carry the promise of the richest blessings which God grants to mankind. They demand a constant striving toward perfection and a continued effort to become more Godlike, for the Holy Ghost is "the gift of God unto all those who diligently seek him."[55] They are so profound that they can be fully understood by man only after he has begun to partake of the influence of the Holy Ghost, for

> As it is written, Eye hath not seen, nor ear heard, neither have entered into the heart of man, the things which God hath prepared for them that love him.
>
> But God hath revealed them unto us by his Spirit: for the Spirit searcheth all things, yea, the deep things of God.
>
> *For what man knoweth the things of a man, save the spirit of man which is in him? even so the things of God knoweth no man, but the Spirit of God.*[56]

Summary

1. The doctrine of spiritual gifts is a basic doctrine of the scriptures. Literally thousands of scriptural passages describe the various gifts and explain the functioning of the Holy Ghost as He aids mankind through them.

---

52. Al. 8:10.
53. Enos 4.
54. Lk. 6:12.
55. I Ne. 10:17.
56. I Cor. 2:9-11.

2. This book is written to help man make contact with the Holy Ghost and to partake of the rich gifts which are available to him.

3. Spiritual gifts serve to
   A. benefit those who love God;
   B. keep men from being deceived by false doctrine;
   C. bless the membership of God's Church;
   D. cause man to walk uprightly before God;
   E. cause man to commune with God;
   F. cause man to consider the end of his salvation; and
   G. characterize those who are true believers.

4. The signs and miracles which are the result of spiritual gifts are identifying characteristics of the true Church of Jesus Christ.

5. Those who seek signs unworthily may receive them, but unto their own condemnation.

6. Man is commanded not to seek external signs, but rather to strive for inward manifestations of the Holy Ghost through spiritual gifts.

7. All members of the Church are promised at least one spiritual gift to be granted by the Holy Ghost. Individuals, through worthy desire, may obtain more than one gift if they wish. Every man is commanded to seek the "best gifts" for him.

8. When man is given a gift of the Spirit he is expected to use and develop it. Failure to do so will result in its loss. He who develops his gifts to the fullest is granted additional gifts even beyond his natural capacity.

9. Suggestions are given as to how one may seek the gifts of the Spirit:
   A. have the desire.

   B. choose goals by the Spirit. It is suggested that a special day be set aside to seek guidance in understanding one's part in God's program of spiritual gifts. Results can be achieved if one will
      1—choose a time to begin;
      2—eliminate routine distractions;

      3—prepare by advance prayer;

      4—stop actions which exclude the Spirit;

      5—know about the gifts of the Spirit in advance;

      6—seek the Spirit by fasting;

      7—resist evil thoughts;

      8—seek inspiration at Church;

      9—try to talk with God;

      10—seek help from close relations and friends; and

      11—learn the methods by which the Holy Ghost communicates.

C. seek spiritual gifts to serve God.

D. strive for the blessings of the Spirit with humility.

E. be free from sin.

F. ask in prayer for help. One's prayer will be more effective if he will

      1—ask in faith;

      2—believe he will receive an answer;

      3—keep the commandments;

      4—pray for what is right;

      5—pray for what is necessary;

      6—pray with real intent;

      7—give thanks; and

      8—pray in "mighty prayer."

CHAPTER II

Recognizing The Guidance of The Spirit

Revealed Aids to Recognizing Revelation

A major problem one encounters as he begins to seek the guidance of the Spirit is his inability to recognize whether thoughts and ideas stem from his own thinking or from the Holy Ghost. Is he receiving inspiration in solving his problems or is he merely making use of his own faculties? Is the dream which he sees inspired or is it the result of too much for supper? Is he talking to himself or hearing the voice of the Holy Ghost? Can he assume that all decisions made in a meeting that was opened with prayer are inspired of God? Most people don't seem to receive great visions or visits from angels; does this mean they are without the guidance of the Spirit? How can one know of a surety when he is being guided by God?

It seems that Oliver Cowdery must have wrestled with the problem of recognizing the guidance of the Spirit, for the most important revelations dealing with the subject were directed to him. Two important items of counsel were revealed to him in the month of April, 1829. The first said,

> Oliver Cowdery, verily, verily, I say unto you, that assuredly as the Lord liveth, who is your God and your Redeemer, even so *surely shall you receive a knowledge of whatsoever things you shall ask in faith, with an honest heart, believing that you shall receive a knowledge* concerning the engravings of old records, which are ancient, which contain those parts of my scripture of which has been spoken by the manifestation of my Spirit.
>
> Yea, behold, *I will tell you in your mind and in your heart by the Holy Ghost, which shall come upon you and which shall dwell in your heart.*
>
> Now, behold, *this is the spirit of revelation;* behold, this is the spirit by which Moses brought the children of Israel through the Red Sea on dry ground.[1]

---

1. D & C 8:1-3.

Here is the key to the nature of a communication granted by the Holy Ghost: it is revealed in both the mind and in the heart. It involves the bestowing of two sensations: a precise, understandable communication to the mind and a physical sensation to the heart or bosom.

The second revelation explaining to Oliver Cowdery the nature of inspiration makes this pattern even clearer:

> Behold, you have not understood; you have supposed that I would give it unto you, when you took no thought save it was to ask me.
>
> But, behold, I say unto you, that *you must study it out in your mind; then you must ask me if it be right, and if it is right I will cause that your bosom shall burn within you; therefore, you shall feel that it is right.*
>
> *But if it be not right you shall have no such feelings, but you shall have a stupor of thought that shall cause you to forget the thing which is wrong;* therefore, you cannot write that which is sacred save it be given you from me.[2]

Each of the two aspects of inspiration should be examined. When the Holy Ghost inspires an individual the recipient is granted a definite message, and he is able to know and understand the intent of the communication. Several scriptural examples serve to illustrate this characteristic. As Philip was going along the road to Gaza he passed the chariot of a high Ethiopian court official. He was impressed to make a specific move: "Then the Spirit said unto Philip, Go near, and join thyself to this chariot."[3] The missionary was able to gain and baptize a convert because of his heeding of the promptings of the Holy Spirit. A similar prompting was given to Peter following a vision which had been granted to the apostle:

> While Peter thought on the vision, the Spirit said unto him, Behold, three men seek thee.
>
> Arise therefore, and get thee down, and go with them, doubting nothing: for I have sent them.[4]

Heeding this prompting enabled Peter to preach the gospel to the household of Cornelius. In each case, the message was distinct.

---

2. D & C 9:7-9.
3. Acts 8:29.
4. Acts 10:19-20.

Oliver B. Huntington described the promptings he received as he attempted to lead a party in escaping from a group of maurading Indians. His impressions were marked by this same characteristic.

> Our lives was the game we were playing for that day, and the responsibility of correct moves was upon me. The thought made me sweat like rain. I told all the men and asked them to ride slowly, very slowly, while I rode up the mountain to see if I could make any discovery. I rode to a good, secure place and there knelt upon the ground and with my whole soul, asked God to show me what to do in this trying time of uncertainty.
>
> I arose and mounted my horse, fully satisfied. I knew how it would terminate. *An impression, a feeling, some would call it, made me understand this: 'Go on; you will come out all right;' that is, keep going as you are going, and you will come around to the right place, was what was meant.*
>
> Some might ask, How did you get that information? I can only tell you that *it was spoken in those words to my soul. It was planted instantly in my understanding by the power of God. It was revealed to my spirit independent of the body.*
>
> I rode down and overtook my fellow-travelers in perfect cheer and told them that we would go on, we were going just right.[5]

A second characteristic of this guidance of the Spirit should be noted also: the message had a definite purpose. Yet another characteristic seems to identify the promptings of the Holy Ghost. Impressions of the Spirit seem to be persistent. They continue to work on an individual's mind until he acknowledges them by either accepting or rejecting them. Thoughts which are not inspiration, however, tend to be more easily forgotten. This is what the Lord explained to Oliver Cowdery, saying if a thought "Be not right you shall have no such feelings, but you shall have a stupor of thought that shall cause you to forget the thing which is wrong.[6]

Three characteristics, then, seem to summarize the nature of any message revealed to a man's mind by the Holy Ghost. Such promptings (1) are a definite message, (2) with a definite purpose, and (3) come persistently until they are either accepted or rejected.

---

5. *Eventful Narratives,* pp. 95-6.
6. D & C 9:9.

The physical sensations associated with the promptings of
the Holy Ghost serve as checking and controlling devices. Without the manifestation of these sensations an individual may well
accept what he believes to be inspiration as only his own thinking
and logic and not necessarily a communication from the Divine.
He is thinking his own thoughts, not receiving new instructions
through the Holy Ghost. The revelation to Oliver Cowdery
defined the dual nature of the physical sensations associated
with inspiration from the Holy Ghost: "If it is right I will cause
that *your bosom shall burn within you; therefore, you shall feel
that it is right.*"[7] Promptings from the Holy Ghost, then, carry
two sensations: a burning within the bosom and a feeling that
the inspired instruction or decision is right.

The burning feeling within the bosom is actual — a reality,
not a figure of speech. Those who have not felt it before should
seek it and learn to recognize and identify it. It should not be
confused with indigestion or heartburn, nor with the feelings
experienced in times of tension or excitement. It is the sensation which was, apparently, felt by the disciples who walked
with the resurrected Christ along the road to Emmaus, who
afterwards commented, *"Did not our heart burn within us*, while
he talked with us by the way, and while he opened to us the
scriptures?"[8] The same feeling was granted to the Nephites when
they heard the voice of the Father, which "Did pierce them that
did hear to the center, insomuch that there was no part of
their frame that it did not cause to quake; yea, it did pierce
them to the very soul, and *did cause their hearts to burn.*"[9]
Nephi was speaking, apparently, of the physical manifestation
of the Spirit when he told of how his father, Lehi, had "Spoken
unto all his household, *according to the feelings of his heart*
and the Spirit of the Lord which was in him."[10]

Many investigators of the gospel have felt this burning feeling as they studied the Book of Mormon. Notice the feelings
experienced by Alice McCracken as she began to study it:

> The next day I found myself stealing every minute I could
> from housework and business to read a couple of verses or a

7. D & C 9:8.
8. Lk. 24:32.
9. 3 Ne. 11:3.
10. 2 Ne. 4:12.

chapter from this appealing book. I didn't bother to look up references or to inquire too deeply about what I didn't understand. I just read to satisfy the hunger.

The following morning I awakened with a wonderful feeling. As it stayed with me during the morning and throughout the day I almost feared to cast about in my mind for a word to describe it lest this beautiful glow would depart. *The only word to describe it was 'blessed.' This desirable feeling of being warm, well cared for, comforted, alert, and completely happy, stayed with me and I KNEW that Joseph Smith must indeed be a prophet of God;* that only through the gift and power of God could he have translated the Book of Mormon. It came as manna from our Eternal Father to a spiritually starved world.[11]

This burning sensation is not always a localized sensation felt only in the bosom, but tends to spread to the entire body. This was expressed by the Seventies who were filled with the Spirit in the Kirtland Temple and arose to bear their testimony.

Many arose and spoke, testifying that they were filled with the Holy Ghost, *which was like fire in their bones,* so that they could not hold their peace, but were constrained to cry hosanna to God and the Lamb, and glory in the highest.[12]

The feeling that the prompting is right is likewise actual and not figurative. The recipient is granted an assurance that God's communication to him is correct and that what has been said will come to pass. In short, "The Spirit beareth record"[13] through this feeling so that the recipient receives a witness of the veracity of the communication. This feeling of "rightness" has been described by various individuals in other terms. Thomas Crowther[14] recorded it as a "certainty":

I will now mention a manifestation I had in answer to prayer. In the spring of 1857, a man by the name of Whittier told me I could use his oxen to plow my lot if I would bring them from the range — telling me where I would find them. I started out early the next morning in search of them, and walked fast until noon without success. I began to get faint and weary,

11. Dorothy South Hackworth, *The Master's Touch* (Salt Lake City: Bookcraft, 1961), p. 266.
12. Joseph Smith, *History of The Church of Jesus Christ of Latter-day Saints* (Second edition, revised; Salt Lake City: The Deseret News, 1954), II, p. 392. Further references to this work will be listed as HC.
13. D & C 59:24.
14. The author's great grandfather.

when I turned to one side into a cedar grove. There I knelt
down and asked the Lord in sincerity to make known to me
where the cattle were. I had not been on my knees more than
two minutes when *a voice said to me — they are up in Coal
canyon. This was not said in a loud voice, but in a pleasant
whisper that filled my heart with a certainty that they were
there.* I arose and went with a light heart about one and a half
miles distant. There I found the cattle lying down, chewing
their cuds.

I mention this circumstance to show that the Lord does
hear and answer prayers when we are humble and sincere.[15]

The same feeling was apparently described by Robert
Aveson as a whispering that "It's all for the best," as he and
his companion were kept from immigrating to America with the
Saints.

We began to shake hands with the Saints, many of whom,
with tears in their eyes, bade us a sad 'good-by.' While thus
engaged the detective seized me by the collar and pulling me
towards the steps, said:

'Come along, we can't wait for you!'

With aching hearts away we went with our box, accompanied by Carter and the detective. Our destination was the
Thames Police Office, which was about a mile distant. On
arriving there, Carter and the detective left as soon as they had
ordered breakfast for us.

There were two men in charge of the office, who took quite
an interest in us and treated us very kindly.

Considering all things, the morning passed away very well.
*Something seemed to be whispering within me, 'It's all for the
best.' I told Richard so, and he said he felt the same.*[16]

If the reader will be tolerant of his doing so, the author
would like to cite several instances from his own personal experience as and when they fit into the outline of this book. The
following is taken from a letter he wrote to his parents on September 8, 1956, while he was serving as District President of the
Panama District, Central American Mission.

---

15. William O. Crowther, *The Crowthers of Fountain Green* (Independence,
    Mo.: Zion's Printing & Publishing Co., 1943), p. 19. The man who wrote
    this family history was the grandfather of the present author.
16. *Eventful Narratives*, p. 26.

Above all things I have learned that the Lord does hear and answer prayer. I have always known that such was the case, but experiences here have shown me that the answer can be immediate and that our prayers can be answered even as we utter them. I might mention two of these instances. Both of them, strangely enough, have to do with baptisms. The first took place about three months ago. When I arrived here I found several applications for baptism completely filled out and signed by the mission president, but with no record of the baptisms ever having been performed. One of these had a note saying that the applicant lived in David, about a hundred miles to the north, and that he would eventually come down to Panama and contact the missionaries, and be baptized. I thought nothing more of the situation for about four months — until the fellow suddenly showed up at Church and asked to be baptized. Well, knowing how much some of my investigators can forget in four months, I arranged to work with him all that week and completely retaught him. The time came for him to be baptized and I still found myself a bit unsure of the situation and hesitant about baptizing him. About five minutes before he was baptized I couldn't remove the hesitancy that I felt about him so I asked the Lord to tell me his will. *As soon as I asked I felt a burning inside and then an overwhelming feeling of peace came over me.* From that day — that minute, I should say — *from that minute on I never felt so much as the shadow of a doubt* as to the fellow's sincerity and worthiness. Even though the fellow lives a hundred miles away from the church and cannot attend the meetings, I know that the life he is living is in accordance with the laws of the gospel. Another instance took place about two weeks ago when the Branch President [Grant Dial] baptized a small child here. One of his counselors and I stood as witnesses and there was a dispute as to whether the wording in the baptism prayer had been correct. We talked it over and none of us were sure, but we were all agreed that if the baptism was to be done over it should be done at that time. We went into one of the classrooms and prayed. I was voice, and as soon as I began to pray *I felt the Spirit of the Lord come over me and once again I knew that the baptism was acceptable to the Lord. I distinctly remember feeling so certain of this that I even asked myself, "Do I need to finish the prayer? I already know the answer to what I am praying about." I felt a complete sense of peace and well-being and assurance that the Lord's requirements had been met. There was no doubt.* As soon as the prayer was over I said that I knew that the ordinance was valid and described the sensations

I had felt, and the same feeling had come at just the same time
to Brother Nilsson. As to whether the wording was correct or
not we don't know, but we do know that the baptism was
accepted and valid. There have been many times before when
I have felt the presence of the Lord's Spirit — I know when He
is guiding me or when I am acting on my own. But this was
the first set of experiences which have been mine in which I've
had an answer even as I spoke. For that reason, even though
to be guided by God is nothing unusual in this day and age,
those simple experiences are important to me and have served
to strengthen my testimony. I know that this is the Church of
Jesus Christ, and that God is guiding his servants in this work!
I know it so strongly that I would gladly die for it. . . . but I
know that the more difficult task will be to live for it.[17]

Although these sensations have been perceived and recorded
in various ways, what is important is that the two sensations
(the burning feeling and the feeling of rightness or surety) are
the signs which tell the recipient that his communication is true
inspiration from the Holy Ghost and not merely his own thinking.

Other Descriptions of the Physical Sensations
Characteristic of the Promptings of the Spirit

Many other terms have been used to describe the physical
and mental sensations people have felt while receiving enlightenment of the Spirit. It is, of course, extremely difficult to describe
in words the nature of a feeling. Perhaps the sensations which
are next described are different perceptions of the feeling of
"rightness" described previously. They may be other sensations
entirely. In either event, they merit careful examination.

1. *Joy and happiness.* Newel Knight described an early conference which he attended by recording the joy they experienced:

> During this time we had much of the power of God mani-
> fested among us and it was wonderful to witness the wisdom
> that Joseph displayed on this occasion, for truly God gave unto
> him great wisdom and power, and it seems to me, even now,
> that none who saw him administer righteousness under such
> trying circumstances, could doubt that the Lord was with him,
> as he acted — not with the wisdom of man, but with the wisdom
> of God, [sic] *The Holy Ghost came upon us and filled our
> hearts with unspeakable joy.*[18]

---

17. Personal file and Missionary Journal of Duane S. Crowther.
18. *Scraps of Biography* (Salt Lake City: Juvenile Instructor Office, 1883),
    p. 65.

The same feeling was experienced by Thomas D. Giles as he was confirmed a member of the Church:

> He bears his solemn testimony now that as soon as the Elders placed their hands upon his head and confirmed him a member of the Church *the power of the Holy Ghost filled his system, brought joy to his heart and gave him an assurance that his sins were forgiven,* for which he had been praying for many years.[19]

Elder Gilbert C. Orme recorded this sensation as he described an encounter with a minister in Australia:

> I was filled with the Holy Spirit and began to preach as I have never preached since. I quoted many passages that I had never read before, and for the next two hours I told this man many things that I had never known before. *My joy was full, and scripture and reason flowed from my lips as a stream of pure water.*[20]

Robert Aveson and his companion, while confined in an English jail for their association with the Saints, also felt this sensation of joy from the Spirit.

> We had been in the cell perhaps two hours, when *a heavenly influence rested upon us.* I said to Richard:
>
> 'How do you feel?'
>
> He replied, 'I feel happy.'
>
> *I told him I never felt so happy in all my life as at that moment, and remarked that I did not care how long we remained in the cell if we could feel like that all the time.*
>
> *It was the holy influence of the Spirit of the Lord that rested upon us.* To us it was a testimony that the gospel we had embraced was true. *Our minds became calm* and we were strengthened in that hour of trial.[21]

A feeling of joy when the Spirit is present is a very common manifestation and is often mentioned in connection with spiritual phenomena.

2. *Peace.* Oliver Cowdery recorded the sensations which were experienced by the prophet Joseph and him when they

---

19. *Early Scenes In Church History* (Salt Lake City: Juvenile Instructor Office, 1882), p. 63.
20. Hackworth, *op. cit.,* p. 144.
21. *Eventful Narratives,* p. 29.

heard the voice of the Redeemer and were visited by John the Baptist. He made special reference to the feeling of peace which they felt as the Savior spoke:

> The Lord, who is rich in mercy and ever willing to answer the consistent prayer of the humble, after we had called upon him in a fervent manner, aside from the abodes of men, condescended to manifest to us His will. *On a sudden, as from the midst of eternity, the voice of the Redeemer spake peace to us*, while the veil was parted and the angel of God came down clothed with glory and delivered the anxiously looked for message, and the keys of the Gospel of repentance. *What joy!* what wonder! what amazement. . . . *Then his voice, though mild, pierced to the center*, and his words, 'I am thy fellow-servant,' dispelled every fear. We listened, we gazed, we admired! 'Twas the voice of the angel from glory' — 'twas a message from the Most High, and *as we heard we rejoiced, while his love enkindled upon our souls*, and we were rapt in the vision of the Almighty. Where was room for doubt? Nowhere; *uncertainty had fled*, doubt had sunk, no more to rise while fiction and deception had fled forever. . . .
>
> I shall not attempt to paint to you the feelings of this heart, nor *the majestic beauty and glory which surrounded us on this occasion;* but you will believe me when I say, that earth, nor men, with the eloquence of time, cannot begin to clothe language in as interesting and sublime a manner as this holy personage. No; nor has this earth power to *give the joy, to bestow the peace, or comprehend the wisdom* which was contained in each sentence as it was delivered by the power of the Holy Spirit![22]

3. *Calmness and Security.* Elder Jack Gardner recorded the feelings he had while being guided by the Holy Ghost as being feelings of calmness and security. He told of his encounter with an evil man during his mission to Virginia:

> He shook with rage, and his voice trembled as he said, 'Don't you come to my place or I will shoot you down like a dog.'
>
> He threatened to tar and feather us and drive us out. I let him know we didn't fear his threats, nor the face of any man, as we were sent there by the authority of God, and if necessary were willing to die for the gospel of Jesus Christ.

---

22. Oliver Cowdery, *The Messenger And Advocate*, 1834. Compare **D & C** 13; JS 2:69.

While I was talking to this evil man, and bearing my testimony to him, *I felt the spirit and power of God so strong within me that I felt as though I were standing above or was lifted from the ground and I shall never forget the calm and secure feeling I had.*[23]

4. *Fearlessness.* Elder George Q. Cannon told how the Spirit caused all fear to vanish.

In attending meeting that day he enjoyed greater liberty than he had at any time previously. *A fearless spirit took possession of him, and the Spirit was able to speak through him as it had not done before.*

The feeling of fear when it rests upon a man, drives away the Spirit of God. The two spirits cannot exist in the same bosom. One must have the mastery. *If the Spirit of God has the mastery, it drives away all fear, and enables a man to speak under its influence with power.* If the spirit of fear has the mastery, the Spirit of God is checked, and the man is not able to tell the people the will and counsel of the Lord.[24]

5. *Heavenly Feeling.* Elder Robert Aveson received his testimony through the Spirit and perceived his sensation as a "heavenly feeling."

That same morning while at work, William conversed with me again on the principles advocated by the Latter-day Saints, and smilingly said:
'You'll have to join the "Mormons." '
While conversing with him *I experienced a heavenly feeling; a mist came over me; I felt within me an influence I had never before realized. The principles and doctrines of the latter-day gospel came clearly before me. The Spirit of the Lord was with me, and I received a testimony of the truth of 'Mormonism' —* a testimony which I shall never forget. *I was supremely happy,* rejoicing with 'joy unspeakable.' I told William I was ready for baptism and asked him to introduce me to the Saints next Sunday.[25]

6. *Active.* While describing a special dedicatory service held in Hawaii, Elder George Q. Cannon commented on the "active" feeling one can receive through the Holy Ghost:

23. Hackworth, *op. cit.,* p. 139.
24. *Gems For The Young Folks* (Salt Lake City: Juvenile Instructor Office, 1881), pp. 42-43.
25. *Eventful Narratives,* pp. 12-13.

Having thus dedicated the land and ourselves to the Lord, one of the Elders spoke in tongues and uttered many comforting promises, and another interpreted. *The spirit of the Lord rested powerfully upon us, and we were filled with exceeding great joy.* I had the satisfaction, afterwards of witnessing the fulfillment of the promise made on that occasion.

The sun was sinking low in the heavens when we got through. Our descent was quickly made, for *we felt joyful, and when men are joyful and the Spirit of God rests upon him, they feel lithe and active.* We had been in the presence of the Lord, and had felt His power, and why should we not be happy?[26]

7. *Message must be given.* Another possible characteristic of the promptings of the Holy Ghost is an overwhelming compulsion to deliver a certain message. He cannot contain the message within him. Elder C. V. Spencer was given this sensation as the Spirit showed him how to overcome an unruly crowd of hecklers.

The idea had become prevalent that Brother Harmon was one of the Twelve. I called on him to speak first. The assembly listened to him for about two minutes. Then Brother Wallace tried it, when a blacksmith by the name of Anguish interrupted him, and Brother Wallace spitefully told him to 'shut your head.' That remark brought matters to a climax. He spoke no more than ninety seconds, and then we had a good representation of what imagination pictures as the pandemonium of hell. I knelt with my back to the congregation and said, 'Father! I have done all I know. If there is anything else you wish me to do, manifest it to me when I get up and I will do it.' As soon as I arose to my feet, a comic song that I used to sing in those days came to my mind, and *I felt as though it wanted to get out of me in all my parts.* I paused a moment, stepped to the front, threw my arms out towards the congregation, and said, 'Boys, it will be a new thing for you to hear a minister sing a comic song in a meeting; but if you will be quiet, I will sing you one.' *I sang it better than ever before or since,* and at the close they gave me a good hearty cheer. I then appealed to them as Englishmen, telling them how Americans treated Englishmen when they came to our country. I continued speaking for one hour, and from the first five minutes the dropping of a pin on the floor could have been heard. At the close many came and shook hands, and in sixpences, shillings, etc., gave me something over $17.00.

---

26. George Q. Cannon, *My First Mission* (Salt Lake City: Juvenile Instructor Office, 1882), p. 17.

When my hands went out towards, and over a part of that congregation I felt power and control go with them as tangibly as I ever felt cold or heat, and I learned this lesson, not to shirk my own responsibilities and run for others to fill my place, let me be ever so weak.[27]

At times when this feeling is experienced, the individual who is voice has no control over the words he speaks. The words just flow from him through the Spirit. This can be illustrated by recording the experience of Brother Scott Williams as he was administered to following a coronary thrombosis:

My wife was told that it was very improbable that I would live for more than a few days; even if by some miracle I should, my heart was the heart of an old man and people in my condition did not live for more than a few years — ten at the most, and were never able to do much physical labor.

My wife immediately asked the branch president and his son, Brothers Brown and Milton to come and administer to me.

---

27. *Labors In The Vineyard* (Salt Lake City: Juvenile Instructor Office, 1884), pp. 20-21. When one speaks under the influence of the Spirit in this manner he is often unable to remember what he said. An example may be found in another experience of Elder Spencer when he was challenged by a group of Protestant ministers:

The meeting commenced about half-past two, p.m., and it was about five o'clock when I entered. At half-past eight the chairman announced that if any member of the unfortunate 'Mormon' Church was present, who had the hardihood and moral courage to attempt a defense after such an overwhelming exposure of their system as had been made that day to the citizens of Norwich, he would be allowed to speak. Of course all eyes had been on me and the invitation was a trap on the part of the ministers. They offered me no way of getting to the pulpit as I was behind five rows of seats, each of which was packed with my opponents and not one offered to allow me to pass. I prayed, put my hands on the sides of the heads of the two ministers in front of me, made an opening and stepped over into their seat; this I did with the others until I reached the pulpit.

A great part of what I said I did not know at the time, nor have I known since, but near the close of my remarks I found myself with my back to the congregation and my face to the preachers. My last words to the latter were, 'You are infidels, and it is you who make infidels, and by your precepts smother the hope of any realizations of the gifts and blessings promised by Christ and His Apostles. *I prophesy, moreover, to you in the name of the Lord Jesus Christ, that your labors of this day and night, shall be the cause of hundreds embracing the gospel I preach.*

After I ceased to speak the chairman undertook to read from the Book of Mormon, but he shook so that it was impossible for him to read. Another man tried to speak, but he was affected in the same way and had to desist. (*Labors In The Vineyard*, p. 24).

In his prayer, Brother Brown told me that the Lord would immediately heal me of my affliction and it would be impossible to find anything wrong with me; that I would be returned to full and active duty in the service; that the Lord had positions of great responsibility in the church awaiting me and that I must prepare myself for them, as I was a favored son of my Heavenly Father. . . . After Brother Brown had completed his prayer, his son said, *'Dad, I've never heard you give such a blessing before.'* *Brother Brown then told us that he had had no control over the words that had come from him.* *We were all rather hesitant about speaking of the feeling we had just had; but when we did, we found that we all had had the same feeling — of others being present in the room and that none of us were in actual physical contact with anything in the room.*[28]

Guidance through the Spirit, when given in this manner, may even go counter to the opinions and beliefs of the person who is voice. Brother Joseph F. Linford found this to be true as he administered to a woman he thought was dying:

Long before Gene was born his mother was in poor health, having been ill for a number of years with a serious heart ailment the doctors could not cure.

Brother Linford was called to administer to her when doctors indicated she couldn't live much longer. He laid his hands on her head *fully convinced that Sister Rich's hours were few.* *He was startled as he commenced the blessing to find himself promising her that she should live to bear a son* who would be a companion to the two little girls who had already come to bless their home. As he spoke the words of the blessing, *a view opened up before Brother Linford's eyes;* and he saw a little boy running and playing with the two little girls.[29]

8. *Attraction.* At times the Spirit manifests Himself by causing one individual to be attracted to another. Jacob Hamblin felt, on one occasion, that he was drawn to a person as he was attempting to choose a man to remain as a missionary in a Moquis Indian village.

I was at a loss to know who to leave with Brother Shelton, and was desirous that it might be made manifest to me. *My mind rested upon Brother Thales Haskell.* I went to him and told him that *he was the only one I could think of* to remain

28. Hackworth, *op. cit.,* pp. 64, 66.
29. *Ibid.,* p. 109.

with Brother Shelton, but he had been out so much that I disliked to mention the subject to him.

He replied that he was the man, for *it had been made known to him that he would be asked to remain before leaving home,* but he had said nothing about it.[30]

9. *Shocks.* At times the impact of the Holy Ghost is perceived as being like an electric shock. Hiram Morris felt this sensation as he came to meet the prophet Joseph Smith.

In the spring of 1844 he made a trip to Nauvoo, Illinois, and was introduced to the Prophet Joseph Smith. Shaking hands, the Prophet asked him if he was a 'Mormon.' 'No sir,' was the reply. 'But you will be,' said the Prophet, laying his hand on his shoulder. *Mr. Morris declared he felt as though an electric shock had passed through him.*[31]

10. *Impending evil.* There are occasions when the Spirit chooses to manifest a warning. In such instances the sensations men feel are likely to be very different from those normally conveyed by the Holy Ghost. They may take the form of a heavy forboding of impending evil. This was experienced by one Mormon Elder as he was directed not to journey on a Mississippi steamboat:

I was never more desirous of pursuing my journey than I was on this occasion, yet soon after going aboard *a feeling of aversion to going on that steamer took possession of me. Instead of a sensation of joy, an undefinable dread, or foreboding of coming evil was exercising an influence over me, that increased in its power every moment, until I could resist no longer,* and snatching up my trunk, I fled with it to shore, just as the deck hands stopped to haul in the gangway, and the boat moved off.

I put my trunk down on the bank of the river, and sat down on it, too weak to stand on my feet longer.

This was a new experience to me, then. What did it mean? One thing was certain, I felt as if I had escaped from some great calamity to a place of safety.

Two days after this I took passage on another steamer for St. Louis, where in due time I arrived in safety. As I walked

30. James A Little, *Jacob Hamblin* (Salt Lake City: Juvenile Instructor Office, 1881), p. 65.

31. Andrew Jenson, *Latter-day Saint Biographical Encyclopedia* (Salt Lake City: Andrew Jenson History Company, 1920), III, 462. See I Ne. 17:53-5.

ashore I met a newsboy crying his morning paper, and among the items of news it contained the most prominent was an account of the ill-fated steamer that I had made my escape from at Evansville, on the Ohio River. I purchased the paper, and found the boat had been snagged in the Mississippi River, below St. Louis, in the night, and sank, with a loss of nearly all that were on board.

The mysterious feeling that impelled me to leave that boat was cleared up to my satisfaction. *There remained not the shadow of a doubt that Providence had interposed between me and the great danger.*[32]

11. *Face shines.* Although this is not an inward feeling which one senses when moved upon by the Holy Ghost, it is a manifestation of the Spirit which has been observed. Elder George Q. Cannon, for instance, recorded how this often took place among the Hawaiian islanders:

The people too, with all their faults and weaknesses, were greatly blessed. *The power of God rested mightily upon them, and many a time their faces would glisten and appear almost white under the influence of the Spirit.* They knew that Jesus was the Son of God and the Savior of the world, and that Joseph Smith and Brigham Young were prophets and servants of God. This knowledge had come to them through obedience to the commandments.[33]

Elder Amasa Potter saw this same glow on the face of his companion as the latter arose to defend them against false charges brought against them in an Australian court.

Our accusers were two merchants, two lawyers and one doctor. They commenced giving in their evidence one by one, and after the judge had heard it all he asked if we had any defense to make, or if we wanted a lawyer. We told him we did not want a lawyer, but we had a defense to make; and as my companion was my senior in age, he arose to make our defense before the court. He commenced on the treaty between England and America. *He had spoken but a few minutes when the Holy Spirit rested upon him in such a way as I had never seen before. His face was very white and he spoke with great power and authority.* The judge looked amazed. The house and yard were full of men who were all silent for one hour. When

---

32. *Gems For the Young Folks,* p. 23.
33. *My First Mission,* p. 53.

he was through we presented our passports from the city of
Washington, our recommendation from the First Presidency of
the Church and our licenses from the parliament of New South
Wales colony.

The judge then arose and said,

'Gentlemen, my decision in this case is that you, the
accusers, who have brought these men before this court under
the pretense of grave charges, have not proved anything against
them. To the prisoners I say, you are honorably acquitted.
You are strangers to us; but I believe you are gentlemen of
honor, or our government would not have given you the docu-
ment that you bear with you. Go your way in peace, and we
are bound to protect you from the ruthless hands of degraded
men. I am sorry that we have put you to so much trouble; but
go in peace.'[34]

12. *Movements of the Spirit can be felt.* One can often,
though not always, feel the entering and leaving of the Spirit
from his body. Newel Knight, for instance, felt the Spirit rest
upon him as he was called to administer to his aunt.

> After the close of the meeting, Brother Hyrum and myself
> intended going to spend the night with one of the Brethren
> who lived a short distance from my uncle's, but as we were ready
> to start, *the Spirit whispered to me that I should tarry there
> at my uncle's all night.* I did so, and retired to bed, where I
> rested till midnight when my uncle came to my room and
> desired me to get up, saying he feared his wife was about to die.
> This surprised me, as she was quite well when I went to bed. I
> dressed myself, and having asked my Heavenly Father to give
> me wisdom, and power to rebuke the destroyer from the habita-
> tion, I went to the room where my aunt lay. She was in a most
> fearful condition; her eyes were closed, and she appeared to be
> in the last agonies of death. Presently she opened her eyes,
> and bade her husband and children farewell, telling them she
> must die for the redemption of this generation, as Jesus Christ
> had died for the generation in His day. Her whole frame shook,
> and she appeared to be racked with the most exquisite pain
> and torment; her hands and feet were cold, and the blood settled
> in her fingers; while her husband and children stood weeping
> around her bed. This was a scene new to me, and I felt she
> was suffering under the power of Satan — that was the same
> spirit that had bound and overpowered me at the time Joseph

34. *Labors In The Vineyard,* pp. 82-3.

cast him out. I now cried unto the Lord for strength and wisdom that we might prevail over this wicked and delusive power. Just at this time my uncle cried aloud to me saying: 'O, Brother Newell, cannot something be done?' *I felt the Holy Spirit of the Lord rest upon me* as he said this, and I immediately stepped forward, took her by the hand, and commanded Satan, in the name of the Lord Jesus Christ, to depart. I told my aunt she would not die, but that she should live to see her children grown up; that Satan had deceived her, and put a lying spirit in her mouth; that Christ had made the only and last atonement for all who would believe on His name; and that there should be no more shedding of blood for sin. She believed and stretched forth her hand, and cried unto me, and Satan departed from her.[35]

Philo Dibble recorded the sensations he had received on the day he was baptized and described the movements of the Spirit within him:

When I came out of the water, I knew that I had been born of water and of the spirit, for *my mind was illuminated with the Holy Ghost.*

I spent that evening at Dr. F. G. Williams'. While in bed that night *I felt what appeared to be a hand upon my left shoulder and a sensation like fibers of fire immediately enveloped my body. It passed from my right shoulder across my breast to my left shoulder, it then struck me on my collar bone and went to the pit of my stomach, after which it left me.* I was enveloped in a heavenly influence, and could not sleep for joy.

The next morning I started home a happy man.[36]

Several years later Brother Dibble was shot by a mob of Missourians, but was miraculously healed. Again he felt the movement of the Spirit within his body.

I bled inwardly until my body was filled with blood, and remained in this condition until the next day at five p.m. I was then examined by a surgeon who was in the Black Hawk war, and who said that he had seen a great many men wounded, but never saw one wounded as I was that ever lived. He pronounced me a dead man.

David Whitmer, however, sent me word that I should live and not die, but I could see no possible chance to recover.

---

35. *Scraps of Biography,* pp. 66-7.
36. *Early Scenes In Church History,* p. 76.

After the surgeon had left me, Brother Newell Knight came to see me, and sat down on the side of my bed. *He laid his right hand on my head but never spoke. I felt the Spirit resting upon me at the crown of my head before his hand touched me, and I knew immediately that I was going to be healed. It seemed to form like a ring under the skin, and followed down my body. When the ring came to the wound, another ring formed around the first bullet hole, also the second and third. Then a ring formed on each shoulder and on each hip, and followed down to the ends of my fingers and toes and left me.* I immediately arose and discharged three quarts of blood or more, with some pieces of my clothes that had been driven into my body by the bullets. I then dressed myself and went out doors and saw the falling of the stars, which so encouraged the Saints and frightened their enemies. It was one of the grandest sights I ever beheld. From that time not a drop of blood came from me and I never afterwards felt the slightest pain or inconvenience from my wounds, except that I was somewhat weak from the loss of blood.[37]

Elder Ben Brown also felt this type of movement as he was administered to in an effort to counteract a severe fever.

While on the lakes, I was attacked by one of the lake fevers prevalent there, and became very ill indeed. I was, however, taken home and put to bed.

The same day two Elders of the Church called in to see me, and finding I was in such a condition, they laid their hands upon me. *While their hands were yet upon my head, I felt the disease remove from my body, commencing at the pit of my stomach, moving gradually upwards towards the hands of the Elders,* and I was made perfectly whole.[38]

Brother Robert A. Barclay felt this same movement of the Spirit within him as he was administered to by Bishop Rudy Luckaw. At this time (1953), Brother Barclay was in the Salt Lake City L.D.S. Hospital, lying partially paralyzed in an iron lung.

After Rudy had sealed the anointing he paused in his prayer so long that my sister Juanita started to cry, fearing there was no blessing for me. Then he said, 'Lucifer has sought to destroy

---

37. *Ibid., pp. 84-5.* This incident is told from Brother Knight's viewpoint in chapter 8 of this book.
38. *Gems For The Young Folks,* p. 64.

you.' He paused again. (He later explained that a power had taken hold of him and attempted to prevent him from giving the blessing that he knew in his heart the Lord had for me. During this pause he had prayed silently to the Lord to release him from this power so that he could speak. The Lord opened up to his mind a vision of a large congregation, and he said he saw me standing among them bearing my testimony to them. Then he was able to go on.) 'This is your blessing,' he continued, and with no hesitation the words came forth. He told me that through the power of the Aaronic priesthood ministering angels would minister unto me, that I would be able to rejoice in my recovery, which would be so rapid that the doctors and nurses would be amazed, and that the hours would no longer be tedious. He said that the Lord had a work for me to do and a mission for me to perform. Then he promised many wonderful things which had such a comforting influence that my heart filled, and I cried through the last half of the blessing.

Now an amazing thing happened. With the words, 'This is your blessing,' *a marvelous power slowly went through me starting where their hands touch my head and proceeding through my body until it reached my feet. After it had passed all pain and nervousness were gone.* From that time on, the blessing took its steady, healing effect.

Rudy later told me that *all the strength had drained from his body*, and he had to hold on to the iron lung for support when he finished.[39]

Verifying Revelation and Inspiration

Man has both the right and the obligation to verify what appears to be revelation and inspiration. He must discern that it is valid and that it seems to be from the proper source. This was Paul's admonition to the Thessalonians, whom he told to "Quench not the Spirit. Despise not prophesyings. *Prove all things; hold fast that which is good.*"[40] Man should test his own inspiration and similarly attempt to evaluate the words of others. This was the example set by the prophet, Alma, who testified,

> Do ye not suppose that I know of these things myself? Behold, I testify unto you that I do know that these things whereof I have spoken are true. And how do ye suppose that I know of their surety?

39. Hackworth, *op. cit.,* p. 49.
40. I Thess. 5:19-21.

Behold, I say unto you they are made known unto me by the Holy Spirit of God. Behold, *I have fasted and prayed many days that I might know these things of myself. And now I do know of myself that they are true; for the Lord God hath made them manifest unto me by his Holy Spirit; and this is the spirit of revelation which is in me.*

And moreover, I say unto you that *it has thus been revealed unto me, that the words which have been spoken by our fathers are true,* even so according to the spirit of prophecy, which is in me, which is also by the manifestation of the Spirit of God.[41]

Without the operation of this testing function in the Church, Satan would have free reign to infiltrate his followers into the ranks of the members. The obligation of all members to confirm by the Spirit the things of the Spirit is a vital force in the maintaining of righteousness, truth, and harmony in the Church. It is also the method whereby members can maintain a strong testimony of the divine calling of their leaders.

The testing process can be carried on successfully only in a spirit of faith, without doubt and pessimism. As Moroni taught,

Whosoever shall believe in my name [Jesus Christ], doubting nothing, unto him will I confirm all my words, even unto the ends of the earth.

And now, behold, who can stand against the works of the Lord? Who can deny his sayings? Who will rise up against the almighty power of the Lord? Who will despise the works of the Lord? Who will despise the children of Christ? Behold, all ye who are despisers of the works of the Lord, for ye shall wonder and perish.

O then despise not, and wonder not, but hearken unto the words of the Lord, and ask the Father in the name of Jesus for what things soever ye shall stand in need. Doubt not, but be believing, and begin as in times of old, and come unto the Lord with all your heart, and work out your own salvation with fear and trembling before him.[42]

Latter-day Saints are not asked to assume blindly that every word, decision, and action of those who hold positions in the various levels of Church activity are performed under inspiration. Many times Church leaders express their own opinions or make decisions based on their own judgment without the aid of revela-

41. Al. 5:45-7.
42. Morm. 9:25-7.

tion. This is as the Lord desires, for He has commanded the Church, saying,

> For behold, *it is not meet that I should command in all things;* for he that is compelled in all things, the same is a slothful and not a wise servant; wherefore he receiveth no reward.[43]

An interesting explanation of this principle was given by Joseph Smith, who recorded in his history that he "visited with a brother and sister from Michigan, who taught that 'a prophet is always a prophet;' but I told them *that a prophet was a prophet only when he was acting as such.*"[44] It often becomes the responsibility of individual members to determine for themselves if what the authority has said is an expression of the will of God or is the authority's personal viewpoint. The former is clearly binding upon the individual, the latter it not.

Not only do present Church officials deserve the privilege of voicing their personal opinions; there are even clear instances of the expression of private opinions in the scriptures. Such opinions should not be accepted as being true without first being tested by the Spirit. Examples may be found in Paul's commentary on married life, which contains such statements as the admission that "I speak this by permission, and not of commandment,"[45] and

> Unto the married I command yet not I, but the Lord, Let not the wife depart from her husband:
> But and if she depart, let her remain unmarried, or be reconciled to her husband: and let not the husband put away his wife.
> *But to the rest speak I, not the Lord:* If any brother hath a wife that believeth not, and she be pleased to dwell with him, let him not put her away.[46]

Paul also said, "Now concerning virgins *I have no commandment of the Lord: yet I give my judgment,* as one that hath obtained mercy of the Lord to be faithful."[47] Certainly these passages show that this portion of the scriptures is not the

---

43. D & C 58:26.
44. HC, V, p. 265.
45. I Cor. 7:6.
46. I Cor. 7:10-12.
47. I Cor. 7:25.

infallible word of God; rather, it is an expression of Paul's opinions.[48] Is this not also the situation found in Alma's comment on the resurrection, in which he tells Corianton, "And now, my son, I do not say that their resurrection cometh at the resurrection of Christ; but behold, *I give it as my opinion,* that the souls and the bodies are reunited, of the righteous, at the resurrection of Christ, and his ascension into heaven."[49] It is, of course, obvious that these passages constitute the exception rather than the rule. Most of the scriptures are clearly the word of God and would abide any test of the Spirit.

Without the testing function being performed, however, man cannot gain a firm and unshakable knowledge and testimony of the divinity of the scriptures. It would seem that Moroni knew this, and for this reason gave his well-known exhortation to mankind to test the validity and truthfulness of the Book of Mormon:

> "And when ye shall receive these things, *I would exhort you that ye would ask God,* the Eternal Father, in the name of Christ, if these things are not true; and if ye shall ask with a sincere heart, with real intent, having faith in Christ, *he will manifest the truth of it unto you by the power of the Holy Ghost.*"[50]

The following are some of the checks man may apply to test the validity of both his own revelation and inspiration and that of others.

1. *Does the speaker claim to have received revelation or inspiration?* This is the easiest test of revelation or inspiration, yet it is rarely, if ever, applied. If an individual sets forth ideas or interpretations which are new, and his listeners wish to evaluate them, it is not amiss for a tactful inquiry to be made of him asking if he believes his new insights are the result of inspiration from on high or whether they are merely his own thinking. The speaker should welcome the privilege either to identify his own thoughts or to bear testimony that he has been blessed with further light and knowledge as a gift of the Spirit. Where no claim for inspiration is made, then the other tests, of course, must be applied.

---

48. See also D & C 74:5.
49. Al. 40:20.
50. Moro. 10:4.

In practice, however, it may not always be possible for a church leader to make a distinction as to which of his decisions are made as a result of direct inspiration and revelation and which result from his own intelligence and experience. Any church official, performing his duty properly, will prayerfully seek the guidance of the Lord continually that all his acts and decisions may be in accord with divine will. Thus the great body of Priesthood officers, schooled in humility, doctrine and administration, guide the Church throughout the earth with substantial freedom from mistakes and wrong decisions. Individuals are not infallible, however, and errors may occur if a man is not humble and in tune with the Spirit. It is not claimed that every decision made by a bishopric, a stake presidency, or other group of Church leaders is inspired. If one has doubt, he may ask the leaders, where appropriate, if they made their decision upon their own judgment or upon direct guidance from the Lord and then test their testimonies by the Spirit. In many cases a bishop issues a call based upon his own considered judgment. The person given the responsibility may nevertheless grow in it, may still seek help and guidance to fulfill it well, and may reap all the joys of faithful service! There are many calls and activities performed without the benefit of specific revelation. Instead, such calls are based on previous revelations and instructions setting a precedent which is to be followed. The Lord proclaimed that He *"will give unto you a pattern in all things, that ye may not be deceived."*[51] Bishops are instructed to interview member boys when they turn twelve years of age and, if they are worthy, to ordain them to the office of deacon. Often the revelation involved is an inclusive commandment on a Church-wide level, not a specific revelation for each boy. It would seem that many missionary calls are similarly initiated. In other words, for some purposes commands are not given on every occasion, rather guidelines are deliniated to bring about the Lord's objectives. This was the message of an early revelation, which said, *"Behold, this is a great and the last commandment which I shall give unto you concerning this matter; for this shall suffice for thy daily walk, even unto the end of thy life."*[52]

2. *Is the message in harmony with the scriptures of the Church?* Isaiah, while speaking of the need to test the revela-

---

51. D & C 52:14.
52. D & C 19:32.

tions of others, proclaimed, "To the law and to the testimony: *if they speak not according to this word, it is because there is no light in them.*"[53] Lehi taught that the "Spirit is the same, yesterday, today and forever."[54] If this is true, then the intent of His revelations will not change. Truth is eternal and unchanging. What was true in the days when the scriptures were written is still true today.

This test is not, however, all-encompassing. It should be recognized that many revelations given today deal with truths which are not mentioned in the standard works. This is a day when God is revealing things which have never before been revealed. Similarly, by revelation to today's Prophet, God may take account of changing circumstances by augmenting or modifying programs or details which were originally set out for previous generations. It would be foolish to maintain that a revelation is false because it speaks of something not mentioned in the written scriptures or changes something shown there to meet modern needs.

3. *Does proper consideration of the message bring the physical sensations which the scriptures say will accompany manifestations of the Spirit?* These sensations, the burning of the bosom and the feeling that the manifestation is right, are essential norms to which spiritual manifestations are to be compared.[55]

These, then, are three means available to members of the Church for verifying revelation and inspiration. It is obvious that each member must have the gifts of the Spirit himself in order to test the inspiration of others. Without the blessing of personal revelation and inspiration, there can be no hope for the process of testing to be valid. Attempts to test without the Spirit become only sources of doubt and confusion and they weaken rather than strengthen the individual's testimony.

Summary

1. Revelation given by the Holy Ghost is given both to one's mind and to one's heart.

2. That which is right may be so indicated by the Spirit by communicating to man a burning within the bosom and a

53. Is. 8:20.
54. 2 Ne. 2:4.
55. D & C 9:8-9.

feeling that it is right. When something is wrong the Holy Ghost can cause the earnest seeker to receive a stupor of thought and to forget the wrong thing.

3. Communications from the Spirit to the mind are characterized by

    A. being a definite message,

    B. having a definite purpose,

    C. being persistent. They continue to be manifested until the individual either accepts or rejects them.

4. A burning sensation in one's bosom usually accompanies the presence of the Holy Ghost. Some people have felt this sensation throughout their body.

5. A feeling of "rightness" also accompanies the manifestations of the Holy Ghost. This is perceived in different ways by different people. It has also been called a feeling of

    A. certainty

    B. joy and happiness

    C. peace

    D. calmness and security

    E. fearlessness

    F. a heavenly feeling

    G. a feeling of activity

    H. an urge to proclaim a message

    I. an attraction

    J. an electric shock.

6. The Holy Ghost sometimes grants warnings by giving people a forboding of impending evil.

7. At times the Holy Ghost is manifested to such a degree that He causes the faces of those under His influence to shine and glow.

8. At times movements of the Spirit within one's body can be felt. This is particularly true with instances of healing.

9. Man should test his own revelation and also attempt to determine whether the words of others are inspired.

10. Testing revelation accomplishes several purposes, including

  A. obeying the commandment to do so.
  B. preventing the infiltration of false teachings into the Church.
  C. enabling members to retain a strong testimony that their leaders are divinely inspired.
  D. allowing Church authorities the privilege of expressing their own ideas and opinions without having people believe that their every word is inspired.

11. There are portions of the scriptures where private opinions are expressed. Such portions are not considered to be doctrinally binding.

12. Inspiration can be tested by asking three questions:

  A. Does the speaker claim to be inspired in his statements?
  B. When a message pertains to items previously revealed in written scripture, does the message conform to the spirit of the scriptures?
  C. Does the message bring the physical sensations which the scriptures say will accompany manifestations of the Spirit?

13. Attempts to test without the Spirit will bring confusion and doubt and will weaken rather than strengthen one's testimony.

Part II

GIFTS OF KNOWLEDGE

CHAPTER III

A Testimony of The Divinity of Jesus Christ Through His Personal Manifestation

Knowledge that Jesus is the Son of God

A deep and abiding testimony that Jesus is the Son of God is one of the most vital and profound gifts of the Spirit. The gift is related not only to the divine Sonship of Jesus, but also to His calling as Savior and Redeemer and to His power and authority as a member of the Godhead.[1] The attaining of this gift is essential for man to fulfill his highest destiny, for *"This is life eternal, that they might know thee the only true God, and Jesus Christ, whom thou hast sent."*[2] The gift of knowledge of the Godhood and divine Sonship of Christ is bestowed upon an individual in one or a combination of four ways:

1. by actual appearance or other manifestation of the Savior himself,

2. by the testimony of God the Father,

3. by revelation through the Holy Ghost, and

4. by testimony born by individuals who have already gained a personal witness of His divinity.

This chapter is devoted to an examination of the first of these four methods.

Personal Visitations of the Resurrected Christ in New Testament Times

The divinity of Jesus was undeniably manifested by His ability to conquer death and achieve a personal resurrection. This was an accomplishment which could not be achieved by one other than a God. No mortal being could have broken the bands of death. Jesus, on numerous occasions following his resurrection,

---

1. D & C 46:13.
2. Jn. 17:3.

demonstrated his divine power over the grave by returning to
earth and appearing to various individuals. These appearances
began when He appeared to Mary Magdalene, near the tomb,
and told her

> Touch me not; for I am not yet ascended to my Father: but
> go to my brethren, and say unto them, I ascend unto my Father,
> and your Father; and to my God, and your God.[3]

Then, as Mary and the other women were running to tell the
Twelve the joyous news, He apparently appeared once again to
them, and this time allowed them to touch Him.

> And as they went to tell his disciples, behold, Jesus met
> them, saying, All hail. And they came and held him by the
> feet, and worshipped him.
> Then said Jesus unto them, Be not afraid: go tell my
> brethren that they go into Galilee, and there shall they see me.[4]

On the same day when it was discovered that Jesus had come
from the tomb He appeared repeatedly to His disciples. He
walked with two of them who were not numbered among the
Twelve on the road to Emmaus. As they walked He "expounded
unto them in all the scriptures the things concerning himself"[5]
and then revealed unto them His true identity and vanished from
their sight. Sometime during this day he appeared to Simon
Peter.[6]

This series of visits on the first day following His resurrection was climaxed by His appearance to ten of His apostles in
the upper room. He invited them to "behold my hands and my
feet, that it is I myself: handle me, and see; for *a spirit hath*

---

3. Jn. 20:17.
4. Mt. 28:9-10. The eleven met with the Savior at an unidentified time in
   Galilee:
   > Then the eleven disciples went away into Galilee, into a mountain
   > where Jesus had appointed them.
   > And when they saw him, they worshipped him: but some doubted.
   > And Jesus came and spake unto them, saying, All power is given
   > unto me in heaven and in earth.
   > Go ye therefore, and teach all nations, baptizing them in the
   > name of the Father, and of the Son, and of the Holy Ghost:
   > Teaching them to observe all things whatsoever I have com-
   > manded you: and, lo, I am with you alway, even unto the end of the
   > world. Amen. (Mt. 28:16-21).
5. Lk. 24:27.
6. Lk. 24:34. I Cor. 15:5.

not flesh and bones, as ye see me have.[7] And then to further prove that he had actually reclaimed his body from the grave, He ate broiled fish and honeycomb before them.[8] What a glorious day this must have been with so many appearances of the Savior! How forceful a testimony that He had conquered death and was truly divine!

Other visits of the Savior followed in the days that ensued. According to the record of Paul, Jesus also appeared to "above five hundred brethren at once,"[9] and then to James.[10] A week after His resurrection He met with the apostles once again. This time He instructed Thomas, who had been absent the week previous, to feel the prints of His wounds, so that there could be no doubt of His having conquered the bands of death.[11] Still later, Jesus appeared to His disciples at the Sea of Tiberias. He helped them to catch a miraculous draught of fishes and then forcefully taught Peter his responsibility to "feed my sheep."[12] There is also on record the Savior's instructions to His disciples on or near the Mount of Olives when He was finally caught up into heaven after being with his followers for almost seven weeks.[13]

Others received the gift of His personal visitation after He had ascended into heaven. Stephen was permitted by the Holy Ghost to see both the Father and the Son. The testimony was left of his vision that

> He, being full of the Holy Ghost, looked up stedfastly into heaven, and *saw the glory of God, and Jesus standing on the right hand of God,*
>
> And said, Behold, I see the heavens opened, and the Son of man standing on the right hand of God.[14]

---

7. Lk. 24:39.
8. Lk. 24:36-43.
9. I Cor. 15:6. Note that I Cor. 15:4-7 gives us clear chronological order for five important appearances of the resurrected Christ. In these five events the Savior appeared first to Peter (Cephas), then to the Twelve, then to over five hundred brethren, then to James, then again to all the apostles.
10. I Cor. 15:7.
11. Jn. 20:24-31.
12. Jn. 21:1-25.
13. Acts 1:9-11. Cf. Lu. 24:45-53.
14. Acts 7:55-56.

The life of Saul of Tarsus was changed on the road to Damascus from the course of persecuting to that of serving God by Christ's question, "Saul, Saul, why persecutest thou me? And He said, Who art thou, Lord? And the Lord said, *I am Jesus* whom thou persecutest. . . ."[15]

Certainly no account of the Savior's appearances in the New Testament could be complete without recording the glorious vision of John the Revelator, who left a vivid and striking description of the resurrected Christ:

> *I was in the Spirit* on the Lord's day, and heard behind me a great voice, as of a trumpet,
>
> Saying, I am Alpha and Omega, the first and the last: . . .
>
> And I turned to see the voice that spake with me. And being turned, I saw seven golden candlesticks;
>
> And in the midst of the seven candlesticks *one like unto the Son of man, clothed with a garment down to the foot, and girt about the paps with a golden girdle.*
>
> *His head and his hairs were white like wool, as white as snow; and his eyes were as a flame of fire;*
>
> *And his feet like unto fine brass, as if they burned in a furnace; and his voice as the sound of many waters.*
>
> And he had in his right hand seven stars: and out of his mouth went a sharp two-edged sword; and *his countenance was as the sun shineth in his strength.*
>
> And when I saw him, I fell at his feet as dead. And he laid his right hand upon me, saying unto me, Fear not; I am the first and the last:
>
> *I am he that liveth, and was dead; and behold I am alive for evermore,* Amen.[16]

Personal Visitations of the Resurrected Christ in Book of Mormon Times

The Savior also appeared to the Saints in the Americas to demonstrate His divinity. To them He gave the commandment:

> Arise and come forth unto me, that ye may thrust your hands into my side, and also that ye may feel the prints of the nails in my hands and in my feet, that ye may know that

---

15. Acts 9:4-5.
16. Rev. 1:10-18.

I am the God of Israel, and the God of the whole earth, and have been slain for the sins of the world.[17]

With this greeting Jesus began His ministry among the Nephites and Lamanites in the Americas. He came from heaven and returned each day for three days, during which He was seen by thousands who gained an undeniable witness of His divinity.[18]

Later, Mormon enjoyed a manifestation while he was still in his youth, for he wrote that "I, being fifteen years of age and being somewhat of a sober mind, therefore *I was visited of the Lord,* and tasted and knew of the goodness of Jesus."[19]

His son, Moroni, also talked with the Savior face to face. While leaving his written testimony for those of the last days to read, Moroni told his readers:

> And now I, Moroni, bid farewell unto the Gentiles, yea, and also unto my brethren whom I love, until we shall meet before the judgment-seat of Christ, where all men shall know that my garments are not spotted with your blood.
>
> And then shall ye know that *I have seen Jesus, and that he hath talked with me face to face,* and that he told me in plain humility, even as a man telleth another in mine own language, concerning these things.[20]

Personal Appearances and Manifestations of the Savior in the Latter Days

After reading the testimonies of the men who saw Christ in their youth, it is not difficult to accept the testimony of Joseph Smith, who as a boy of fourteen was also granted a visit by the Savior:

> I saw a pillar of light exactly over my head, above the brightness of the sun, which descended gradually until it fell upon me.
>
> It no sooner appeared than I found myself delivered from the enemy which held me bound. When the light rested upon me, *I saw two Personages, whose brightness and glory defy all description, standing above me in the air.* One of them spake

17. 3 Ne. 11:14.
18. 3 Ne. Chapters 11-28.
19. Morm. 1:15.
20. Eth. 12:38-39.

unto me, calling me by my name and said, pointing to the other — This is My Beloved Son. Hear Him![21]

Others who were prominent in the restoration of the Church were given visitations, visions, or communications from the Lord Jesus Christ. Consider the testimony of David Whitmer, one of the three witnesses to the Book of Mormon, in which he told how Jesus spoke to Joseph Smith, Oliver Cowdery and himself in June of 1829, as they were being shown the Book of Mormon plates by an angelic being.

> Joseph, Oliver and I were sitting just here on a log, when we were overshadowed by a light. It was not like the light of the sun, nor like that of a fire, but more glorious and beautiful. It extended away round us, I cannot tell how far, but in the midst of this light about as far off as he sits (pointing to John C. Whitmer, sitting a few feet from him), there appeared, as it were, a table with many records or plates upon it, besides the plates of the Book of Mormon, also the sword of Laban, the directors (i.e., the ball which Lehi had) and the interpreters. I saw them just as plain as I see this bed (striking the bed beside him with his hand), and *I heard the voice of the Lord, as distinctly as I ever heard anything in my life, declaring that the records of the plates of the Book of Mormon were translated by the gift and power of God.*[22]

During the first conference of the Church, on June 9, 1830, a series of remarkable manifestations were granted to the Saints assembled in Fayette, New York. Among these was the choice vision which was opened up to Newel Knight, who had been a baptized member of the Church for less than two weeks:

---

21. Joseph Smith 2:16-17. Of the instruction which he received on this occasion, Joseph later wrote:

    I was enwrapped in a heavenly vision, and *saw two glorious personages, who exactly resembled each other in features and likeness, surrounded with a brilliant light which eclipsed the sun at noon day.* They told me that all religious denominations were believing in incorrect doctrines, and that none of them was acknowledged of God as His Church and kingdom: and *I was expressly commanded 'to go not after them,'* at the same time receiving a promise that the fullness of the Gospel should at some future time be made known unto me. (HC, IV, p. 536).

22. Jenson, I, p. 266. This testimony was given to Apostles Orson Pratt and Joseph F. Smith on September 7, 1878. See also *The Testimony of Three Witnesses* which is published in the front of the Book of Mormon.

I saw the heavens opened, *I beheld the Lord Jesus Christ seated at the right hand of the Majesty on High,* and it was made plain to my understanding that the time would come when I should be admitted into His presence, to enjoy His society for ever and ever.[23]

An awe-inspiring manifestation of both the Savior and God the Father was granted a year later to Joseph Smith and Sidney Rigdon.[24] On February 16, 1832, while they were working together on a translation of the Bible at Hiram, Ohio, they saw the vision which they thus reported:

We, Joseph Smith, Jun., and Sidney Rigdon, *being in the Spirit* on the sixteenth day of February, in the year of our Lord one thousand eight hundred and thirty-two —

By the power of the Spirit our eyes were opened and our understandings were enlightened so as to see and understand the things of God. . . .

The Lord touched the eyes of our understandings and they were opened and the glory of the Lord shone round about.

And *we beheld the glory of the Son, on the right hand of the Father, and received of his fulness;* . . .

And saw the holy angels, and them who are sanctified before his throne, worshipping God, and the Lamb, who worship him forever and ever.

And now, after the many testimonies which have been given of him, this is the testimony, last of all, which we give of him: *That he lives!*

---

23. *Scraps of Biography,* p. 53. Joseph Smith also made an entry in his history concerning the event, as follows:

Among the rest was Brother Newel Knight, who had to be placed on a bed, being unable to help himself. By his own account of the transaction, he could not understand why we should lay him on the bed, as he felt no sense of weakness. He felt his heart filled with love, with glory, and pleasure unspeakable, and could discern all that was going on in the room; when all of a sudden a vision of the future burst upon him. He saw there represented the great work which through my instrumentality was yet to be accomplished. *He saw heaven opened, and beheld the Lord Jesus Christ, seated at the right hand of the majesty on high,* and had it made plain to his understanding that the time would come when he would be admitted into His presence to enjoy His society for ever and ever. When their bodily strength was restored to these brethren, they shouted hosannas to God and the Lamb, and rehearsed the glorious things which they had seen and felt, whilst they were yet in the spirit. (HC, I, p. 85).

24. At this time, Sidney Rigdon held no calling of prominence in the Church. He was not called to the presidency of the Church until more than a year later.

For we saw him, even on the right hand of God; and we heard the voice bearing record that he is the Only Begotten of the Father —[25]

The Savior chose to make His appearance to the leaders of the Church gathered in the School of the Prophets on March 18, 1833. On this occasion, the Prophet Joseph promised the group that the 'pure in heart should see a heavenly vision.' Then, following a short period of secret prayer,

> The promise was verified; for many present had the eyes of their understanding opened by the Spirit of God, so as to behold many things. I then blessed the bread and wine, and distributed a portion to each. *Many of the brethren saw a heavenly vision of the Savior,* and concourses of angels, and many other things, of which each one has a record of what he saw.[26]

A series of appearances of the Savior are recorded in connection with the completion of the Kirtland Temple in early 1836. On January 21, 1836, in a meeting of the Church presidency and patriarch, a number of glorious visions were given. Twice during the meeting the Savior manifested Himself in visions. These visions were subsequently recorded by Joseph Smith in his history in these words:

> The heavens were opened upon us, and *I beheld the celestial kingdom of God, and the glory thereof,* whether in the body or out I cannot tell. I saw the transcendent beauty of the gate through which the heirs of that kingdom will enter, which was like unto circling flames of fire; also *the blazing throne of God, whereon was seated the Father and the Son.* I saw the beautiful streets of that kingdom, which had the appearance of being paved with gold. . . . I saw the Twelve Apostles of the Lamb, who are now upon the earth, who hold the keys of this last ministry, in foreign lands, standing together in a circle, much fatigued, with their clothes tattered and feet swollen, with their eyes cast downward, and *Jesus standing in their midst, and they did not behold Him.* The Savior looked upon them and wept.[27]

The group who had experienced these blessings with the Prophet then called in the bishoprics and High Council of Kirtland and Zion (Jackson County, Missouri) and again the Savior was seen.

---

25. D & C 76:11-12, 19-23.
26. HC, I, pp. 334-35.
27. HC, II, pp. 380-81.

The visions of heaven were opened to them also. *Some of them saw the face of the Savior,* and others were ministered unto by holy angels and the spirit of prophecy and revelation was poured out in mighty power; and loud hosannas, and glory to God in the highest, saluted the heavens, for we all communed with the heavenly host. And I saw in my vision all the Presidency in the celestial kingdom of God, and many others that were present.[28]

A week later, on January 28, Joseph Smith held a meeting to organize the Quorum of Seventy. Once again the Savior appeared in vision.

President Zebedee Coltrin, one of the seven presidents of the Seventy, *saw the Savior extended before him, as upon the cross, and a little after, crowned with glory upon his head above the bsightness* [sic] *of the sun.*

After these things were over, and a glorious vision, which I saw, had passed, I instructed the seven presidents to proceed and anoint the Seventy, . . .

I retired to my home, filled with the Spirit, and my soul cried hosanna to God and the Lamb, through the silent watches of the night; and while my eyes were closed in sleep, *the visions of the Lord were sweet unto me, and His glory was round about me.*[29]

Various other groups were blessed with abundant outpouring of the gifts of the Spirit during the meetings that followed. It

---

28. HC, II, p. 382.
29. HC, II, p. 387. Elder Harrison Burgess in his *Sketch of a Well-Spent Life,* left this account of the meeting:

> The Lord blessed His people abundantly in that Temple with the Spirit of prophecy, the ministering of angels, visions, etc. I will here relate a vision which was shown to me. It was near the close of the endowments. I was in a meeting for Instruction in the upper part of the Temple, with about a hundred of the High Priests, Seventies, and Elders. The Saints felt to shout, "Hosannah!" and the Spirit of God rested upon me in mighty power and I beheld the room lighted up with a peculiar light such as I had never seen before. It was soft and clear and the room looked to me as though it had neither roof nor floor to the building and I beheld the Prophet Joseph and Hyrum Smith and Roger Orton enveloped in the light: Joseph exclaimed aloud, "I behold the Savior, the Son of God." Hyrum said, "I behold the angels of heaven." Brother Orton exclaimed, "I behold the chariots of Israel." All who were in the room felt the power of God to that degree that many prophesied, and the power of God was manifest, the remembrance of which will remain with me while I live upon the earth. *(Labors in the Vineyard,* p. 67).

was apparently not for another two months, however, that the
Savior chose to return. Then, on March 30th, at a meeting of
over three hundred stake and general authorities held in the
Temple, He again appeared:

> The brethren continued exhorting, prophesying, and speaking
> in tongues until five o'clock in the morning. *The Savior made
> His appearance to some, while angels ministered to others, and
> it was a Pentecost and an endowment indeed,* long to be remem-
> bered, for the sound shall go forth from this place into all the
> world, and the occurrences of this day shall be handed down
> upon the pages of sacred history, to all generations; as the day
> of Pentecost, so shall this day be numbered and celebrated as
> a year of jubilee, and time of rejoicing to the Saints of the
> Most High God.[30]

The following Sunday, April 3, He again appeared in the
Temple. On this occasion His coming was shielded from all but
Joseph Smith and Oliver Cowdery, who had just knelt in prayer
at the Temple pulpit.

> The veil was taken from our minds, and the eyes of our under-
> standing were opened.
>
> *We saw the Lord standing upon the breastwork of the
> pulpit, before us; and under his feet was a paved work of pure
> gold, in color like amber.*
>
> *His eyes were as a flame of fire; the hair of his head was
> white like the pure snow; his countenance shone above the
> brightness of the sun; and his voice was as the sound of the
> rushing of great waters,* even the voice of Jehovah, saying:
>
> I am the first and the last; I am he who liveth, I am he
> who was slain; I am your advocate with the Father.[31]

There are occasions on record in which members of the
Church have seen the Savior in dreams. Orson F. Whitney,
well-known writer, lecturer, and historian, had such an experience
while laboring as a missionary in Pennsylvania in 1876. At this
time the twenty-one-year-old youth had deviated from his
missionary calling and had made a two-week journey to Washington, D.C. to visit Congress, Mt. Vernon, and other points of
historical importance. He had written his impressions of these
places to a Salt Lake City newspaper and found himself more

30. HC, II, pp. 432-33.
31. D & C 110:1-4.

interested in his newspaper correspondence than in his missionary labors. About this time he received the following remarkable dream, which became a molding influence in his life:

I thought I was in the garden of Gethsemane, a witness of the Savior's agony. I seemed to be standing behind a tree in the foreground of the picture, from which point I could see without being seen. The Savior, with the Apostles Peter, James and John, entered the garden through a little wicket gate at my right, where he stationed them in a group, telling them to pray. He then passed over to my left, but still in front of me, where he knelt and prayed also. His face, which was towards me, streamed with tears, as he besought the Father to let the cup pass, and added, 'not my will but thine be done.' Having finished his prayer, he arose and crossed to where the Apostles were kneeling fast asleep. He shook them gently, they awoke and he reproved them for their apathy. Again he bade them pray, and again crossed to his place and prayed, returning as before to find them sleeping. This happened three times, until I was perfectly familiar with his face, form, and movements. *He was much taller than ordinary men, and though meek, far more dignified than any being I had ever beheld; and he wore a look of ineffable tenderness and compassion, even while reproving His disciples. My heart went out to him as never before to anybody or anything; I loved him with all my soul.* I wept at seeing him weep, and felt for him the deepest sympathy. Then all of a sudden the circumstances changed, though the scene remained the same. Instead of before the crucifixion, it was after. The Savior and the three Apostles, whom he had beckoned to him, now stood in a group at the left, and were about to take their departure, ascending into heaven. I could endure it no longer, but rushed out from behind the tree, fell at his feet, clasped him around the knees and begged him to take me also. With a look of infinite tenderness, as of a father or an elder brother, he stooped, lifted me up and embraced me, saying as he did so in the kindest and gentlest manner possible, while slowly shaking his head and sweetly smiling, 'No, my son, these can go with me; for they have finished their work; but you must stay and finish yours!' *Still I clung to him and the contact was so real that I felt the warmth of his bosom as I rested upon it.* Gazing up into his face, I once more besought him, 'Well promise me that I will come to you at the last.' Again he smiled sweetly, and there was a look as if he would have gladly granted my request had it been wise to do so. He then said, 'That will depend entirely upon yourself.' I awoke with a sob, and it was morning. This dream made a wonderful impression upon me, paving the way to my thorough conversion, which soon followed. Among the things it taught me was not to sleep at my post, and to regard first the duties of my mission, and not to allow anything to interfere with them."[32]

Another missionary, who later became a member of the Quorum of the Twelve Apostles, also saw Jesus in a dream. This manifestation was given to Elder Melvin J. Ballard:

"When I was doing missionary work with some of our brethren, laboring among the Indians, seeking the Lord for light to decide certain matters pertaining to our work there, and receiving a witness from Him that we were doing things according to His will, *I found myself one evening in the dreams of the night, in that sacred building, the Temple.* After a season of prayer and rejoicing, I was informed that I should have the privilege of entering into one of those rooms, to meet a glorious Personage, and as I entered the door, *I saw, seated on a raised platform, the most glorious Being my eyes have ever beheld, or that I ever conceived existed in all the eternal worlds.* As I approached to be introduced, he arose and stepped towards me with extended arms, and *he smiled as he softly spoke my name.* If I shall live to be a million years old, I shall never forget that smile. He took me into his arms and kissed me, pressed me to His bosom, and blessed me, *until the marrow of my bones seemed to melt!* When he had finished, I fell at His feet, and as I bathed them with my tears and kisses, *I saw the prints of the nails in the feet of the Redeemer of the world. The feeling that I had in the presence of Him who hath all things in His hands, to have His love, His affection, and His blessings was such that if I ever can receive that of which I had but a foretaste, I would give all that I am, all that I hope to be, to feel what I then felt!*"[33]

President David O. McKay was also privileged to see the Lord Jesus Christ:

I then fell asleep, and beheld in vision something infinitely sublime. In the distance I beheld a beautiful white city. Though far away, yet I seemed to realize that trees with luscious fruit, shrubbery with gorgeously-tinted leaves, and flowers in perfect bloom abounded everywhere. The clear sky above seemed to

---

32. Jenson, I, pp. 660-61.
33. Bryant S. Hinckley, *Sermons and Missionary Services of Melvin Joseph Ballard* (Salt Lake City: Deseret Book Company, 1949), p. 156.

reflect these beautiful shades of color. I then saw a great concourse of people approaching the city. Each one wore a white flowing robe, and a white headdress. Instantly my attention seemed centered upon their Leader, and though I could see only the profile of his features and his body, I recognized him at once as my Savior! *The tint and radiance of his countenance were glorious to behold! There was a peace about him which seemed sublime — it was divine!*

The city, I understood, was his. It was the City Eternal; and the people following him were to abide there in peace and eternal happiness.

But who were they?

As if the Savior read my thoughts, he answered by pointing to a semicircle that then appeared above them, and on which were written in gold the words:

'These Are They Who Have Overcome The World — Who Have Truly Been Born Again!'[34]

On September 2, 1898, Lorenzo Snow was visited by the Savior in the Salt Lake Temple. The visit was occasioned by the death of President Wilford Woodruff earlier in the day. Elder Snow at this time was president of the Quorum of the Twelve and had gone into the Temple to seek guidance as to how the affairs of the Church should best be conducted in that time of sorrow. He related his experience to his granddaughter, Alice Young Pond, later, and it is her record which has been transmitted:

"One evening when I was visiting Grandpa Snow in his room in the Salt Lake Temple, I remained until the doorkeepers had gone and the nightwatchman had not yet come in, so Grandpa said he would take me to the main front entrance and let me out that way. He got his bunch of keys from his dresser.

"After we left his room and while we were still in the large corridor, leading into the Celestial room, I was walking several steps ahead of Grandpa when he stopped me, saying: 'Wait a moment, Allie. I want to tell you something. It was right here that the Lord Jesus Christ appeared to me at the time of the death of President Woodruff. He instructed me to go right ahead and reorganize the First Presidency of the Church at once and not wait as he had done after the death of the previous presidents, and that I was to succeed President Woodruff.'

34. Clare Middlemiss, *Cherished Experiences from the writings of President David O. McKay* (Salt Lake City: Deseret Book Company, 1955) p. 102.

"Then Grandpa came a step nearer and held out his left hand and said: '*He stood right here, about three feet above the floor. It looked as though He stood on a plate of solid gold.*'

"*Grandpa told me what a glorious personage the Savior is and described His hands, feet, countenance and beautiful White Robes, all of which were of such a glory of whiteness and brightness that he could hardly gaze upon Him.*

"Then Grandpa came another step nearer me and put his right hand on my head and said: Now, granddaughter, I want you to remember that this is the testimony of your grandfather, that he told you with his own lips that *he actually saw the Savior here in the Temple and talked with Him face to face.*'[35]

The Savior To Appear to the Humble

Thus it is seen that the gift of knowledge of the divinity of Christ has often been granted by personal visitations or manifestations of Jesus Himself. This gift is promised to those who diligently seek it. Men have seen Him in visions and dreams. They have often recorded their joy as they saw Him and have shown it to be worth far more than all man's material possessions.

This is a blessing which is available to all who would truly seek it, as the Lord wills it. He has shown himself not only to Prophets, but to ordinary members of the Church, to missionaries, to new converts, to young men.

Verily I say unto you that it is your privilege, and a promise I give unto you that have been ordained unto this ministry, that inasmuch as you strip yourselves from jealousies and fears, and humble yourselves before me, for ye are not sufficiently humble, *the veil shall be rent and you shall see me and know that I am* — not with the carnal neither natural mind, but with the spiritual.

For no man has seen God at any time in the flesh, except quickened by the Spirit of God.

Neither can any natural man abide the presence of God, neither after the carnal mind.

Ye are not able to abide the presence of God now, neither the ministering of angels; wherefore, continue in patience until ye are perfected.[36]

35. N. B. Lundwall (comp.), *Temples of the Most High* (10th ed. enlg.; Salt Lake City: Bookcraft, n.d.) p. 149.
36. D & C 67:10-13.

The Master's promise of His willingness to manifest Himself unto men is found also in the Bible, where the Savior taught that

> He that hath my commandments and keepeth them, he it is that loveth me: and he that loveth me shall be loved by my Father, and I will love him, and *will manifest myself to him.*
>
> Judas saith unto him, not Iscariot, Lord, how is it that thou wilt manifest thyself unto us, and not unto the world?
>
> Jesus answered and said unto him, If a man love me, he will keep my words: and my Father will love him, and *we will come unto him, and make our abode with him.*[37]

Summary

1. A testimony of the divinity of Jesus is a gift of the Spirit.

2. This testimony must be gained if one is to obtain eternal life in the celestial kingdom.

3. A testimony of Jesus is granted to man in one or a combination of four ways:

    A. by actual appearance or other manifestation of the Savior,

    B. by the testimony of God the Father,

    C. by revelation through the Holy Ghost, and

    D. by the testimonies borne by others.

4. The divinity of Jesus was manifested by his ability to conquer death and return to life through the resurrection process.

5. Jesus made numerous appearances to his followers in Palestine after His resurrection as recorded in the New Testament.

6. The resurrected Christ also appeared to the people of the Americas, as recorded in the Book of Mormon. His visits for three days in succession to the Nephites and Lamanites in the land Bountiful, plus his appearances to Mormon and Moroni are cited in the chapter.

7. Many of the appearances and other communications of the Savior in the last days were cited.

---

37. Jn. 14:21-23.

8. A composite description drawn from the testimonies of those who have seen the resurrected Savior would describe Him as having

    A. a dignified bearing,

    B. snow white hair,

    C. eyes like a flame of fire,

    D. a countenance which radiates a brilliant light which eclipses the noon-day sun,

    E. a pavement of gold beneath his feet,

    F. nail prints in His hands and feet,

    G. exactly the same features and likeness as God the Father,

    H. a voice as of the sound of many rushing waters,

    I. the ability to cry, smile, kiss, and embrace,

    J. the ability to stand motionless in the air.

9. To see the Savior causes one to feel a sense of peace and sublimity. It is described as being a feeling worth more than all man can be or possess.

10. The Savior has granted His self-manifestations to many members of the Church without restrictions as to Church position, Priesthood authority, age, experience, or walk of life.

11. It should be noted that a significant percentage of the recorded appearances of Jesus have been to children in their middle "teens" or younger.

12. No man can see the Savior in the flesh unless he is quickened by the Spirit of God.

13. The Savior has promised that He will manifest Himself unto those who keep His commandments and who love Him.

CHAPTER IV

A Testimony of The Divinity of Jesus Christ Through Belief in The Witness of Others

While some individuals have been so richly blessed as to have seen the resurrected Savior, it is probable that most people will gain their testimony of His divinity by hearing and accepting the testimony of others. The ability to gain a testimony in this manner is of itself a rich blessing. It too comes as a gift of the Spirit. As the Lord revealed in the *Doctrine and Covenants*, to some it is given to "know that Jesus Christ is the Son of God, and that he was crucified for the sins of the world. *To others it is given to believe on their words,* that they also might have eternal life if they continue faithful."[1] This chapter will examine the manner in which testimony of Christ's divinity has been borne by (1) God the Father (2) the Holy Ghost, and (3) Church officials and other members of the Church.

Knowledge of Christ's Divinity Through the Testimony of God the Father

Certainly it would be a marvelous experience to hear the voice of the Father testifying to the divine sonship of His Only Begotten just as it would be to witness an appearance of the resurrected Christ. Such testimony is even less common than the self-manifestations of Jesus Christ. Like the appearances of the Savior, such manifestations from the Father are given at His choosing rather than man's. To the recipients they come as gifts from the Divine, and what choice gifts they are!

An important factor in the father-son relationship of Jesus and His Eternal Father is the willingness of the latter to testify of the divinity of His firstborn Son. Jesus asserted this willingness to a group of Pharisees who were doubting His words because they were not supported by the testimony of others.

---

1. D & C 46:13-14.

He told His challengers, "I am not alone, but I and the Father that sent me. It is also written in your law, that the testimony of two men is true. I am one that bear witness of myself, and *the Father that sent me beareth witness of me.*"[2] What other testimony could be more valid than that of God the Father! More than any mortal being, He knows of the blessings and divinity which He has bestowed upon Jesus, "For as the Father hath life in himself; *so hath he given to the Son to have life in himself; And hath given him authority* to execute judgment also, because he is the Son of man."[3] It was because of this relationship that the Savior proclaimed, "All things are delivered to me of my Father: and no man knoweth who the Son is, but the Father."[4]

It should be noted that most of the communications from the Father which men have received have filled the specific purpose of confirming the divine Sonship of Jesus. Such was the testimony given at the Savior's baptism, at which a voice from heaven proclaimed, *"This is my beloved Son, in whom I am well pleased."*[5] A similar witness was given to Peter, James, and John at the time of Christ's transfiguration: While he [Peter] yet spake, behold, a bright cloud overshadowed them: and behold a voice out of the cloud, which said, *This is my beloved Son, in whom I am well pleased; hear ye him.*"[6]

The voice of the Father was heard in answer to Jesus' prayer following His triumphal entry into Jerusalem. Because He knew that the time for His trial and suffering was very near, Jesus prayed for help from above. In doing so He said, "Father glorify thy name." A voice from heaven responded with the words, *"I have both glorified it, and will glorify it again."*[7]

God the Father testified of the divinity of His Son to the righteous inhabitants of the Americas just before the Savior

---

2. Jn. 8:16-18.
3. Jn. 5:26-27.
4. Lk. 10:22.
5. Mt. 3:17.
6. Mt. 17:5.
7. Jn. 12:28. These words from the Father were also in the nature of a testimony of the divinity of Jesus, for the account continues:
   The people therefore, that stood by, and heard it, said that it thundered: others said, An angel spake to him.
   Jesus answered and said, *This voice came not because of me, but for your sakes.* (Jn. 12:29-30).

descended to them from the heavens. Once more His witness to the people was, *"Behold my beloved Son, in whom I am well pleased, in whom I have glorified my name — hear ye him."*[8]

Again, with this pattern of scriptures as a background, the Father's words to Joseph Smith in the latter days become more beautiful and meaningful. Now once more the voice of God the Father has been heard to bear witness of the divinity of Jesus Christ, saying, *"This is My Beloved Son. Hear Him!"*[9]

The testimony of the Father is the second way in which the gift of a deep and undeviating testimony of the divinity of Jesus is bestowed upon man. It is the rarest of the four methods being considered. Care should be taken in regard to this gift, however, for such a manifestation carries with it a tremendous responsibility.

If we receive the witness of men, *the witness of God is greater: for this is the witness of God which he hath testified of his Son.*

He that believeth on the Son of God hath the witness in himself: *he that believeth not God hath made him a liar; because he believeth not the record that God gave of his Son.*

And this is the record, that God hath given to us eternal life, and this life is in his Son.

He that hath the Son hath life, and he that hath not the Son of God hath not life.[10]

Knowledge of Christ's Divinity Through the Witness of the Holy Ghost

"For behold, and lo, *the Lord is God, and the Spirit beareth record*, and the record is true, and the truth abideth forever and ever. Amen."[11] The Holy Ghost attests not only to the divinity

---

8. 3 Ne. 11:7. The description of the Father's voice which is given in this chapter is interesting:

> And it came to pass that while they were thus conversing one with another, they heard a voice as if it came out of heaven; and they cast their eyes round about, for they understood not the voice which they heard; and *it was not a harsh voice, neither was it a loud voice;* nevertheless, and notwithstanding it being a small voice *it did pierce them that did hear to the center, insomuch that there was no part of their frame that it did not cause to quake; yea it did pierce them to the very soul, and did cause their hearts to burn.* (3 Ne. 11:3).

9. JS 2:17.
10. I Jn. 5:9-12.
11. D & C 1:39.

of Christ, but it also is He "which manifesteth that Jesus was
crucified by sinful men for the sins of the world, yea, for the
remission of sins unto the contrite heart."[12] It is also through the
Holy Spirit that Jesus is "declared to be the Son of God with
power, according to the spirit of holiness, by the resurrection
from the dead."[13]

It would seem that such a manifestation of the Spirit is
what produced the undisputable testimony of Simeon, who recognized the divinity of the baby Jesus when the Savior first was
brought to the Temple:

> And behold, there was a man in Jerusalem, whose name
> was Simeon: and the same man was just and devout, waiting
> for the consolation of Israel: and the Holy Ghost was upon him.
>
> *And it was revealed unto him by the Holy Ghost, that he
> should not see death, before he had seen the Lord's Christ.*
>
> And he came by the Spirit into the temple: and when the
> parents brought in the child Jesus, to do for him after the
> custom of the law,
>
> Then took he him up in his arms, and blessed God, and
> said,
>
> Lord, now lettest thou thy servant depart in peace, accord-
> ing to thy word:
>
> For mine eyes have seen thy salvation.[14]

In like manner John the Baptist, who was filled with the
Holy Ghost from his mother's womb,[15] had the gift of knowledge
that Jesus is the Son of God.

> And John bare record, saying, *I saw the Spirit descending
> from heaven like a dove, and it abode upon him.*
>
> And I knew him not: but he that sent me to baptize with
> water, the same said unto me, Upon whom thou shalt see the
> Spirit descending, and remaining on him, the same is he which
> baptizeth with the Holy Ghost.
>
> And I saw, and bare record that this is the Son of God.[16]

Modern day experiences also tell of the manner in which the
Holy Ghost bears witness of the divinity of Christ. Consider

12.   D & C 21:9.
13.   Rom. 1:4.
14.   Lk. 2:25-30.
15.   D & C 84:27.
16.   Jn. 1:32-34.

the experience of Lorenzo Snow at the time of his baptism
(June 1836). Upon joining the Church he diligently sought to
obtain a personal testimony and retired to a secret place to seek
the Lord in humble prayer. This is his account of his experience:

> I had no sooner opened my lips in an effort to pray than
> I heard a sound just above my head like the rushing of silken
> robes; and immediately *the Spirit of God descended upon me,
> completely enveloping my whole person, filling me from the
> crown of my head to the soles of my feet, and oh, the joyful
> happiness I felt!* No language can describe the almost instan-
> taneous transition from a dense cloud of spiritual darkness into
> a refulgence of light and knowledge, as it was at that time
> imparted to my understanding. *I received a perfect knowledge
> that God lives, that Jesus Christ is the Son of God, and of
> the restoration of the Holy Priesthood, and the fulness of the
> gospel. It was a complete baptism — a tangible immersion in
> the heavenly principle or element, the Holy Ghost;* and even
> more physical in its effects upon every part of my system than
> the immersion by water.[17]

The Holy Ghost does not only bear direct witness of the
divinity of Christ. He also reveals that certain individuals are
true representatives of the Savior and that their testimony of
the Savior may be accepted and believed. This gift was often
manifested, for instance, to those who met the prophet Joseph
Smith for the first time. Amasa M. Lyman, who later became a
member of the Quorum of the Twelve, wrote of his first meeting
with the prophet while he [Amasa] was a youth of nineteen:

> This . . . afforded me an opportunity to see the man of
> God. Of the impressions produced I will here say, although
> there was nothing strange or different from other men in his
> personal appearance, yet, when he grasped my hand in that cor-
> dial way (known to those who have met him in the honest sim-
> plicity of truth), I felt as one of old in the presence of the Lord;
> my strength seemed to be gone, so that it required an effort on
> my part to stand on my feet; but in all this there was no fear,
> but the serenity and peace of heaven pervaded my soul, and
> *the still small voice of the spirit whispered its living testimony
> in the depths of my soul, where it has ever remained, that he
> was the Man of God.*[18]

---

17. Jenson, I, p. 27.
18. Jenson, I, p. 97.

It must be recognized that the Holy Ghost is instrumental in any testimony which a man may gain of the divinity of Jesus, whether that testimony may come by appearance of the Savior, the witness of God the Father, through belief on the word of others, or through personal study and promptings. This was the apostle Paul's understanding when he wrote, "Wherefore I give you to understand, that no man speaking by the Spirit of God calleth Jesus accursed: and that *no man can say that Jesus is the Lord, but by the Holy Ghost*.[19]

Though man may receive his testimony from various sources, yet it is the Holy Ghost working within the individual which makes him receptive to the influence of the others. If the individual is not prepared to receive the testimony of others by the Holy Ghost, then even an appearance of the Savior would be of relatively little value to him. Nor is he able to read and study and strengthen his knowledge and testimony. As Nephi wrote,

> When a man speaketh by the power of the Holy Ghost *the power of the Holy Ghost carrieth it unto the hearts of the children of men.*
>
> But behold, there are many that harden their hearts against the Holy Spirit; that it hath no place in them; wherefore, *they cast many things away* which are written and esteem them as things of naught.[20]

Just as a warning accompanied the promise of a witness from the Father, the scriptures also caution man about forfeiting a testimony obtained through the Holy Ghost. Paul wrote to the Hebrews that

> It is impossible for those who were once enlightened, and have tasted of the heavenly gift, and were made partakers of the Holy Ghost,
>
> And have tasted the good word of God, and the powers of the world to come,
>
> *If they shall fall away, to renew them again unto repentance;* seeing they crucify to themselves the Son of God afresh, and put him to an open shame.[21]

---

19. I Cor. 12:3. Joseph Smith taught that this passage should be translated "no man can *know* that Jesus is the Lord, but by the Holy Ghost." (HC, IV, p. 603).
20. 2 Ne. 33:1-2.
21. Heb. 6:4-6.

The Holy Ghost may reveal a testimony of Jesus with such convincing power, such conclusiveness, as to place the recipient beyond the range of doubt. Such a testimony is even more binding upon an individual than receiving an appearance of the Savior, and to deny it is considered blasphemy against the Holy Ghost, which is unpardonable:

> Wherefore I say unto you, All manner of sin and blasphemy shall be forgiven unto men: but the blasphemy against the Holy Ghost shall not be forgiven unto men.

> And whosoever speaketh a word against the Son of man, it shall be forgiven him: *but whosoever speaketh against the Holy Ghost, it shall not be forgiven him, neither in this world, neither in the world to come.*[22]

Knowledge of Christ's Divinity Through Belief on the Words of Others

To some God sees fit to grant a testimony of Christ in a different form than through direct revelation from the Spirit, the Son, or the Father. Many people are given the ability to know that Jesus is a divine Being through their belief on the words of others. Such a blessing is carefully designated as being a gift of the Spirit,[23] although it is not always accompanied by special revelation or spiritual manifestation. It is a choice gift, however, for the Savior held that those who gained their knowledge of His divinity through this gift were more blessed than those to whom He appeared. To his followers in the Americas He said,

> Blessed are ye if ye shall believe in me and be baptized, after that ye have seen me and know that I am.

> And again, *more blessed are they who shall believe in your words because that ye shall testify that ye have seen me, and that ye know that I am.* Yea, blessed are they who shall believe in your words, and come down into the depths of humility and be baptized, for they shall be visited with fire and with the Holy Ghost, and shall receive a remission of their sins.[24]

---

22. Mt. 12:31-32. See also D & C 132:27; 76:31-35, 44-46; Heb. 6:4-6; HC, VI, pp. 314-315; Joseph Fielding Smith, *Answers to Gospel Questions,* Vol. I, p. 78.
23. D & C 46:14.
24. 3 Ne. 12:1-2.

Testimony of Christ From the Scriptures

Many people gain their testimony of Jesus after prayerful study of the scriptures. The Book of Mormon is particularly dedicated to the convincing of mankind that Jesus is the Christ and that salvation comes through Him. Nephi, as he began the record, set this pattern and design for the book with the statement that *"the fulness of mine intent is that I may persuade men to come unto the God of Abraham, and the God of Isaac, and the God of Jacob, and be saved."*[25] He made a solemn proclamation to all the world of the relationship of the Book of Mormon to the truths the Savior taught:

> And now, my beloved brethren, and also Jew, and all ye ends of the earth, hearken unto these words and believe in Christ; and if ye believe not in these words believe in Christ. And *if ye shall believe in Christ ye will believe in these words, for they are the words of Christ, and he hath given them unto me;* and they teach all men that they should do good.
>
> And if they are not the words of Christ, judge ye — for Christ will show unto you, with power and great glory, that they are his words, at the last day; and you and I shall stand face to face before his bar; and ye shall know that I have been commanded of him to write these things, notwithstanding my weakness.[26]

The Bible also is written to bring men to believe in Christ. The admonition of Jesus concerning this record was to "search the scriptures; for in them ye think ye have eternal life: and *they are they which testify of me.*[27] This formula of scriptural study which leads to conversion was followed by the Saints in Paul's day, "In that they received the word with all readiness of mind, and *searched the scriptures daily, whether those things were so. Therefore many of them believed;* also of honourable women which were Greeks, and of men, not a few."[28]

Testimony of Christ from the Prophets

Just as the study of the scriptures can aid man in gaining a testimony of Christ, so also can such a testimony follow from the heeding of the words of living prophets. To each generation God

---

25. 1 Ne. 6:4. See also 1 Ne. 19:17-18.
26. 2 Ne. 33:10-11.
27. Jn. 5:39.
28. Acts 17:11-12.

sends men who are His representatives, called to preach and testify of the divinity of the Savior. The voice of the prophets of today is a vital force in bearing witness of Christ. Those who heed their words can partake of this gift of the Spirit through belief in their message.

Throughout history the major theme of the prophets has been the divinity of Christ. Indeed, "None of the prophets have written, nor prophesied, save they have spoken concerning this Christ."[29] And throughout history the prophets have declared the word of Christ to their generation, conversions often following from among their hearers through the gift of the Spirit. Abinadi testified:

> Behold I say unto you, that *whosoever has heard the words of the prophets, yea, all the holy prophets who have prophesied concerning the coming of the Lord* — I say unto you, that all those who have hearkened unto their words, and believed that the Lord would redeem his people, and have looked forward to that day for a remission of their sins, *I say unto you, that these are his seed, or they are the heirs of the kingdom of God.*[30]

Conversion Through the Preaching and Example of Believers

Certainly there are many people who have gained their testimony of Christ's divinity through their discussions and relationship with individuals who are already converted. Every Church member should remember his responsibility given in the Lord's commandment: "Behold, I sent you out to testify and warn the people, and it *becometh every man who hath been warned to warn his neighbor.* Therefore, they are left without excuse, and their sins are upon their own heads."[31] In this day of "every member a missionary" the failure to preach "Jesus Christ and him crucified"[32] is enough to cause an individual to reap the Lord's displeasure. He has said that

> *With some I am not well pleased, for they will not open their mouths, but they hide the talent which I have given unto them, because of the fear of man.* Wo unto such, for mine anger is kindled against them.

---

29. Jac. 7:11.
30. Mos. 15:11.
31. D & C 88:81-82.
32. I Cor. 2:2.

> And it shall come to pass, if they are not more faithful unto me, it shall be taken away, even that which they have. . . .
>
> Behold, *they have been sent to preach my gospel among the congregations of the wicked;* wherefore, I give unto them a commandment, thus: Thou shalt not idle away thy time, neither shalt thou bury thy talent that it may not be known.[33]

Those members of the church who fail to set a good example would do well to consider the seriousness of hampering the Lord's work. They may be like Corianton, to whom his father, Alma, said, *"When they saw your conduct they would not believe in my words."*[34] It would be much better if such individuals would remember Paul's admonition to *"be thou an example of the believers, in word, in conversation, in charity, in spirit, in faith, in purity."*[35]

Knowledge of Jesus' divinity through direct means and belief in His divinity through acceptance of the witness borne by others are two of the fundamental gifts which God bestows on man. To one a spiritual manifestation or appearance of Deity is given which shows him the divinity of Jesus. To another the path lies with careful listening to and evaluation of the words of those about him and through diligent and prayerful study of the scriptures. At times the two gifts are shown together and may be contrasted. Such is the case in the instance of the Samaritan woman at the well whom Jesus taught and converted. She went and taught her friends, and brought them to hear the Master. Many believed her words, but others were not converted until they saw Jesus Himself:

> And many of the Samaritans of that city *believed on him for the saying of the woman,* which testified, He told me all that ever I did.
>
> So when the Samaritans were come unto him, they besought him that he would tarry with them: and he abode there two days.
>
> *And many more believed because of his own word;*
>
> And said unto the woman, *Now we believe, not because of thy saying: for we have heard him ourselves, and know that this is indeed the Christ, the Savior of the world.*[36]

---

33. D & C 60:2-3, 13.
34. Al. 39:11.
35. I Tim. 4:12.
36. Jn. 4:39-42.

Just as the two gifts may be contrasted, it must be noted that they can accompany one another. The individual who gains a testimony of the divinity of Jesus by one gift is often blessed and given a strengthening of his testimony through the second gift. Both gifts are choice offerings of the Spirit and are well worthy of a place as goals in following the admonition to "seek ye earnestly the best gifts."

Summary

1. To some individuals is granted the spiritual gift of a testimony of the divinity of Jesus through belief on the testimony of others.

2. There are several instances on record in the scriptures in which God the Father has spoken from the heavens to bear witness of the divine nature of His son Jesus.

3. The Holy Ghost testifies that Jesus is divine, that He was crucified for the sins of the world, and that He was resurrected from the dead.

4. Although man may gain a knowledge of the divinity of Christ from several sources, the testimony of the truthfulness of that knowledge comes only through the Holy Ghost. His is the only power by which men can know that Jesus is the Lord.

5. To rebel against a sure knowledge of the divinity of Christ which has been granted by the Holy Ghost is a grievious sin for which there is no pardon.

6. The scriptures are written to convince mankind that Jesus is the Christ. A testimony of His divinity may be obtained through the means of scriptural study.

7. The labor and message of the prophets down through the ages has been to convince men of the divinity of Christ. A testimony may be obtained through faithful acceptance of their words.

8. Every member of the Church has the responsibility to preach the good news of Christ's divinity to those with whom

he is associated. Each member should set a proper example so that others will heed his words.

9. The gifts of a manifestation of Christ and of belief in his divinity through the testimony of others may be granted at the same time.

CHAPTER V

Godly Knowledge

Knowledge the Key to the Celestial Kingdom

Among the most coveted of all the gifts of the Spirit is the gift of knowledge. Throughout history, man has sought for knowledge of the world around him; for understanding of the marvels of nature; for the ability to comprehend art, history, economics, science; and myriads of other endeavors of the mind. For some types of knowledge man must rely on the guidance of the Holy Ghost. Such knowledge is granted to many only in accordance with the will of God and with man's individual efforts to obtain it. For obtaining knowledge man must always pay a price of time and effort. The shortness of his mortal span limits him, and compels him to choose the knowledge which best deserves his earnest inquiry. This gift of the Spirit is of great value to man as he seeks to make this choice, for it leads him to direct his efforts toward the things of God and to those principles which will lead him toward exaltation. Through this gift he seeks to obtain *"the keys of the kingdom, which consist in the key of knowledge."*[1]

Knowledge of God and His Plans for Mankind

It was Samuel the Lamanite who centered the definition of knowledge in religious principles, for he taught that men must be *"brought to the true knowledge, which is the knowledge of their Redeemer."*[2] The knowledge of God and his program for mankind must be the central theme of life, the hub of the wheel from which all else radiates. This was basic to the teaching and philosophy of the great and righteous King Benjamin, who taught that

> *As ye have come to the knowledge of the glory of God, or if ye have known of his goodness and have tasted of his love,* and have received a remission of your sins, which causeth such

---

1. D & C 128:14.
2. Hel. 15:13.

exceeding great joy in your souls, even so I would that ye
should remember, and always retain in remembrance, the great-
ness of God, and your own nothingness, and his goodness and
long-suffering towards you, unworthy creatures, and humble
yourselves even in the depth of humility, calling on the name
of the Lord daily, and standing steadfastly in the faith of that
which is to come, which was spoken by the mouth of the angel.

And behold, I say unto you that if ye do this ye shall always
rejoice, and be filled with the love of God, and always retain a
remission of your sins; and *ye shall grow in the knowledge of
the glory of him that created you, or in the knowledge of that
which is just and true.*[3]

Knowledge of God is a foundation stone, a basic building
block upon which all other knowledge and spiritual growth must
be predicated. Peter knew this; he taught that grace and peace
come from this knowledge. The way is then paved for man to
enter into the kingdom of heaven. Knowledge of God is the
first step, which precedes even faith:

Grace and peace be multiplied unto you, *through the knowledge of God, and of Jesus our Lord.*

According as his divine power hath given unto us all things
that pertain unto life and godliness, *through the knowledge of
him that hath called us to glory and virtue:*

Whereby are given unto us exceeding great and precious
promises: that by these ye might be partakers of the divine
nature, having escaped the corruption that is in the world
through lust.

And beside this, giving all diligence add to your faith
virtue; and to virtue *knowledge;*

And to knowledge *temperance;* and to temperance *patience;*
and to patience *godliness;*

And to godliness *brotherly kindness;* and to brotherly kindness *charity.*

*For if these things be in you, and abound, they make you
that ye shall neither be barren nor unfruitful in the knowledge
of our Lord Jesus Christ.*

But he that lacketh these things is blind, and cannot see
afar off, and hath forgotten that he was purged from his old sins.

---

3. Mos. 4:11-12.

Wherefore the rather, brethren, give diligence to make your calling and election sure: for if ye do these things, ye shall never fall:

For so an entrance shall be ministered unto you abundantly into the everlasting kingdom of our Lord and Savior Jesus Christ.[4]

It seems that it was the process of building upon the knowledge of God to which Paul referred when he spoke of the Savior and said that *"in every thing ye are enriched by him, in all utterance, and in all knowledge."*[5]

Knowledge of Good and Evil

Another type of knowledge has been given by God to man which also aids him in progressing toward exaltation. As Samuel the Lamanite taught,

Whosoever perisheth, perisheth unto himself; and whosoever doeth iniquity, doeth it unto himself; for behold, ye are free; ye are permitted to act for yourselves; for behold, *God hath given unto you a knowledge and he hath made you free.*

He hath given unto you that ye might know good from evil, and he hath given unto you that ye might choose life or death; and ye can do good and be restored unto that which is good, or have that which is good restored unto you; or ye can do evil, and have that which is evil restored unto you.[6]

A fundamental principle of the Gospel of Jesus Christ is that man has been given the knowledge of good and evil and that he is free to act and choose on the basis of that knowledge. It seems that few have stopped to consider that this knowledge is also a gift to man — a gift of the Spirit.[7] According to the Lord, this gift was first given to man in the Garden of Eden. He said, *"I gave unto them their knowledge,* in the day I created them; and in the Garden of Eden, gave I unto man his agency."[8]

Godly Knowledge to Stabilize Faith

Knowledge is revealed by the Holy Ghost for various purposes. One of the most important is that revealed knowledge serves to stabilize one's faith in the restored gospel and in the

---

4. II Pet. 1:2-11.
5. I Cor. 1:5.
6. Hel. 14:30-31.
7. I Cor. 12:8; D & C 46:18; Moro. 10:10.
8. Moses 7:32.

Church. It is recorded, for instance, that such a manifestation was granted to the mother of David Whitmer during the difficult period when Joseph Smith and Oliver Cowdery were translating the Book of Mormon while living in the Whitmer home. David Whitmer stated that a heavenly messenger appeared to her and showed her the Book of Mormon plates.

> . . . My mother was going to milk the cows, when she was met out near the yard by the same old man (judging by her description of him), who said to her: 'You have been very faithful and diligent in your labors, but you are tired because of the increase in your toil; *it is proper, therefore, that you should receive a witness that your faith may be strengthened.' Thereupon he showed her the plates.* My father and mother had a large family of their own, the addition to it, therefore, of Joseph, his wife Emma and Oliver very greatly increased the toil and anxiety of my mother. And although she had never complained she had sometimes felt that her labor was too much, or at least she was perhaps beginning to feel so. *This circumstance, however, completely removed all such feelings and nerved her up for her increased responsibilities.*[9]

Apparently a similar manifestation of the Book of Mormon plates was granted to strengthen the faith of Harrison Burgess in the year 1833. At this time he was a young man of nineteen and had belonged to the Church for less than a year:

> On the third Sabbath in May while speaking to a congregation I declared that I knew that the Book of Mormon and the work of God were true. The next day while laboring in the field something seemed to whisper to me, "*Do you know the Book of Mormon is true?*" *My mind became perplexed and darkened, and I was so tormented in spirit that I left my work and retired into the woods. The misery and distress that I there experienced cannot be described.* The tempter all the while seemed to say, "Do you know the Book of Mormon is true?' I remained in this situation about two hours. Finally I resolved to know, by exercising faith similar to that which the brother of Jared possessed, whether I had proclaimed the truth or not, and commenced praying to the God of heaven for a testimony of these things. *Suddenly a glorious personage clothed in white stood before me and exhibited to my view the plates from which the Book of Mormon was taken.*[10]

---

9. Jenson, I, p. 267. The "old man" apparently was Moroni.
10. *Labors in the Vineyard,* pp. 65-66.

Elder Thomas Ball, who later became patriarch of the Summit Stake, was granted a dream in 1848 in Whitwick, Leicestershire, England. The purpose of this dream seemed to be to strengthen and stabilize his faith.

> Soon after joining the Church he had rather an impressive dream, which portrayed to him some scenes of Church history, and the personalities of the Prophet Joseph Smith and his Brother Hyrum, laying in their coffins, and others. In his dream a hymn was sung to him, the tune and words of which he was utterly unacquainted with. The dream having impressed him greatly he called the next day upon a Sister Bailey, to whom he related the dream and kindly asked her to sing over what Church hymn tunes she could think of. She did so, and at length came to the hymn commencing with "When we came to the place where the two martyrs lay." "That is the very tune and the very words that I heard in my dream," he said. He had never heard them before.[11]

Godly Knowledge to Show the Will of God

Just as the Holy Ghost reveals knowledge from on high to stabilize man's faith, He also reveals godly knowledge to indicate to man the will and desires of the Divine. Newel K. Whitney was one who learned the Lord's will through revelation. While living in Kirtland, Elder Whitney was called by the prophet Joseph Smith to serve as the presiding bishop over the Eastern branches of the Church. The thought of the great magnitude of the responsibility was overwhelming to him, and he doubted his ability to fulfill the calling successfully. In desperation he appealed to the prophet,

> 'I cannot see a Bishop in myself, Brother Joseph; but if you say it's the Lord's will, I'll try.' 'You need not take my word alone,' answered the Prophet, kindly, *'Go and ask Father for yourself.'* Newel felt the force of this mild rebuke, but determined to do as he was advised. His humble, heartfelt prayer was answered. *In the silence of night and the solitude of his chamber he heard a voice from heaven: 'Thy strength is in me.' The words were few and simple, but they had a world of meaning. His doubts were dispelled like the dew before the dawn.* He straightway sought the Prophet, told him he was satisfied, and was willing to accept the office to which he had been called.[12]

---

11. Jenson, II, p. 259.
12. Jenson, I, p. 224.

Another example of the manner in which the Holy Ghost
has revealed knowledge indicating the will of God is the revelation given to Mary Smith Ellsworth in a women's meeting held
in Lehi, Utah, in the fall of 1903. At this time, a strong feeling
had been developing among the young against the practice of
rearing large families. The following was revealed to Sister Ellsworth through the gift of tongues:

> I, the Lord, love the women of Zion above all other women
> for their willingness to bear the souls of choice spirits in these
> latter days, and when they have finished their missions on
> earth they will be thrice welcome in my Kingdom, and crowned
> above all other women.[13]

Godly Knowledge to Further God's Work

Many times godly knowledge is imparted unto man to aid
in furthering the Lord's work. A good instance of this can be
found in the manifestation granted to many of the Saints shortly
after the death of Joseph the Prophet. Sidney Rigdon had
returned from the East and was seeking to take control of the
Church, while the Quorum of the Twelve asserted that the
authority was vested in them. On August 8, 1848, a meeting of
the Church was held at Nauvoo to decide to whom the allegiance
of the Church would be given. At this meeting God revealed His
will by causing the mantle of the Prophet to fall over the President of the Twelve, Brigham Young, as he addressed the congregation. Although the people knew it was Brigham Young,
he appeared and spoke like Joseph Smith. Many who were
present left their testimonies of this sign. Typical is the record
left by Jacob Hamblin, who wrote

> On the 8th of August, 1844, I attended a general meeting
> of the Saints. Elder Rigdon was there, urging his claims to the
> presidency of the Church. His voice did not sound like the
> voice of the true shepherd. When he was about to call a vote
> of the congregation to sustain him as President of the Church,
> Elders Brigham Young, Parley P. Pratt and Heber C. Kimball
> stepped into the stand.

> Brigham Young remarked to the congregation: 'I will
> manage this voting for Elder Rigdon. He does not preside here.

---

13. German E. Ellsworth and Mary Smith Ellsworth (comp.) and John
    Orval Ellsworth (ed), *Our Ellsworth Ancestors* (Salt Lake City: Utah
    Printing Company, 1956) p. 58. Sister Ellsworth was the grandmother
    of the author's wife.

This child' (meaning himself) 'will manage this flock for a season.' *The voice and gestures of the man were those of the Prophet Joseph.*

The people with few exceptions, visibly saw that the mantle of the prophet Joseph had fallen upon Brigham Young. To some it seemed as though Joseph again stood before them.

I arose to my feet and said to a man sitting by me, 'That is the voice of the true shepherd — the chief of the Apostles.'[14]

Other instances of godly knowledge being revealed to further the Lord's work are known. The mother of Elder Melvin J. Ballard wrote of an experience which occurred in Logan, Utah, on May 19, 1844. The Logan Temple had been dedicated the day previous and President John Taylor had said that those members who were worthy and who desired to go through the Temple might do so the next day. Concerning the experience of her family, Sister Ballard wrote,

My husband being a bishop, was very busy writing out recommends to all who wished to go through the temple, when my daughter, Ellen, came in and asked for her father. I told her that her father was busy and asked her to give the newspaper, which she had in her hand, to me so that I might give it to him. She said: 'No, the man who gave the paper to me told me to give it to no one but Father.' I let the child take the paper to her father, and when he looked it over, he was greatly surprised for *he saw that the paper had been printed in Berkshire, England, his birthplace, and was only four days from the press.* He was so amazed at such an incident that he called Ellen and asked her where the man was who had given her the paper. She said that she was playing on the sidewalk with other children when two men came down the street walking in the middle of the road. One of them called to her, saying: 'Come here, little girl.' She hesitated at first, for there were other little girls with her. Then he pointed to

---

14. *Jacob Hamblin,* pp. 19-20. Similar references are legion. The event was so well known that many ceased to describe it in detail. Edmund Lovell Ellsworth, in his autobiography, wrote:
    I was present at the meeting which heard President Sidney Rigdon. I plainly saw the mantle of Priesthood fall upon President Young with its power and spirit. The testimony of this was given to most of the congregation. (*Our Ellsworth Ancestors,* pp. 89-90).
    William Carbine, who was only nine years old at the time, later wrote, "Though I was only a boy, I remember it distinctly, and I told my mother that the Prophet was not dead, for I had seen him on the stand' (Jenson, III, p. 41).

her and said: 'You.' She went out, and he gave her the paper and told her to give it to her father. *This paper contained about sixty names of the dead acquaintances of my husband, giving the dates of their birth and death. My husband was baptized for the men, and I for the women, and all of the work was done for them. Again I felt the Lord was mindful of us in blessing us abundantly.*[15]

Godly knowledge to further the Lord's work was revealed to President German E. Ellsworth, president of the Northern States Mission, in June of 1907. At this time President Ellsworth was visiting the Sacred Grove and the Hill Cumorah in the company of George Albert Smith for the purpose of purchasing the Joseph Smith homestead for the Church. While waiting for the title to be cleared, President Ellsworth frequently walked the three miles from Palmyra to Cumorah to pray and meditate there. One morning, at sunrise, a voice from beyond the veil spoke to him and told him to "*Push the distribution of the record taken from this hill; it will help bring the world to Christ.*"[16]

---

15. Hinckley, *Sermons and Missionary Experiences of Melvin J. Ballard*, p. 18.
16. *Our Ellsworth Ancestors*, p. 55. Details as to how he carried out this command have been summarized as follows:
   German followed the admonition by injecting enthusiasm and inspiration for the value of the God-given Book of Mormon as a witness for Christ. A postcard picture of the Hill Cumorah with this statement was sent to all Northern States missionaries and to all Mission Presidents. German E. was invited to visit all U. S. missions in order to spark the wider use of the Book of Mormon as a missionary medium. At one mission, Apostle George Albert Smith said, 'President Ellsworth, you haven't said a thing I wanted you to say. Get up and give them your conviction that there is no missionary book equal to the Book of Mormon, the one given by the Lord for the convicing of both Jew and Gentile that Jesus is the Christ.' (The Book of Mormon was the exclusive book used by early missionaries from 1830-1837).
   President Joseph F. Smith sent for President Ellsworth to spend a day with Elder Melvin J. Ballard before going as a new Mission President to the Northwestern States Mission in order to encourage the wider use of the Book of Mormon in that Mission. From a few hundred copies shipped to the Missions of the Church (at 37½ cents per copy) from the Desert News in Salt Lake City, a Chicago edition of ten thousand from new plates was printed at a cost of 27 cents, including new plates. This was followed by a fifteen thousand edition at 24 cents per copy, and then many additions (sic) of twenty-five thousand at 18 cents per copy over the years, and finally a one hundred thousand-copy edition of the same quality was printed in Chicago at 12½ cents per copy just prior to the establishing of Zion's Printing Company in Indepen-

This revelation changed the course of the missionary program of the Church for many years, for President Ellsworth effected a new proselyting approach based upon the use of the Book of Mormon which spread rapidly to other missions.

Godly Knowledge to Increase Personal Understanding

Revelation is often given to help individuals understand the nature and true meaning of events which influence their lives. Godly knowledge helps man to recognize the influence of the Almighty in shaping his life. Heber J. Grant wrote of such a revelation which was given to his twelve-year-old daughter at the time of the passing of Sister Grant:

> About one hour before my wife died, I called my children into her room and told them that their mother was dying and for them to bid her good-bye. One of the little girls, about twelve years of age, said to me: 'Papa, I do not want my mama to die. I have been with her in the hospital in San Francisco for six months. Time and time again when mama was in distress, you have administered to her, and she has been relieved of her pain and quietly gone to sleep. I want you to lay hands upon my mama and heal her.'
>
> 'I told my little girl that we all had to die sometime, and that I felt assured in my heart that her mother's time had arrived. She and the rest of the children left the room.
>
> I then knelt down by the bed of my wife (who by this time had lost consciousness) and I told the Lord I acknowledged His hand in life, in death, in joy, in sorrow, in prosperity, or adversity. I thanked Him for the knowledge I had that my wife belonged to me for all eternity, that through the power and authority of the priesthood here on the earth that I could and would have my wife forever if I were only faithful as she had been. But I told the Lord that I lacked the strength to have my wife die and have it affect the faith of my little children in the ordinances of the Gospel of Jesus Christ; and *I supplicated the Lord with all the strength that I possessed that He would give to that little girl of mine a knowledge that it was His mind and His will that her mama should die.*

---

dence, Missouri to which place all Book of Mormon plates and all plates for various tracts and books that had been printed in Chicago were shipped, from which place millions of books and tracts were printed. (p. 56) President Ellsworth was the grandfather of the author's wife, and husband of Mary Smith Ellsworth, mentioned earlier in the chapter.

Within an hour my wife passed away, and I called the children back into the room. My little boy, about five and one-half or six years of age, was weeping bitterly, and the little girl twelve years of age took him in her arms and said: *'Do not weep, Heber; since we went out of this room, the voice of the Lord from Heaven has said to me, in the death of mamma, the will of the Lord shall be done.'*[17]

President Grant also told of another situation which occurred in connection with the death of his son:

'My last son died of a hip disease. I had built great hopes that he would live to spread the Gospel at home and abroad and be an honor to me. About an hour before he died I had a dream that his mother, who was dead, came for him, and that she brought with her a messenger, and she told this messenger to take the boy while I was asleep. In the dream I thought I awoke, and I seized my son and fought for him and finally succeeded in getting him away from the messenger who had come to take him, and in so doing I dreamed that I stumbled and fell upon him.

'I dreamed that I fell upon his sore hip, and the terrible cries and anguish of the child drove me nearly wild. I could not stand it, and I jumped up and ran out of the house so as not to hear his distress, I dreamed that after running out of the house I met Joseph E. Taylor and told him of these things.

He said: 'Well, Heber, do you know what I would do if my wife came for one of her children — I would not struggle for that child; I would not oppose her taking that child away. *If a mother who had been faithful had passed beyond the veil, she would know of the suffering and the anguish her child may have to suffer. She should know whether that child might go through life as a cripple and whether it would be better or wiser for that child to be relieved from the torture of life.* And when you stop to think, Brother Grant, that the mother of that boy went down into the shadow of death to give him life, she is the one who ought to have the right to take him or leave him.'

I said, 'I believe you are right, Brother Taylor, and if she comes again, she shall have the boy without any protest on my part.'

After coming to that conclusion I was waked by my brother, B. F. Grant, who was staying that night with us. He

---

17. Bryant S. Hinckley, *Heber J. Grant, Highlights in The Life of a Great Leader* (Salt Lake City: Deseret Book Co., 1951) p. 243.

came into the room and told me that the child was dying. I
went in the front room and sat down. There was a vacant
chair between me and my wife who is now living, and *I felt the
presence of that boy's deceased mother sitting in that chair.*
I did not tell anybody what I felt, but I turned to my wife and
said, 'Do you feel anything strange?'

'*Yes, I feel assured that Heber's mother is sitting between
us waiting to take him away.*'[18]

Elder Alonzo A. Hinckley was called on a mission to Holland
in 1897 and left behind a wife who was expecting her second
child. When the time for the arrival of the child drew near,
Elder Hinckley grew very apprehensive and was filled with
anxiety concerning the well-being of his loved ones. Yet he was
blessed with a dream concerning his family and was able to write
the following letter to them:

November 18, 1897. I have never received better news
than I have received from you this morning. I am so happy
and relieved of anxiety that I actually am beside myself. I cannot keep from laughing when I meet any one, and tell them of
my good fortune. I am the most thankful man in Holland; and
I tell you, it did not take me long to get on my knees and
pour out my heart in gratitude to God for his mercies unto us.

I have had such a lovely dream. *I have been with you all
— seen you, my dear wife, and the little newcomer, and all
those kind ones who have surrounded you. I saw you made
comfortable and happy.* It seemed that I was in a hurry to get
off again for Holland. But I first thanked all, with my heart
so full of love that I gathered you all in my arms and embraced
you, and then took one more peek in the door at Rose (his
wife) and the children, and then landed back in Holland. Was
this not a beautiful dream for one in my mood?[19]

The Lord aided Benjamin Brown, an early convert, to bring
his wife to the waters of baptism. For a year and a half following Brother Brown's entrance into the Church his wife had
opposed the work, saying that the Church was poor and had a
bad reputation among her acquaintances. Then the following
manifestation was given to her, together with the revelation of
godly knowledge to her husband:

She dreamed one night that a large company of visitors
had come to her house, for whom she had to prepare supper. On

18. *Ibid.*, pp. 246-48.
19. Hinckley, *Faith of our Pioneer Fathers*, p. 234.

going into her buttery to procure the necessary food to cook, she could only find a small potato, about the size of a robin's egg, lying on a wooden trencher. However, with small stock she commenced, and by some wonderful means converted this little affair into a splendid preparation of pies, puddings, etc.

When they were ready she stood still, wondering how it had all been done, for, as may be supposed, it puzzled her sorely to conceive how, from a small potato, and that on a wooden trencher, she had produced such an elegant entertainment.

Just at this moment while she was thus marveling, *I was awakened from my sleep, with a command sounding in my ears that I was to say to my wife, 'Don't you remember hearing that you should not despise the day of small things?' I was to speak at once, without waiting. So I awoke her, and without any preface did as I was bid.*

The wonderful concurrence of these words with her dream, and the self-evident interpretation of it, referring as it did to her past conduct (for one of the principal reasons of the opposition she felt to my joining the Church was, that she considered it disgraced her to have her husband belong to a Church that was so poor, and everywhere spoken against), so impressed itself upon her mind, with other confirmations, that she was baptized, and has remained firm to the Church ever since.[20]

In each of these instances, revelation of special knowledge from heaven was given to enable the recipient to better understand the nature of important events in their lives.

Knowledge a Preparation for the Hereafter

A powerful lesson is to be gained from the experience of the brother of Jared when he saw the Lord. Because he had a perfect knowledge of God, all other Godly knowledge was opened to him:

> *And because of the knowledge of this man he could not be kept from beholding within the veil;* and he saw the finger of Jesus, which when he saw, he fell with fear; for he knew that it was the finger of the Lord; and he had faith no longer, for he knew, nothing doubting.
>
> *Wherefore, having this perfect knowledge of God, he could not be kept from within the veil;* therefore he saw Jesus; and he did minister unto him. . . .

---

20. *Gems for the Young Folks,* pp. 63-64.

And when the Lord had said these words, he showed unto the brother of Jared all the inhabitants of the earth which had been, and also all that would be; and he withheld them not from his sight, even unto the ends of the earth.

For he had said unto him in times before, that if he would believe in him that he could show unto him all things — it should be shown unto him; *therefore the Lord could not withhold anything from him*, for he knew that the Lord could show him all things.[21]

As it was with the brother of Jared, so it may be with others who would seek to grow through their knowledge of God. Man's growth in knowledge is vital to his well-being in the hereafter, for

Whatever principle of intelligence we attain unto in this life, it will rise with us in the resurrection.

And if a person gains more knowledge and intelligence in this life through his diligence and obedience than another, he will have so much the advantage in the world to come.[22]

Doctrinal Truths Revealed for Individual Progress

It is fundamental to Latter-day Saint belief that every worthy member of the Church who seeks it is entitled to receive understanding and knowledge through the Holy Ghost. This revelation often takes the form of clarification of scriptural teachings or insights into the eternal plan which exceed in scope the stated doctrine of the Church. Such instruction and revelation is intended to increase the knowledge and faith of the person to whom it is revealed but is not intended for the instruction of the general membership of the Church, who may not yet be ready to receive the new teaching. Knowledge of eternal principles which is revealed to individual Church members (while placing added responsibility through added knowledge upon the recipient) does not become the doctrine of the Church, nor does it become binding upon the entire membership of the Church. Nevertheless, it is eternal truth which brings its recipient closer to perfection and exaltation as he applies it in his own life.

Numerous examples of revelations in which Godly knowledge has been imparted to individual members of the Church can be found and cited as examples. It was Lorenzo Snow to whom the

21. Eth. 3:19-20, 25-26.
22. D & C 130:18-19.

profound truism, "As man now is, God once was; as God now is, man may be," was first revealed. The inspiration was given to him when he was twenty-seven years old, a school teacher in Portage County, Ohio.

> This sublime truth was not then known to the Latter-day Saints. It had not been taught by the Prophet, and Brother Snow wisely kept the matter to himself, except that he confided in his sister Eliza R. Snow and President Brigham Young. The latter also cautioned him not to confide the matter to others.[23]

Shortly thereafter he was called on a mission to England, where he labored for three years. It was not until the completion of his mission that he was approached by Brigham Young who "informed Brother Snow that the doctrine he had mentioned concerning God and man was true, the Prophet Joseph Smith having taught it to the Twelve."[24] Here is a choice example of Godly knowledge which was given to an individual but which was not at that time intended for the entire membership of the Church. When the people as a whole were ready, the Prophet became the spokesman for the Lord in presenting the doctrine.

A similar example is found in Joseph Smith's treatment of the remarkable vision granted to Newel Knight during the first conference of the Church (Fayette New York, June 9, 1830). During the conference, Brother Knight was overcome by the Spirit and was laid on a bed, "When all of a sudden a vision of the future burst upon him. He saw there represented the great work which through my instrumentality was yet to be accomplished."[25] Although Newel apparently saw the future course and fate of the Church and made his vision known to Joseph, the Prophet chose to refrain from writing the details into his record. He seemingly regarded the vision as a blessing intended for its recipient only, and not for the entire Church.

How should an individual treat personal revelations concerning doctrinal matters which are granted to him? He should recognize that the revelation was intended for himself and those close to him, and not for Church officials or other members. The advice of Elder John A. Widtsoe should be heeded in this respect:

---

23. Jenson, I, pp. 27-28.
24. Jenson, I, p. 28.
25. HC, I, 85.

Divine manifestations for individual comfort may be received by every worthy member of the Church. In that respect all faithful members of the Church are equal. Such manifestations most commonly *guide the recipients to the solution of personal problems;* though, frequently, *they also open the mind to a clearer comprehension of the Lord's vast plan of salvation.* They are cherished possessions, and should be so valued by those who receive them. In their very nature, they are sacred and should be so treated. *If a person who has received such a manifestation by dream, vision, or otherwise, feels impressed to relate it beyond his immediate family circle, he should present it to his bishop, but not beyond.* The bishop then may decide upon its further use, if any, or may submit it to those of higher authority for action. The gift was a personal one, not for the Church as a whole; and *the recipient is under obligation, in harmony with the established order, not to broadcast it over the Church.*[26]

Certainly it is not the responsibility of lay members to attempt to change the doctrines or policies of the Church by contacting the General Authorities and "setting them straight." If the Lord has policy or doctrinal instructions for the entire Church, He will reveal them to his prophets and have them carried out on a Church-wide level. When individuals are seemingly prompted to "steady the ark" by attempting to correct the prophets called to preside over the Church, it is very possible that they are receiving false revelations from the evil one, Lucifer. Such was the case with Hiram Page, who found a strange stone and began to receive revelations through it. Of him Joseph Smith wrote,

> To our great grief, however, we soon found that Satan had been lying in wait to deceive, and seeking whom he might devour. Brother Hiram Page had in his possesson [sic] a certain stone, by which he had obtained certain "revelations" concerning the upbuilding of Zion, the order of the Church, etc. all of which were entirely at variance with the order of God's house, as laid down in the New Testament, as well as in our late revelations. As a conference meeting had been appointed for the 26th day of September, I thought it wisdom not to do much more than to converse with the brethren on the subject, until the conference should meet. Finding, however, that many, especially

26. John A. Widtsoe, *Evidences and Reconciliations* (Salt Lake City: Bookcraft, 1960) pp. 98-99.

the Whitmer family and Oliver Cowdery, were believing much in the things set forth by this stone, we thought best to inquire of the Lord concerning so important a matter; and before conference convened, we received the following:

> . . . And again thou shalt take thy brother, Hiram Page, between him and thee alone, and *tell him that those things which he hath written from that stone are not of me, and that Satan deceiveth him;*
>
> *For behold, these things have not been appointed unto him, neither shall anything be appointed unto any of this church contrary to the church covenants.*
>
> *For all things must be done in order, and by common consent in the church, by the prayer of faith.*[27]

In this same revelation, given through Joseph Smith to Oliver Cowdery, the Lord clearly established the relationship between revelations intended for the entire Church and inspiration given to individuals for their private betterment. Concerning revelations for the Church He said,

> But behold, verily, verily, I say unto thee, *no one shall be appointed to receive commandments and revelations in this Church excepting my servant Joseph Smith, Jun.,* for he receiveth them even as Moses.
>
> And *thou shalt be obedient unto the things which I shall give unto him,* even as Aaron, to declare faithfully the commandments and the revelations, with power and authority unto the Church.[28]

To guide others who were receiving revelation but were not called to serve as the prophet for the Church, He gave this counsel to Oliver:

> And if thou art led at any time by the comforter to speak or teach, or at all times by the way of commandment unto the Church, thou mayest do it.
>
> *But thou shalt not write by way of commandment, but by wisdom.*
>
> *And thou shalt not command him who is at thy head, and at the head of the church;*

---

27. HC, I, 109-110; D & C 28:11-13.
28. D & C 28:2-3.

For I have given him the keys of the mysteries and the revelations which are sealed, until I shall appoint unto them another in his stead.[29]

Church Strengthened Through Revelation to Individual Members

It should not be assumed, however, that God shapes the destiny of the Church only through revelations to His prophet. There have been many occasions in the history of the Church when individuals have been prompted to undertake projects which have later been of great value to the Church. These projects reflect inspiration to lay members rather than initial guidance of the Lord to His prophet. Was this not the case with Richard Ballantyne, who took the initiative and organized the first Sunday School in the winter of 1849, after first seeking permission from his bishop? In describing what prompted him to undertake such a project he wrote,

> *I was early called to this work by the voice of the spirit, and I have felt many times that I have been ordained to this work before I was born,* for even before I joined the Church, I was moved upon to work for the young. Surely no more joyful nor profitable labor can be performed by an Elder.[30]

There can be little doubt that his past experience as a Sunday School teacher in the Relief Presbyterian Church in Scotland before his conversion to the restored gospel also helped him to envision the great growth that a Sunday School program could accomplish. Not for eighteen years, until 1867, did the Church adopt his program and organize the association which later became known as *The Deseret Sunday School Union.*[31] From his story it can be seen that the Lord, at times, will inspire individuals to perform deeds which precede, rather than follow, revelation for the entire Church given to General Authorities.

A similar conclusion might be drawn from the history of the organization of the Primary Association, which had its beginning in August 1878, in Farmington, Utah. In this instance a woman living in that area, Aurelia S. Rogers,

---

29. D & C 28:4-7.
30. Jenson, I, p. 705.
31. Sunday School Handbook, Deseret Sunday School Union, 1964) p. 94.

Perceived the need for weekday religious education of boys and girls. *Her interest led to a consultation with President John Taylor, Eliza R. Snow, and Emmeline B. Wells, and others where* a decision was made to organize "The Primary Association.'[32]

Again the need was sensed and an initial plan was formulated by an individual member of the Church which was later accepted for use by the entire Church.

Several Latter-day Saint missionary plans have also followed the same course in gaining acceptance, and yet have become sources of much growth and development to the cause of Mormondom. The Anderson plan, The Great Lakes Mission plan, and the current plan which had its beginning in the Northwestern States Mission — these have all played a vital part in the rapid growth of the Church in recent years. Yet they were the result of inspiration given originally to missionaries laboring in their fields of endeavor rather than to the Prophets of the Church.

The Lord has said,

> *For behold, it is not meet that I should command in all things; for he that is compelled in all things, the same is a slothful and not a wise servant; wherefore he receiveth no reward.*
>
> *Verily I say, men should be anxiously engaged in a good cause, and do many things of their own free will and bring to pass much righteousness;*
>
> *For the power is in them, wherein they are agents unto themselves. And inasmuch as men do good they shall in nowise lose their reward.*
>
> But he that doeth not anything until he is commanded, and receiveth a commandment with a doubtful heart, and keepeth it with slothfulness, the same is damned.[33]

The responsibility to be engaged constantly in bringing to pass much righteousness is an important one, and it rests upon the shoulders of every Latter-day Saint. It is an impossibility for the person who is continually seeking to obey this calling not to receive revelation or inspiration which will cause him to undertake projects, large or small, which will be for the betterment of

---

32. William E. Berrett, *The Restored Church* (10th ed. Salt Lake City, Deseret Book Co., 1964) p. 352.
33. D & C 58:26-29.

his fellow man. But when such prompting comes, let the recipient act with prudence. If the activity about which he has been prompted concerns a ward or a stake then let him counsel with his bishop or stake president, telling him of his promptings and proposal. Then let him rely on the spirit of discernment and the inspiration of his presiding authority as to the further disposition and approval of the matter.[34]

Summary

1. Since man is limited in the time available for seeking knowledge while here on the earth, he would do well to center his efforts in seeking godly knowledge.

2. God has given man two basic types of knowledge:
   A. knowledge of God and His plans for mankind,
   B. knowledge of good and evil.
3. Godly knowledge is given to fulfill four major purposes:
   A. to stabilize man's faith,
   B. to manifest God's will,
   C. to further God's work, and
   D. to increase man's personal understanding of particular events.

It is possible for man to gain so much godly knowledge that God will no longer keep him from seeing beyond the veil.

4. Godly knowledge leads to other knowledge, both sacred and secular.

5. Doctrinal truths are often revealed to worthy individuals to aid them in their individual progress. Such truths often take the form of clarifications of scriptural teachings or insights into the eternal plan which exceed in scope the stated doctrine of the Church.

6. When an individual receives a doctrinal revelation which goes beyond the stated doctrines of the Church, he would do well

---

34. This places tremendous responsibility on the presiding authority to discern and recognize the promptings which the individual has received, in order to keep over-all direction in harmony with all that the Lord has revealed and to strengthen the faith of the individuals whom the Lord has inspired. It is neither safe nor wise for him to assume that inspiration always comes automatically to the presiding officials and not to the individual members.

to keep the knowledge to himself until such time as the Lord reveals it to the entire Church through His prophets.

7. Satan attempts to confound members of the Church by injecting false ideas and teachings into people's minds and then leading them to challenge Church leaders in doctrinal disputes.

8. Church members who are anxiously engaged in a good cause may expect revelation concerning ways in which they may further God's work. If such promptings involve programs which may be of use to the Church, they should bring the matter to the appropriate local Church official and let him prayerfully consider the project. Such undertakings, when guided by the Spirit, may bring to pass much good and may strengthen the Church.

9. A heavy responsibility is placed upon Church officials to test such programs and promptings through the gift of discernment bestowed upon them. Things of the Spirit are recognized through the Spirit.

10. The gift of godly knowledge may be forfeited through lack of use.

11. Growing in knowledge makes man responsible for rendering greater obedience to God.

CHAPTER VI

Godly Wisdom

Godly Wisdom the Proper Use of Godly Knowledge

Wisdom, or the wise and proper use of knowledge, is also a gift of the Spirit.[1] God wants man to know of Him and to attain godly wisdom. His invitation is made to man to "hearken ye together and let me show unto you even my wisdom — the wisdom of him whom ye say is the God of Enoch, and his brethren."[2] *That person has godly wisdom who has and knows God's commandments and keeps them.*[3] Such wisdom is based on a love of Christ, for the Savior taught that "he that hath my commandments, and keepeth them, he it is that loveth me: and he that loveth me shall be loved of my Father, and I will love him, and will manifest myself to him."[4]

Perhaps the best definition of godly wisdom is found in the fatherly advice given by Alma to his son, Helaman: "O, remember, my son, and *learn wisdom in thy youth; yea, learn in thy youth to keep the commandments of God.*"[5]

The Old Testament contains repeated exhortations to center wisdom in the keeping of God's commandments. To his people Moses said,

> Behold, I have taught you statutes and judgments, even as the Lord my God commanded me, that ye should do so in the land whither ye go to possess it.
>
> *Keep therefore and do them; for this is your wisdom and your understanding in the sight of the nations, which shall hear all these statutes, and say, Surely this great nation is a wise and understanding people.*[6]

---

1. I Cor. 12:8; D & C 46:17; Moro. 10:9.
2. D & C 45:11.
3. D & C 1:24-28.
4. Jn. 14:21.
5. Alma 37:35.
6. Deut. 4:5-6.

This theme was repeated by the Psalmist, who wrote that *"The fear of the Lord is the beginning of wisdom: a good understanding have all they that do his commandments: his praise endureth for ever."*[7] A similar teaching came from the giver of Proverbs. His counsel was that "The fear of the Lord is the beginning of wisdom; and the knowledge of the holy is understanding."[8]

Godly wisdom, then consists of knowing and keeping God's commandments and carrying out His divine will to further His work.

Wise Actions Prompted by The Spirit

There are numerous examples of people who, as they are laboring to fulfill God's commandments, have received revelation as to how they may act most wisely and prudently in their callings. Such revealed wisdom, at times, changes the entire program of the Church. The guidance given to the apostle, Wilford Woodruff in 1877, was of this nature.

All the Latter-day Saints understand that we build temples for the purpose of administering ordinances for the dead as well as for the living.

The Lord has opened the way in a remarkable manner for many of the members of the Church to obtain records of the names of their dead for several generations.

I had also obtained a record of somewhat over 3,000 of my father's and mother's families.

After the dedication of the temple at St. George, President Young appointed me to preside over it. When we commenced work in the temple *I began to reflect: 'How can I redeem my dead, I have some 3,000 names of the dead who have been baptized for, and how can I get endowments for them?'*

I had none of my family there, and if they had been there they would not have been able to get endowments for so many.

While praying to the Lord to show me how to redeem my dead, the Spirit of God rested upon me, and the voice of the Spirit said to me, 'Go and call upon the sons and the daughters of Zion in St. George, to come into the temple of the Lord and get their endowments for your dead; and it shall be acceptable unto me, saith the Lord.'

7. Ps. 111:10.
8. Pro. 9:10.

This filled my soul with joy, and I saw that it opened a field as wide as eternity for the salvation of our dead and the redemption of man, that we might magnify our calling as saviors upon Mount Zion.

On my birthday, March 1, 1877, the day that I was 70 years old, 154 sisters at St. George went into the temple to get endowments for the same number of the female portion of my dead.

This principle was received by President Young and adopted from that hour, and through the kindness of friends I have had nearly 2,000 of my friends receive endowments in the temple of the Lord; and thousands of others have received the same blessings in the same way.

President Young received revelations in that temple, and there are yet many revelations to be received in the last days, concerning the redemption of the dead and many other subjects, but they will all be manifest in due time through the proper authority unto the Church and kingdom of God.[9]

Many experiences of early L. D. S. pioneers among the Indians show the fruits of revealed wisdom. Oliver B. Huntington recorded an example of such inspired wisdom in connection with an excursion which was stopped by a maurading Indian party:

We soon moved on south a few miles; but *feeling forbodings of evil,* stopped about 2 p.m., on a fine, grassy place near a spring and sent Mr. Davis ahead to reconnoitre the country, which was mostly clear and open to the end of the valley, about twelve miles distant. He rode cautiously about five miles when, on looking over his left shoulder, he saw an Indian on foot running towards the road behind and dropping into the grass as Davis looked around. He instantly wheeled his horse and sped for camp. Just as he started back an Indian on horseback started from some willows near by to cut off his retreat, but that racehorse outran the Indian pony, although the latter had the advantage.

When these facts were known in camp every man prepared for the worst. We had chosen an open piece of ground where we could not be surprised in daylight. We were preparing an

9. *Leaves from My Journal,* pp. 92-93. It should be noted that this is another example showing that revelation comes to those who have the specific need and preparation for it, and not always from the head of the Church. In this instance the guidance came from the apostle and the prophet, upon learning of it, concurred.

early supper so as to have it over before any surprise might be undertaken. Just as we were sitting down to eat, seven Indians on horseback rode slowly towards our camp, came past our horses which were grazing near and dismounted, near our fires. We saluted them kindly with 'how-de-do,' and they replied. They were all dressed in coats, pants, overcoats, caps, etc., and rode well-shod horses, excepting one short, thick-set Indian, about twenty-three years old, who wore buckskin pants, a hickory shirt, a Panama hat and with his hair cut short and straight around his neck; he was very wide between the eyes, rode a very large mare without a saddle. He came to my mess where I, my nephew and Natsab [the Indian interpreter] were just sitting down to eat, and shook hands.

We sat with guns and pistols in our laps. I told all our company to be very careful, as this one could talk English. The interpreter tried to talk with him, but to no effect until he spoke in the Snake language, when he answered some. They were observing our actions, habits, etc., and making their calculations how and when to take our scalps. I felt that under the Panama hat was a dreadful chief for blood and plunder, and that he could talk English; and I was right in my judgment or feelings.

As soon as the interpreter and I were done eating, we walked around the horses after cautioning the men. *While driving the animals a little nearer camp, he asked me if I had noticed a secret sign, a strange motion, the Indian made as he shook hands with us, and he showed it to me*, stating that he believed these Indians were of the tribe and party who had done so many murders on the Humboldt, among the California gold seekers, and that he believed they were banded with whites by secret oaths, signs and pass-words. *Immediately after he told this I felt a strange but bright sensation come over my mind and I could see with my heart, or my spirit could see without my eyes. I told him we would leave the horses and go quickly to camp, where he should go up to that Indian (the chief), give him the same sign he had given us, and that we would then be safe among them.*

He did this and the effect was astonishing. The Indian shook hands and hugged him heartily.

I gave further instructions to the interpreter what to say about a certain man whom we knew lived on the Humboldt River, where so much murdering had been done, and with whom I went to school in Nauvoo. Every word had its effect, as I anticipated, and the chief understood that this man who lived

on the Humboldt, and whom very many believed to be the cause
of all the murdering done there for money and plunder, was our
friend from boyhood; but the opposite might be said to be
nearly true, as we held no sympathy in common, although we
had been boys together. The chief called that man his "daddy,"
meaning father.[10]

Elder Jacob Hamblin was given wisdom from God which
shaped his life and made him an ambassador of peace among the
Indians. In his early life he was sent as head of a company to
destroy a band of Indians which had repeatedly molested the
settlers around Tooele, Utah. During this journey he was
prompted with an understanding which later saved his life on
several occasions.

We surprised them near a large mountain between Tooele
and Skull Valleys. They scattered in the foot hills, and the
company divided to the right and left to keep them from the
mountains. I rode my horse as far as he could go on account
of the difficulties of the ground, then left him, and secreted
myself behind a rock in a narrow pass, through which I presumed
some of the Indians would attempt to escape. I had not been
there long before an Indian came within a few paces of me.

I leveled my rifle on him, and it missed fire. He sent an
arrow at me, and it struck my gun as I was in the act of re-
capping it; he sent the second, and it passed through my hat;
the third barely missed my head; the fourth passed through my
coat and vest. As I could not discharge my gun, I defended
myself as well as I could with stone. The Indian soon left the
ground to me.

I afterwards learned that as he went on, he met two others
of our company and passed them safely, *as their guns also
missed fire.* When the company gathered back to the place from
which they scattered, we learned that *not one was able to discharge his gun when within range of an Indian.* One of the company received a slight arrow wound, which was the only injury
inflicted.

In my subsequent reflections, it appeared evident to me
that a special providence had been over us, in this and the two
previous expeditions, to prevent us from shedding the blood of
the Indians. *The Holy Spirit forcibly impressed me that it
was not my calling to shed the blood of the scattered remnant*

10. *Eventful Narratives,* pp. 80-81.

of Israel, but to be a messenger of peace to them. It was also made manifest to me that if I would not thirst for their blood, I should never fall by their hands. The most of the men who went on this last expedition, also received an impression that it was wrong to kill these Indians.[11]

At times godly wisdom is revealed to help people solve urgent personal problems with which they are unable to cope without divine aid. This type of wisdom was granted to Amanda Smith at the time of the Haun's Mill Massacre. At this time, an armed mob had suddenly come down upon the Saints at Haun's Mill and brutally murdered many of them. Sister Smith's husband and son were killed and another son was tragically wounded:

> The fountain of tears was dry; the heart overburdened with its calamity, and all the mother's sense absorbed in its anxiety for the precious boy which God alone could save by his miraculous aid. The entire hip joint of my wounded boy had been shot away. Flesh, hip bone, joint and all had been ploughed out from the muzzle of the gun, which the ruffian placed to the child's hip through the logs of the shop and deliberately fired. We laid little Alma on a bed in our tent and I examined the wound. It was a ghastly sight. I knew not what to do. . . . 'O my Heavenly Father,' I cried, 'what shall I do? Thou seest my poor wounded boy and knowest my inexperience. Oh Heavenly Father, direct me what to do!' *And then I was directed as by a voice speaking to me.* The ashes of our fire was still smouldering. We had been burning the bark of the shag-bark hickory. *I was directed to take those ashes and make a lye and put a cloth saturated with it right into the wound.* It hurt, but little Alma was too near dead to heed it much. Again and again I saturated the cloth and put it into the hole from which the hip joint had been ploughed, and each time mashed flesh and splinters of bone came away with the cloth; and the wound became as white as chicken's flesh. Having done as directed I again prayed to the Lord and *was again instructed as distinctly as though a physician had been standing by speaking to me.* Near by was a slippery-elm tree. *From this I was told to make a slippery-elm poultice and fill the wound with it.* My eldest boy was sent to get the slippery-elm from the roots, the poultice was made, and the wound, which took fully a quarter of a yard of linen to cover, so large was it, was properly dressed. . . . I removed the wounded boy

---

11. *Jacob Hamblin,* pp. 28-29.

to a house, some distance off, the next day, and dressed his hip; *The Lord directing me as before. I was reminded that in my husband's trunk there was a bottle of balsam.* This I poured into the wound, greatly soothing Alma's pain. 'Alma, my child,' I said, 'you believe that the Lord made your hip?' 'Yes mother.' 'Well, the Lord can make something there in place of your hip, don't you believe he can, Alma?' 'Do you think that the Lord can, mother?' inquired the child in his simplicity. 'Yes my son,' I replied, *'he has showed it all to me in a vision.'* Then I laid him comfortably on his face and said: 'Now you lay like that, and don't move, and the Lord will make you another hip.' So Alma laid on his face for five weeks, until he was entirely recovered — a flexible gristle having grown in place of the missing joint and socket, which remains to this day a marvel to physicians. On the day that he walked again I was out of the house fetching a bucket of water, when I heard screams from the children. Running back, in affright, I entered, and there was Alma on the floor, dancing around, and the children screaming in astonishment and joy. It is now nearly forty years ago, but Alma has never been the least crippled during his life, and he has traveled quite a long period of the time as a missionary of the gospel and a living miracle of the power of God.[12]

Another type of revealed wisdom was given in a dream to Sister Millie B. Farrimond, of Clearfield, Utah. She recorded her dream in this manner:

Among the gifts of the spirit which have been mine is the gift to dream true dreams, many of them being inspirational ones. I have seen many things in them which have later come to pass. I wish to share one of these experiences with you, hoping that it may benefit someone. . . .

Many times in our youth we are led to do foolish and even dangerous things, some of which are misleading to others. This was the case of a very young girl. People misjudged her and a terrible scandal arose. There was much malicious gossip. I was greatly troubled about the things I heard, not knowing for sure as to their truthfulness. Then one night I dreamed I saw Satan. He had set a trap for this beautiful girl. I saw him standing there by his terrible trap; he had his eyes on the girl and was beckoning to her. She seemed not to see the danger and was about to enter the trap when all of a sudden she realized the mistake and turned and ran away in the opposite

---

12. Jenson, II, pp. 793-96.

direction. I saw Satan in his anger and disappointment at his unsuccessful attempt to catch her in his trap, sending out a most vicious looking bulldog after her. The dog overtook her and tore her to tiny bits. I could see those tiny particles flying in all directions, and yet the girl stood there before me: I wondered at the meaning of it. Then I heard a voice say, *'The bulldog you see is Satan's most vicious tool. It is known as malicious gossip. What you saw him tear into tiny bits and scatter to the far winds and you thought was the girl, is her reputation.'* I shall never forget the pain in my heart as I looked upon this little girl stripped of her reputation which had been a part of her as her very body, and saw the look of helplessness and anguish in her very body, and saw the look which came to me to know she was still innocent of the things she had been so harshly accused of.

I was very grateful for this dream, because I was now able to go to that young girl and give her the honest friendship and support that she needed so desperately in her struggle — to prove to her that there were those who knew her innocence. With this extra strength she was able to combat her problem with greater spirit, and the devil's campaign was defeated.[13]

Seeking the Wisdom of Heaven

As with the other gifts, man is commanded to seek for godly wisdom. A promise of reward is made to those who find it: *"Seek not for riches but for wisdom, and behold, the mysteries of God shall be unfolded unto you, and then shall you be made rich. Behold, he that hath eternal life is rich."*[14] It is sought by asking of God: *"Therefore, he that lacketh wisdom, let him ask of me, and I will give him liberally and upbraid him not."*[15] Such requests of God must be made in deepest humility if they are to be effective:

Let him that is ignorant *learn wisdom by humbling himself and calling upon the Lord his God,* that his eyes may be opened that he may see, and his ears opened that he may hear;

For my Spirit is sent forth into the world to enlighten the humble and contrite, and to the condemnation of the ungodly.[16]

But man must do more than merely ask, for wisdom implies the previous acquisition of knowledge. As the prophet Daniel taught,

---

13. Hackworth, *op. cit.,* pp. 210-11.
14. D & C 6:7.
15. D & C 42:68; See James 1:5-6.
16. D & C 136:32-33.

God "giveth wisdom unto the wise, and knowledge to them that know understanding."[17] The gaining of wisdom is also conditioned on obedience to the commandments, as is set forth in the closing verses of the Lord's law of health, the Word of Wisdom:

> And all saints who remember to keep and do these sayings, walking in obedience to the commandments, shall receive health in their navel and marrow to their bones;
>
> *And shall find wisdom and great treasures of knowledge, even hidden treasures.*[18]

Godly Wisdom Versus the Foolishness of Men

The scriptures continually differentiate between wisdom in the things of God and the pseudo-wisdom often demonstrated in the affairs of man. The first is held to be of great value while the latter is continually depreciated. Paul made this differentiation when he wrote to the Corinthians:

> For it is written, I will destroy the wisdom of the wise, and will bring to nothing the understanding of the prudent.
>
> Where is the wise? where is the scribe? where is the disputer of this world? *hath not God made foolish the wisdom of this world?*
>
> *For after that in the wisdom of God the world by wisdom knew not God, it pleased God by the foolishness of preaching to save them that believe. . . .*
>
> Because the foolishness of God is wiser than men; and the weakness of God is stronger than men.[19]

And he also told them:

> And my speech and *my preaching was not with enticing words of man's wisdom, but in demonstration of the Spirit and of power:*
>
> That your faith should not stand in the wisdom of men, but in the power of God.
>
> Howbeit we speak wisdom among them that are perfect: yet not the wisdom of this world, nor of the princes of this world, that come to nought:

17. Dan. 2:21.
18. D & C 89:18-19.
19. I Cor. 1:19-21, 25.

But we speak the wisdom of God in a mystery, even the hidden wisdom, which God ordained before the world unto our glory.[20]

It was King Limhi who commented on the unwillingness of men to learn the things of God and to seek His guidance. He exclaimed, "How blind and impenetrable are the understandings of the children of men; for they will not seek wisdom, neither do they desire that she should rule over them!"[21]

Paul saw that the weakness of worldly wisdom was that men who possess it often become vain. It is better that man find glory in service to God than in worldly honors:

Let no man deceive himself. *If any man among you seemeth to be wise in this world, let him become a fool, that he may be wise.*

For the wisdom of this world is foolishness with God. **For** it is written, He taketh the wise in their own craftiness.

And again, The Lord knoweth the thoughts of the wise, that they are vain.

Therefore let no man glory in men. For all things are yours.[22]

Summary

1. Godly wisdom consists of knowing the will and commandments of God and obeying them.

2. Wise actions, or godly wisdom, are often prompted by the Holy Ghost and are then a gift of the Spirit.

3. It is sometimes difficult to differentiate between the gifts of godly knowledge and godly wisdom. Godly knowledge is an understanding and comprehension of God's plan and teachings. Godly wisdom in its revealed form is primarily instruction in how to apply godly knowledge.

4. Man is commanded by God to seek wisdom. He can learn wisdom by humbling himself and calling upon the Lord.

---

20. I Cor. 2:4-7.
21. Mos. 8:20.
22. I Cor. 3:18-21.

5. Wisdom is given to those who have previously acquired knowledge. Applying knowledge to one's life increases the opportunity for one to receive further guidance through the Spirit.

6. The gaining of wisdom is also conditional on obedience to God's commandments.

7. Earthly wisdom holds little value when compared with godly wisdom. Man is commanded not to place his faith in earthly wisdom for it is regarded as foolishness by God.

Part III

GIFTS OF FAITH

CHAPTER VII

Faith

Seeking Faith — The Beginning of the Path

Almost anyone who has taught children knows of the many questions they have to ask about the gospel. He knows also of the desire that the young have to grow and progress. Many of them are anxious to start along the path to exaltation, yet they do not know how to begin. They want to know about God; they want to have faith in Him; they want to be prompted and led in their actions by the Holy Ghost; but they do not have these feelings and experiences and they do not know how to begin to seek them. All they have is desire!

Alma met a group of people with exactly this problem. They knew nothing. All they had was desire. He was equal to the task that confronted him and he started them down the path. He told them,

> If ye will awake and arouse your faculties, even to an *experiment upon my words*, and exercise a particle of faith, yea, *even if ye can no more than desire to believe, let this desire work in you*, even until ye believe in a manner that ye can give place for a portion of my words.[1]

Alma knew that he would have to plant an idea in their minds — a good idea, a fruitful one, one that would grow. He told them what the results would be:

> Now, we will compare the word unto a seed. Now, if ye give place, that a seed may be planted in your heart, behold, if it be a true seed, or a good seed, *if ye do not cast it out by your unbelief, that ye will resist the Spirit of the Lord, behold, it will begin to swell within your breasts; and when you feel these swelling motions, ye will begin to say within yourselves — It must needs be that this is a good seed*, or that the word is good, for it beginneth to enlarge my soul; yea, it beginneth to enlighten my understanding, yea, it beginneth to be delicious to me.

---

1. Al. 32:27.

Now behold, would not this increase your faith? I say unto you, Yea; nevertheless it hath not grown up to a perfect knowledge. . . .

And now, behold, because ye have tried the experiment, and planted the seed, and it swelleth and sprouteth, and beginneth to grow, ye must needs know that the seed is good.[2]

Alma was wise enough to know that his tree of faith could not be left unattended; it would have to be properly cared for and nourished:

And behold, as the tree beginneth to grow, ye will say: Let us nourish it with great care, that it may get root, that it may grow up, and bring forth fruit unto us. And now behold, if ye nourish it with much care it will get root, and grow up, and bring forth fruit.

But if ye neglect the tree, and take no thought for its nourishment, behold it will not get any root; and when the heat of the sun cometh and scorcheth it, because it hath no root it withers away, and ye pluck it up and cast it out.

Now, this is not because the seed was not good, neither is it because the fruit thereof would not be desirable; but it is because your ground is barren, and ye will not nourish the tree, therefore ye cannot have the fruit thereof.

And thus, if ye will not nourish the word, looking forward with an eye of faith to the fruit thereof, ye can never pluck of the fruit of the tree of life.[3]

Alma's message, then, was that if man will plant the seed of desire to know about God, if he will not cast it out by unbelief nor resist the promptings of the Holy Ghost, and if he will nourish this seed, faith will be given him as a gift of the Spirit.[4] Perhaps Paul clarified how the seed may be nourished when he wrote that "faith cometh by hearing, and hearing by the word of God."[5] Moroni also knew how faith was to be nourished, for he knew the way it grew among his people. "Wherefore, by the ministering of angels, and by every word which proceeded forth out of the mouth of God, men began to exercise faith in Christ; and thus by faith, they did lay hold upon every good thing; and thus it was until the coming of Christ."[6]

---

2. Al. 32:28-29, 33.
3. Al. 32:37-40.
4. 1 Ne. 10:17.
5. Ro. 10:17; D & C 35:19.
6. Moro. 7:25.

Faith a Hope in Things Unseen

Classic definitions of faith are given in the scriptures. One is by Alma, another is by Paul. They are similar in their meanings. Alma said that "faith is not to have a perfect knowledge of things; therefore *if ye have faith ye hope for things which are not seen, which are true.*"[7] Paul's definition was that "*faith is the substance of things hoped for, the evidence of things not seen.*"[8] Moroni also commented on the nature of faith and emphasized that man's faith must be proven before he may begin to reap its benefit: "I would show unto the world that *faith is things which are hoped for and not seen;* wherefore, dispute not because ye see not, for *ye receive no witness until after the trial of your faith.*"[9]

Paul knew how essential the gift of faith is. He emphasized its importance when he declared, "But *without faith it is impossible to please him:* for he that cometh to God must believe that he is, and that he is a rewarder of them that diligently seek him."[10] A modern revelation also stresses that man is completely limited and unable to progress without faith:

Ask the Father in my name, in faith believing that you shall receive, and you shall have the Holy Ghost, which manifesteth all things which are expedient unto the children of men.

And *if you have not faith, hope, and charity you can do nothing.*[11]

The Results of Faith

No other gift of the Spirit carries with it such rich promises for far-reaching results as does the gift of faith. The following are among the many things man can accomplish if he cultivates this gift and receives its full benefits.

1. *Faith brings results to man's prayers.* This was the testimony of Enos, to whom God had said, "Whatsoever thing ye shall ask in faith, *believing that ye shall receive* in the name of Christ, ye shall receive it."[12]

---

7. Al. 32:21.
8. Heb. 11:1.
9. Eth. 12:6.
10. Heb. 11:6.
11. D & C 18:18-19.
12. Enos. 15.

2. *Faith brings to man the manifestations of the Holy Ghost.* Jarom saw the results of faith which was free from vanity in his day: "And there are many among us who have many revelations, for they are not all stiffnecked. And *as many as are not stiffnecked and have faith, have communion with the Holy Spirit,* which maketh manifest unto the children of men, according to their faith."[13] This was also the way Lehi received his promptings, for

He spake by the power of the Holy Ghost, which power he received by faith on the Son of God — and the Son of God was the Messiah who should come — I Nephi, was desirous also that I might see, and hear, and know of these things, by the power of the Holy Ghost, which is *the gift of God unto all those who diligently seek him,* as well in times of old as in the time that he should manifest himself unto the children of men.[14]

3. *Faith leads to repentance,* and they combine to *bring about the mercies of the atonement.* Amulek taught,

And behold, this is the whole meaning of the law, every whit pointing to that great and last sacrifice; and that great and last sacrifice will be the Son of God, yea, infinite and eternal.

And thus he shall bring salvation to all those who shall believe on his name; this being the intent of this last sacrifice, to bring about the bowels of mercy, which overpowereth justice, and bringeth about means unto men that they may have *faith unto repentance.*

And thus mercy can satisfy the demands of justice, and encircles them in the arms of safety, while he that exercises no faith unto repentance is exposed to the whole law of the demands of justice; therefore *only unto him that has faith unto repentance is brought about the great and eternal plan of redemption.*

Therefore may God grant unto you, my brethren, that ye may begin to exercise your faith unto repentance, that ye begin to call upon his holy name, that he would have mercy upon you.[15]

4. *Faith brings about the forgiveness of sins,* as in the case of Enos, who wrote that

My soul hungered; and I kneeled down before my Maker, and I cried unto him in mighty prayer and supplication for mine

13. Jarom 4.
14. 1 Ne. 10:17.
15. Al. 34:14-17.

own soul; and all the day long did I cry unto him; yea, and when the night came I did still raise my voice high that it reached the heavens.

And there came a voice unto me saying: Enos, *thy sins are forgiven thee, and thou shalt be blessed.*

And I, Enos, knew that God could not lie; wherefore, my guilt was swept away.

And I said: Lord, how is it done?

And he said unto me: *Because of thy faith in Christ,* whom thou hast never before heard nor seen. And many years pass away before he shall manifest himself in the flesh; wherefore, go to, *thy faith hath made thee whole.*[16]

King Benjamin also taught that faith leads to the forgiveness of sins, and asserted that "when that time cometh, none shall be found blameless before God, except it be little children, *only through repentance and faith* on the name of the Lord God Omnipotent."[17]

5. *Faith strengthens both man and his work.* The case of Nephi, who was seized by his brethren and bound while they plotted to take away his life, demonstrates the strengthening power of faith. Nephi prayed, saying

O Lord, *according to my faith which is in thee, wilt thou deliver me from the hands of my brethren; yea, even give me strength that I may burst these bands with which I am bound.*

And it came to pass that when I had said these words, behold, the bands were loosed from off my hands and feet, and I stood before my brethren, and I spake unto them again.[18]

Nephi also found that faith influenced the workings of the Liahona, a special director which had been provided for his people by the Lord:

And it came to pass that I, Nephi, beheld the pointers which were in the ball, that *they did work according to the faith and diligence and heed which we did give unto them.*

And there was also written upon them a new writing, which was plain to be read, which did give us understanding concerning the ways of the Lord; and it was written and changed from

16 Enos 4-8.
17. Mos. 3:21.
18. 1 Ne. 7:17-18.

time to time, *according to the faith and diligence which we gave unto it.* And thus we see that by small means the Lord can bring about great things.[19]

The Lord has ever promised His servants that *"the weakness of their words will I make strong in their faith,* unto the remembering of my covenant which I made unto thy fathers."[20]

6. *By faith signs are shown to true believers* and they are thus distinguished from others:

Faith cometh not by signs, but signs follow those that believe.

Yea, *signs come by faith,* not by the will of men, nor as they please, but *by the will of God.*

Yea, *signs come by faith, unto mighty works, for without faith no man pleaseth God;* and with whom God is angry he is not well pleased; wherefore, unto such he showeth no signs, only in wrath unto their condemnation.[21]

7. *Through faith mighty miracles are performed.* Moroni told of just such an event when he prayed,

O Lord, thy righteous will be done, for I know that thou workest unto the children of men according to their faith; for the brother of Jared said unto the mountain Zerin, Remove — and it was removed. And if he had not had faith it would not have moved; wherefore *thou workest after men have faith.*[22]

8. Most important of all, *faith leads its possessor to eternal life.* All men are commanded to strive for "receiving the end of your faith, even the salvation of your souls."[23]

Two "Roll Calls" of Faith — Some Examples

The sacred records are full of examples of the power of the gift of faith. It would be challenging to consider them all in detail, but space limitations forbid such a project. Paul, however, lists in summary form a great many instances of the manifestation of this power among the characters in Biblical history:

Now faith is the substance of things hoped for, the evidence of things not seen.

---

19. 1 Ne. 16:28-29.
20. 2 Ne. 3:21.
21. D & C 63:9-11.
22. Eth. 12:29-30.
23. I Pet. 1:9.

For by it the elders obtained a good report.

Through faith we understand that the worlds were framed by the word of God, so that things which are seen were not made of things which do appear.

By faith *Abel* offered unto God a more excellent sacrifice than Cain, by which he obtained witness that he was righteous, God testifying of his gifts; and by it he being dead yet speaketh.

By faith *Enoch* was translated that he should not see death; and was not found, because God had translated him: for before his translation he had this testimony, that he pleased God.

But *without faith it is impossible to please him: for he that cometh to God must believe that he is, and that he is a rewarder of them that diligently seek him.*

By faith *Noah*, being warned of God of things not seen as yet, moved with fear, prepared an ark to the saving of his house; by the which he condemned the world, and became heir of the righteousness which is by faith.

By faith *Abraham*, when he was called to go out into a place which he should after receive for an inheritance, obeyed; and he went out, not knowing whither he went.

By faith he sojourned in the land of promise, as in a strange country, dwelling in tabernacles with Isaac and Jacob, the heirs with him of the same promise:

For he looked for a city which hath foundations, whose builder and maker is God.

Through faith also *Sara* herself received strength to conceive seed, and was delivered of a child when she was past age, because she judged him faithful who had promised.

Therefore sprang there even of one, and him as good as dead, so many as the stars of the sky in multitude, and as the sand which is by the sea shore innumerable.

These all died in faith, not having received the promises, but having seen them afar off, and were persuaded of them, and embraced them, and confessed that they were strangers and pilgrims on the earth.

For they that say such things declare plainly that they seek a country.

And truly, if they had been mindful of that country from whence they came out, they might have had opportunity to have returned.

But now they desire a better country, that is, an heavenly: wherefore God is not ashamed to be called their God: for he hath prepared for them a city.

By faith *Abraham*, when he was tried, offered up Isaac: and he that had received the promises offered up his only begotten son,

Of whom it was said, That in Isaac shall thy seed be called:

Accounting that God was able to raise him up, even from the dead, from whence also he received him in a figure.

By faith *Isaac* blessed Jacob and Esau concerning things to come.

By faith *Jacob*, when he was a dying, blessed both the sons of Joseph; and worshipped, leaning upon the top of his staff.

By faith *Joseph*, when he died, made mention of the departing of the children of Israel; and gave commandment concerning his bones.

By faith *Moses*, when he was born, was hid three months of his parents, because they saw he was a proper child; and they were not afraid of the king's commandment.

By faith Moses, when he was come to years, refused to be called the son of Pharoah's daughter;

Choosing rather to suffer affliction with the people of God, than to enjoy the pleasures of sin for a season;

Esteeming the reproach of Christ greater riches than the treasures in Egypt: for he had respect unto the recompence of the reward.

By faith he forsook Egypt, not fearing the wrath of the king: for he endured, as seeing him who is invisible.

Through faith he kept the passover, and the sprinkling of blood, lest he that destroyed the firstborn should touch them.

By faith *they passed through the Red sea as by dry land:* which the Egyptians assaying to do were drowned.

By faith *the walls of Jericho fell down,* after they were compassed about seven days.

By faith the harlot *Rahab* perished not with them that believed not, when she had received the spies with peace.

And what shall I more say? for the time would fail me to tell of *Gedeon,* and of *Barak,* and of *Samson,* and of *Jephthae;* of *David* also, and *Samuel,* and of the prophets:

Who through faith subdued kingdoms, wrought righteousness, obtained promises, stopped the mouths of lions,

Quenched the violence of fire, escaped the edge of the sword, out of weakness were made strong, waxed valiant in fight, turned to flight the armies of the aliens.

Women received their dead raised to life again: and others were tortured, not accepting deliverance; that they might obtain a better resurrection:

And others had trial of cruel mockings and scourgings, yea, moreover of bonds and imprisonment:

They were stoned, they were sawn asunder, were tempted, were slain with the sword: they wandered about in sheepskins and goatskins; being destitute, afflicted, tormented;

(Of whom the world was not worthy:) they wandered in deserts, and in mountains, and in dens and caves of the earth.

And these all, having obtained a good report through faith, received not the promise:

God having provided some better things for us, that *they without us should not be made perfect.*[24]

A similar listing of men of great faith was prepared by Moroni, who drew his examples from the history of his people in the Book of Mormon:

For if there be no faith among the children of men God can do no miracle among them; wherefore, he showed not himself until after their faith.

Behold, it was the faith of *Alma* and *Amulek* that caused the prison to tumble to the earth.

Behold, it was the faith of *Nephi* and *Lehi* that wrought the change upon the Lamanites, that they were baptized with fire and with the Holy Ghost.

Behold, it was the faith of *Ammon* and his brethren which wrought so great a miracle among the Lamanites.

Yea, and even all they who wrought miracles wrought them by faith, even those who were before Christ and also those who were after.

And it was by faith that the *three disciples* obtained a promise that they should not taste of death; and they obtained not the promise until after their faith.

24. Heb. 11.

And neither at any time hath any wrought miracles until after their faith; wherefore they first believed in the Son of God.

And there were many whose faith was so exceeding strong, even before Christ came, who could not be kept from within the veil, but truly saw with their eyes the things which they had beheld with an eye of faith, and they were glad.

And behold, we have seen in this record that one of these was the *brother of Jared;* for so great was his faith in God, that when God put forth his finger he could not hide it from the sight of the brother of Jared, because of his word which he had spoken unto him, which word he had obtained by faith.

And after the brother of Jared had beheld the finger of the Lord, because of the promise which the brother of Jared had obtained by faith, the Lord could not withhold anything from his sight; wherefore he showed him all things, for he could no longer be kept without the veil.[25]

Latter-day Examples of Faith

There is a vast multitude of incidents recorded in L.D.S. Church history of people receiving answers to their prayers of faith. Their abundance makes it difficult to choose which true stories would be of greatest benefit to the reader. The roll calls of faith cited previously have served to remind the reader of mighty acts of faith which have moved mountains, held back the waters of the sea, overcome cities, etc. Perhaps a series of incidents showing how the Lord has helped to provide for the temporal needs of His people in the furthering of His cause or in their day-to-day living would be appropriate in this context. A typical incident of this type is the blessing extended to John Taylor during his mission to the Isle of Man in 1840.

While laboring on the Isle of Man he had secured the printing of some tracts, which he wrote in reply to the falsehoods circulated by ministers and others regarding the character and doctrines taught by the Prophet Joseph Smith. When the tracts were ready the printer would not deliver them until every penny was paid which was due him. Elder Taylor did not have sufficient to meet the demand, and being very anxious to obtain the tracts went immediately into a private room, and, kneeling down, *told the Lord in plain simplicity exactly how much he needed to pay for the matter he had published in defense of*

25. Eth. 12:12-21.

his cause. In a few minutes after his prayer was offered a young man came to the door, and upon being invited to enter handed Elder Taylor an envelope and walked out. The young man was unknown to him. The envelope contained some money and a little note which read: 'The laborer is worthy of his hire,' and no signature was placed thereon. In a few minutes later a poor woman engaged as a fish vender came to the house and offered a little money to assist him in his ministerial labors. He told her there was plenty of money in the world and he did not wish to take her money. She insisted that the Lord would bless her the more and she would be happier if he would accept it, whereupon he received the offering, and to his surprise the poor woman's mite, added to what the young man had given him, made exactly the amount sufficient to pay the printer the balance due him.[26]

Another such instance is the experience of Brother L............,[27] which took place shortly after he immigrated to America from England in 1844. It took place during the two year period in which he helped to construct the Nauvoo Temple:

> Many a time he felt the pangs of hunger, and went to his work fasting rather than join with his family in eating the last ration of food in their possession, but the Lord sustained him by His Spirit, gave him joy in his labors and provided a way for more food to be obtained to sustain the lives of himself and his family.
>
> He and his young wife had a habit of appealing to the Almighty in prayer when in an extremity, and they invariably found comfort in so doing, and generally had their prayers answered.
>
> Upon one occasion, their infant child was dangerously sick, and they felt the want of twenty-five cents to procure some medicine with. Where to get it they did not know, and so, as usual, *they prayed to the Lord to open their way to obtain it. They felt an assurance on arising from their knees that their prayer would be answered, but they knew not how.* Soon afterwards the husband happened to feel some hard substance in the waistband of his pants, and called his wife's attention to it, wondering what it could be. The pants were almost new. They had been made to order for him only a short time before.

26. Jenson, I, p. 16.
27. In several of the books of the Juvenile Instructor's "Faith Promoting" series, names of the individuals whose experiences are cited are witheld. Nevertheless, the instances are set forth as true experiences.

There was no hole in the band, and it seemed that, whatever it was, it must have been inserted between the pieces of cloth when the pants were being made, and yet he thought it strange that he had not discovered it before.

To solve the mystery, a few stitches were cut, and the waistband opened, when lo! there were two new ten cent pieces and one five cent piece — just the amount of money they required to buy medicine with.

Lest the money might have been lost by the tailor who made the pants, a very poor man who lived neighbor to them, he took it to him and asked him, but that impecunious individual said he knew it could not be his, for he had never had a cent of money in his possession for months.

They accepted it as a gift from the Lord, bought the medicine their child needed and he was soon well.[28]

As the same brother was crossing the plains he again experienced an act of providence which rewarded his faith and helped him in his journey:

A rather remarkable case of special providence occurred when Brother L............ was crossing the plains, coming to Salt Lake Valley. His shoes gave out, and his feet became very sore from having to walk so much while driving his ox team, etc. Early one morning, when he, in company with another brother, were out hunting for their cattle, he exclaimed to his companion as he limped and hobbled over the rocky ground, 'Oh! I do wish the Lord would send me a pair of shoes!'

He had not walked many rods after expressing this wish when he saw something lying a short distance ahead of him, and called the attention of his companion to it, who remarked that it must be the bell and strap lost off one of the oxen, but to the inexpressible joy of Brother L............, he found, on approaching the object, that it was a new pair of shoes, which had evidently never been worn, and which he found, on trying them on, to fit him as well as if they had been made for him. He thanked the Lord for them, for he felt that it was through His merciful providence that they had been left there, and went on his way rejoicing. The shoes did him good service.[29]

Prayers of faith asking for aid in times of suffering and distress have often been answered. Typical is the case of Jacob Hamblin, who had been driven out of Nauvoo in February, 1846:

28. *Fragments of Experience,* pp. 84-85.
29. *Ibid.,* p. 87.

I was taken sick, and sent for my family to return to me. My wife and two children were taken sick the day after their arrival. We found shelter in a miserable hut, some distance from water.

One day I made an effort to get some water for my suffering family, but failed through weakness. Night came on, and my family were burning with fever and calling for water.

These very trying circumstances called up some bitter feelings within me. It seemed as though in this, my terrible extremity, the Lord permitted the devil to try me, for just then a Methodist class leader came along, and remarked that I was in a very bad situation. He assured me that he had a comfortable house that I could move into, and that he had plenty of everything, and would assist me if I would renounce 'Mormonism.' I refused, and he passed on.

I afterwards knelt down and asked the Lord to pity us in our miserable condition, and to soften the heart of some one to administer to us in our affliction.

About an hour after this, a man by the name of William Johnson came with a three gallon jug full of water, set it down and said: 'I came home this evening, weary, having been working with a threshing machine during the day, but, when I lay down I could not sleep; *something told me that you were suffering for water.* I took this jug, went over to Custer's well and got this for you. I feel now as though I could go home and sleep. I have plenty of chickens and other things at my house, that are good for sick people. When you need anything I will let you have it.' I knew this was from the Lord in answer to my prayer.[30]

The answering of the fervent prayers of young children has been one manner in which the gift of faith has been granted. Elder Ephraim Lambert told of a childhood incident which influenced his life. At this time his family were participating in the colonization of Kamas, Utah:

When my brother and I were about eight years of age, and were herding sheep, we lost a lamb on a certain occasion. We searched and hunted, but failed to find it, and we were afraid to go home without it, as our father was quite strict with his children. Having been taught the principle of prayer, we made up our mind to pray to the Lord, and ask Him to direct us, so that we could find the lost animal. Consequently, we knelt down and

---

30. *Jacob Hamblin*, p. 22.

prayed, each in turn, and when we arose to our feet, we saw
the lost lamb standing close by and in plain view. This may
appear like a trifling affair to some, but *it was the means of
creating a faith in me through which the Lord has subsequently
blesed* [sic] *me abundantly and preserved my life.* Often, when
I have been alone on the tops of high mountains, have I knelt
down and lifted up my voice in thanksgiving to the Lord for
the many manifestations of His goodness towards me.[31]

An experience given to Elder John Parry shortly after his
conversion to the Church in 1846 taught him that the blessings
of the gift of faith come from praying with true faith and not
with just an insincere, formal prayer:

> After joining the Church Elder Parry was often troubled
> in his sleep by evil spirits. Upon one occasion he inquired of
> the president of the Liverpool branch why it was that he was
> thus annoyed. The Elder replied that some persons were
> troubled more than others, and told him to use the following
> words in his prayers before retiring to rest: 'O God, the Eternal
> Father, I ask Thee in the name of Thy Son, Jesus Christ, to
> give Thine angels charge concerning me this night and allow
> not the powers of darkness to molest my spirit nor body.'
>
> He did this, and was troubled with evil spirits no more,
> until one night, feeling very sleepy, he uttered a hasty, formal
> prayer and went to bed. During the night he was almost over-
> come by the power of evil spirits, which were visible. Unable
> to utter a word, he prayed fervently in his mind to the Lord
> to release him. In an instant the heavens appeared to him to
> open, and he saw an angel descend towards him. The personage
> took hold of him and raised him up a little, and immediately
> the powers of darkness disappeared.
>
> Elder Parry asked the angel why it was that the Lord
> permitted the evil one to abuse him in such a manner, to which
> he replied: '*Because thou didst not pray from the heart, but
> with thy lips.*'[32]

Faith and the Full Manifestation of God's Power

The gift of faith must be woven into the fabric of an individual's life and become an integral part of him, for "*the just
shall live by faith.*"[33] It is basic to Latter-day Saint belief that

---

31. Jenson, I, p. 477.
32. *Early Scenes in Church History*, p. 45.
33. Heb. 2:4, Rom. 1:17.

man may so perfect his mortal faith that God will grant complete power to him — that everything which he commands will be brought to pass. Implied in this perfection of faith is man's willingness to be guided by the Spirit in what he asks, to seek for nothing that is contrary to the will of God. One of the few individuals to whom God wanted this complete and absolute power was the prophet Nephi, to whom the Lord said,

> Blessed art thou, Nephi, for those things which thou hast done; for I have beheld how thou hast with unwearyingness declared the word, which I have given unto thee, unto this people. And thou hast not feared them, and hast not sought thine own life, but hast sought my will, and to keep my commandments.
>
> And now, because thou hast done this with such unwearyingness, behold, I will bless thee forever; and *I will make thee mighty in word and in deed, in faith and in works; yea, even that all things shall be done unto thee according to thy word,* for thou shalt not ask that which is contrary to my will.[34]

Another individual who apparently was granted the full manifestation of God's power through his faith was the prophet Jacob. He knew that to gain such power his faith had to combine with knowledge, with the workings of the Spirit, and with a full acknowledgment of God's goodness. He wrote that

> *We search the prophets, and we have many revelations and the spirit of prophecy; and having all these witnesses we obtain a hope, and our faith becometh unshaken,* insomuch that we truly can command in the name of Jesus and the very trees obey us, or the mountains, or the waves of the sea.
>
> Nevertheless, the Lord God showeth us our weakness that we may know that it is by his grace, and his great condescensions unto the children of men, that we have power to do these things.[35]

How great a goal this is for every man who seeks to serve the Lord! How glorious it would be to become such a trusted servant of the Master that all power would be granted unto one for the futherance of His work! Yet how great a task it must be to perfect oneself to that degree, and what great temptations must lie in wait for those who draw near to this goal! Man can

---

34. Hel. 10:4-5.
35. Jac. 4.6-7.

do only that which Alma taught: plant the seed, nourish it carefully, and seek the gift of faith, the guidance of the Spirit, and the opportunity to humbly serve the Lord.

Lack of Faith a Retarding Force

There are those who forfeit the richest of blessings because of their lack of faith in the Savior and his power. In His own day He encountered men who would not accept Him, and their unbelief in some instances prevented Him from manifesting His power. When He visited His own village, for instance, the people said,

> Is not this the carpenter, the son of Mary, the brother of James, and Joses, and of Juda, and Simon? and are not his sisters here with us? and they were offended at him.
>
> But Jesus said unto them, A prophet is not without honour, but in his own country, and among his own kin, and in his own house.
>
> *And he could there do no mighty work,* save that he laid his hands upon a few sick folk, and healed them.
>
> And he marvelled because of their unbelief.[36]

On another occasion the Master had to rebuke His disciples because they were unable to cast out an evil spirit. The Savior told them that it was "because of your unbelief: for verily I say unto you, *If ye have faith as a grain of mustard seed, ye shall say unto this mountain, Remove hence to yonder place; and it shall remove; and nothing shall be impossible unto you.*"[37]

Later, when His apostles were marveling at the withering of the fig tree which had been cursed by the Master, He again emphasized the great power which could be theirs if they would only "doubt not:"

> Verily I say unto you, *If ye have faith, and doubt not,* ye shall not only do this which is done to the fig tree, but also if ye shall say unto this mountain, Be thou removed, and be thou cast into the sea; it shall be done.
>
> *And all things, whatsoever ye shall ask in prayer, believing, ye shall receive.*[38]

---

36. Mk. 6:3-6.
37. Mt. 17:20.
38. Mt. 21:21-22.

Peter was granted power which enabled him to walk on the water, but the elements of doubt and fear robbed him of his power and he plunged into the sea, for

> When he saw the wind boisterous, he was afraid; and beginning to sink, he cried, saying, Lord, save me.
>
> And immediately Jesus stretched forth his hand, and caught him, and said unto him, O thou of little faith, wherefore didst thou doubt?[39]

Through the centuries the unwillingness of Thomas to believe in the resurrection of Jesus has caused the term "doubting Thomas" to be one of derision and belittlement. The Christ's contrasting of his "seeing is believing" attitude with the sightless faith of others should be a lesson to every man:

> Then saith he to Thomas, Reach hither thy finger, and behold my hands; and reach hither thy hand, and thrust it into my side: and *be not faithless, but believing.*
>
> And Thomas answered and said unto him, My Lord and My God.
>
> Jesus saith unto him, Thomas, because thou hast seen me, thou hast believed: *blessed are they that have not seen, and yet have believed.*[40]

In these latter days, lack of faith is still a retarding force which prevents man from rendering service in the kingdom. That person who lacks faith finds himself restrained and unable to render service. A modern revelation says,

> Now, as you have asked, behold, I say unto you, keep my commandments, and *seek to bring forth and establish the cause of Zion.*
>
> Behold, I speak unto you, and also to all those who have desires to bring forth and establish this work;
>
> *And no one can assist in this work except he shall be humble and full of love, having faith, hope, and charity, being temperate in all things, whatsoever shall be entrusted to his care.*[41]

---

39. Mt. 14:30-31.
40. Jn. 20:27-29.
41. D & C 12:6-8.

Summary

1. He who seeks the gift of faith can gain it by accepting a portion of the word of God and applying it to see if it is true. This portion of God's word will be like a seed which will grow and swell within him and will become "delicious" unto him.

2. The seed of faith must be nourished or it will die. It can be nourished by learning more of the word of God and by applying this knowledge.

3. Faith comes to an individual as a gift of the Spirit.

4. Faith is a hope for things which cannot be seen at the time but which are true.

5. It is impossible to please God without faith.

6. Faith achieves numerous results:
   A. it brings answers to prayer.
   B. it brings the manifestations of the Holy Ghost.
   C. it leads to repentance.
   D. it makes available the mercies of Christ's atonement.
   E. it brings the forgiveness of sins.
   F. it strengthens both man and his work.
   G. it brings signs to true believers.
   H. it allows mighty miracles to be performed.
   I. it leads its possessor to eternal life.

7. Faith is a major theme of the scriptures. Numerous examples from Holy Writ can be cited of this gift of the Spirit.

8. God will provide for the wants and needs of the faithful in instances when they are unable to provide for themselves.

9. Man should strive to perfect his faith so that it is an unconscious, everyday characteristic of his life. "The just shall live by faith."

10. To achieve a perfection of faith man must combine with his belief knowledge, the workings of the Spirit, and a full acknowledgment of God's goodness.

11. Lack of faith is a retarding influence. Man is commanded to be not faithless, but believing. An accepting rather than a skeptical attitude is basic to the acquisition of the gift of faith.

CHAPTER VIII

Faith To Heal Others

The Healing Power of Jesus and His Followers

It was by the pool of Bethesda in the outskirts of Jerusalem that the Master found a man who lacked even the strength to dip himself in the water. Though this man had been in a helpless condition for thirty-eight years, Jesus commanded him to "Rise, take up thy bed, and walk,"[1] and the man immediately received the strength to do so.

While teaching in the synagogue, the Savior encountered a woman with an infirmity which had forced her to walk in a bent-over position for eighteen years. To her he stated simply, "Woman, thou art loosed from thine infirmity,"[2] and immediately she was made straight.

A soldier who tried to arrest Jesus was challenged and struck; his ear was sliced from his head. Yet a mere touch of the Savior's hand served to restore the ear.[3]

Such was, and is, the power of the Son of God. Whether he healed by "the application of higher law" or by "controlling the elements of nature" or by some other logical process, we do not know, and any explanation as to how He performed the wondrous deed can be at best pure speculation. But others were made well at his command. It would seem that this power to heal was power which he possessed in and of himself; it was a power of Godhood, and Jesus was, in truth, God.

Mortal men today, with all their technical knowledge, have not yet found any scientific method of duplicating the Master's feats of healing. Throughout the long years, however, men have been able, upon occasions, to tap the power of Godhood and to perform feats similar to those Jesus did by using the same source of power. This was as Christ intended, for He told his apostles,

1. Jn. 5:1-16.
2. Lk. 13:10-17.
3. Lk. 22:50-51.

"Verily, verily, I say unto you, *He that believeth on me, the works that I do shall he do also; and greater works than these shall he do.*"[4]

Peter, while entering the temple, found a man who had been born lame. He took compassion on him and said, "Silver and gold have I none; but such as I have give I thee: In the name of Jesus Christ of Nazareth rise up and walk."[5] Stretching forth his hand, he pulled the lame man to his feet and immediately the man's feet and ankle bones received the strength necessary for him to walk and leap.

While laboring in Lydda, Peter found Aeneas, who had been confined to bed with palsy for eight years. The simple words "Aeneas, Jesus Christ maketh thee whole: arise and make thy bed"[6] caused the man to be made well and to rise from his bed immediately.

Paul also tapped this power of Godhood. While shipwrecked on the isle of Melita, he lodged at the home of Publius, whose father lay sick of fever and of a bloody flux. To help him, "Paul entered in, and prayed, and laid his hands on him, and healed him. So when this was done, others also, which had diseases in the island, came, and were healed."[7]

By what power were these great miracles performed? It would appear that Peter and Paul were blessed with the gift of the Holy Spirit which gave them the faith to heal.

Four Factors In The Gift of Healing

It was James who wrote,

> Is any sick among you? let him call for the elders of the church; and let them pray over him, anointing him with oil in the name of the Lord:
> And *the prayer of faith shall save the sick, and the Lord shall raise him up.*[8]

Although on a few occasions the pattern has been modified, the method outlined by James is the norm. This was the manner

---

4. Jn. 14:12.
5. Acts 3:6.
6. Acts 9:34.
7. Acts 28:8-9.
8. Jas. 5:14-15.

in which many healings were performed by Christ's apostles, for they "anointed with oil many that were sick, and healed them."[9] In the last days the same pattern has been set forth by the Lord. A revelation given in 1831 commanded, "Lay your hands upon the sick, and they shall recover."[10] This pattern is well established in the Church today.

The gift of healing apparently involves four forces. The first force is the *faith of those who perform the ordinance.*[11] This is a gift of God and must come through the ministrations of the Holy Ghost. Yet those who perform the ordinance can encourage the presence of the Spirit, with the resulting strengthening of their faith, through several specific actions. The first is the earnest seeking of the Spirit through prayer, for the aid of that Being is "the gift of God unto all those who diligently seek him."[12] Christ promised that "whatsoever ye shall ask the Father in my name, which is right, believing that ye shall receive, behold it shall be given unto you."[13] Also, the power of fasting and prayer in behalf of the needy individual may be necessary. This was the essential ingredient which was lacking when the disciples made an unsuccessful attempt to cure a lunatic man. When they asked Jesus why their efforts were to no avail, he told them,

9. Mk. 6:13.
10. D & C 66:9.
11. It is well to review the instructions given for administering to the sick:
    Administration should be made at the request of the sufferer or some one vitally concerned, so that it may be done in answer to faith. One of the Elders called in should pour oil on the crown of the head and anoint the sick person and while anointing pray to the Father in the name of Jesus Christ for the restoration of the health of the sick brother or sister, but he should not seal the anointing. Oil for this anointing should be pure olive oil which has been consecrated for the purpose. Giving consecrated oil internally is not a part of the administration and should not be done.
    Two or more Elders shall lay their hands on the head of the sick person, after he or she has been anointed, and one of the Elders shall be voice in the sealing of the anointing. After sealing the anoint-ing, the one speaking may add such blessing upon the head of the sick person as the Spirit of the Lord may dictate, doing all in the name of Jesus Christ, and by virtue of the Holy Priesthood. It is permissible, if the Spirit of the Lord should indicate that it should be done, for the brethren to kneel in prayer before the administration, but this is not an essential part of the ordinance of administering to the sick. (John A. Widstoe, (comp.) Priesthood and Church Govern-ment in the Church of Jesus of Latter-day Saints (Salt Lake City, Utah: Deseret Book Company, 1950) pp. 356-57.)
12. I Ne. 10:17.
13. 3 Ne. 18:20.

Because of your unbelief: for verily I say unto you, If ye have faith as a grain of mustard seed, ye shall say unto this mountain, Remove hence to yonder place; and it shall remove; and nothing shall be impossible unto you.

Howbeit *this kind goeth not out but by prayer and fasting.*[14]

The second force involved is the *priesthood.* It would seem that this was the power being conferred by the Savior, when he "gave them power against unclean spirits, to cast them out, and to heal all manner of sickness and all manner of disease."[15] If the power of the priesthood is defined as the authorization to perform deeds in the name of Christ, then the healings performed by the twelve disciples among the Nephites may be regarded as acts of that power:

And there were great and marvelous works wrought by the disciples of Jesus, insomuch that they did heal the sick, and raise the dead and cause the lame to walk, and the blind to receive their sight, and the deaf to hear; and *all manner of miracles did they work among the children of men; and in nothing did they work miracles save it were in the name of Jesus.*[16]

In addition to the first two powers enumerated, the other elements have a bearing on the outcome of the administration. One is the *faith to be healed on the part of the individual receiving the administration.*[17] To be healed at the hands of the servants of God one must possess the necessary faith to warrant the special blessings of God being manifested in his behalf. In some situations, such as the healing of tiny babies, people who are unconscious, etc., the need for this faith is seemingly met by the faith of members of the family and other close associates. The remaining element is the *will of God that the individual be healed.* This is the final and governing power which must control all healing processes.

And the elders of the church, two or more, shall be called, and shall pray for and lay their hands upon them in my name; and *if they die they shall die unto me, and if they live they shall live unto me.*

Thou shalt live together in love, insomuch that thou shalt weep for the loss of them that die, and more especially for those

---

14. Mt. 17:20-21.
15. Mt. 10:1.
16. 4 Ne. 5.
17. This will be considered in the next chapter.

that have not hope of a glorious resurrection.

And it shall come to pass that those that die in me shall not taste of death, for it shall be sweet unto them;

And they that die not in me, wo unto them, for their death is bitter.

And again, *it shall come to pass that he that hath faith in me to be healed, and is not appointed unto death, shall be healed.*[18]

Miracles with the Gift of Healing

Man working as God's instrument can actually bring to pass miracles by properly exercising this gift of healing. It is possible to restore life and good health to individuals, instantly or over a period of time, when the afflicted are beyond the hope of doctors and medical technics. They who scoff at this premise forfeit their claim to this gift. Miraculous healings are more than mere coincidence, more than psychological changes in the mind of the sick person, and more than fortunate blunders. Consider a few examples which are far beyond the realm of chance. Benjamin Brown left this record of an administration he performed:

> One of the fourteen persons converted at Portland was a young man named Jesse W. Crosby, and, as it may prove interesting to many of the Saints, I will relate something that particularly affected him, occurring in his history.
>
> He had been engaged with his brother and brother-in-law, in felling trees in a wood. The trees grew very close together, and one which they cut down had, in falling, struck another, and broken off one of its limbs, which hung suspended by the other branches.
>
> It is a very common thing in forest country, to see dry, detached limbs hanging in this way for months, and sometimes years, without falling. This one was about ten or eleven feet long, and as thick as a man's thigh, and very high up the tree.
>
> Not apprehending danger, Jesse was working without his hat, just under this branch. Suddenly, a movement, caused by the wind, shook the tree, and the loose branch fell from a hight [sic] of at least sixty feet, striking him on the crown of his head, crushing him to the earth. The violence of the blow broke in a portion of his skull, forming a hollow about as large as the palm of a man's hand. His neck and shoulders were also much

---

18. D & C 42:44-48.

injured. Altogether, a more deplorable object I never saw in
my life.

He was carried home by his friends, most of whom were
members of the Church, and his father, who was not a member,
procured a doctor, who pronounced Jesse's case desperate,
unless, on removing the broken part of the skull, it should be
found that the skin of the brain was still entire, when, by using
a silver plate over the exposed portion, a chance might still
exist of his life.

The doctor proceeded to cut Jesse's head for that purpose,
but was stopped by his mother, who strongly objected to this
experiment, and sent for me to administer to him.

I was then eight miles off, and at the time of my arrival
he had not spoken, nor scarsely indicated any signs of life.
Going into the room where he lay, I found it filled with the
neighbors, who were mostly enemies of the Church. Sneers and
jeers of 'Here comes the Mormon, we'll soon see whether he can
heal now,' saluted my ears on all sides.

*From a sign which I had received while on my way, I knew
Jesse would recover,* and being reminded, on account of the
reason given in the previous remarks, that such people should
not be privileged to behold a manifestation of the power of
God, I, like Peter of old, cleared the house of all but Jesse's
relatives, and administered to him in the name of the Lord.
Jesse then recovered sufficiently to speak, after which he fell
into a peaceful sleep, and, before morning, was altogether better.

In less than four days from the time of receiving this terrible
accident, from which there seemed no human probability that he
could recover, or, if he did, only to survive the loss of reason,
he was again at work in the woods hauling timber, the wound
being entirely healed up.

Since then, he, as an Elder of this Church, has been on
missions to various parts of the world, including England, and
has also fulfilled a mission to Nova Scotia.[19]

Several miraculous healings were performed by Elder Martin
H. Peck to preserve the health of his family. One such incident
served to convert the family doctor:

There was a doctor by the name of Harvey Tate living
neighbor to Brother Peck in Ohio, who became somewhat interested in the doctrines of the Latter-day Saints, and for the
purpose of learning more concerning them made a visit to his

---

19. *Gems for The Young Folks*, pp. 68-70.

house. While he was there Brother Peck's son James was brought home with a broken arm, caused by his falling from a tree. The fracture was about three inches above the wrist joint, and so complete that his arm formed a right angle at the place where it was broken. The doctor set and bandaged it, and the boy was put in bed. The pain was so great, however, that he could scarcely endure it, and after the doctor had gone he begged his father to 'bless' him, saying he knew that would cure him.

Brother Peck accordingly administered to him and the pain immediately ceased. He slept well during the night and on getting up the next morning played about with his fellows as if nothing had ever been the matter with his arm, not even having it in a sling. The next day he was sent to the doctor to show him his arm, and when he entered his house, the doctor noticed, to his surprise, that the boy took hold of a chair with his lame hand and lifted it forward to sit down upon. Taking the little fellow by the hand, he then asked him if he felt any pain in his arm or hand, and the boy answered frankly that he did not. The doctor bent his fingers and saw that he had free use of them, then examined his hand and wrist and saw that there was no sign of swelling, and declared that it was the power of God which had healed the broken limb, for nothing else could have done it in so short a time. This incident probably influenced Dr. Tate in favor of the Latter-day Saints, as he soon afterwards joined the Church.[20]

Elder Peck also had occasion to effect a miraculous cure for another of his sons:

While journeying to Missouri with the 'Kirtland Camp,' Brother Peck's son, Edwin, had his leg accidentally run over by a heavily loaded wagon, on a very hard road. When he was picked up the limb appeared to be flattened as if almost crushed to a pulp, and the flesh was laid open. Brother Peck had seen the power of God manifested in so many instances then, and he had such confidence in the Almighty hearing and answering his prayers, that he never thought of summoning a surgeon, but immediately administered to the boy and then placed him in the wagon. In an hour afterwards he examined his leg and found that it was entirely well, the only sign of the injury left being a slight scar which had the dry and scaly appearance of an old sore, long since healed up. The place was not even discolored.

20. *Early Scenes in Church History* pp. 72-73.

There were numbers of witnesses to this miracle, many of whom are living to-day.[21]

Another instance of rapid healing was recorded by Thomas D. Giles, a Welsh convert. Brother Giles told that

> A friend of his, named David Davis, who was living in Merthyr, was almost crushed to a pulp by the roof of a coal mine falling upon him. When he was dug out Elder William Phillips and some other brethren laid their hands upon him and promised him that he should live and be healed. *While their hands were upon his head, his broken ribs and other bones were heard coming together with a noise which was quite perceptible.* Brother Davis, who was a truthful, honest man, lived to travel about Wales and testify of this miracle and follow his daily labor as if no such accident had ever occurred. He afterwards emigrated to the United States, and is perhaps yet alive.[22]

These are merely samples of the numerous healings which have occurred at the hands of Latter-day Saints. These particular examples are cited because they involved badly broken bones and open wounds, injuries which are so obvious that the unbeliever cannot attribute them to psychological change within the mind of the victim.

Those Who Seek To Use Faith To Heal Must Be Worthy of The Gift

To enjoy the gift of faith to heal others it is essential that every individual involved be worthy and living a good life. An experience of Elder Abel Evans, an early missionary to Wales, illustrates this point:

> When Elder Evans was crossing the Atlantic in charge of a company of Saints emigrating to Utah, a terrible epidemic in the nature of a fever broke out on the ship, and threatened the destruction of all on board. He felt that their only hope lay in securing the favor of the Almighty, and determined to muster all the faith he could in appealing to the Lord. He called together four Elders of experience who were on board, and asked them to retire with him to the hold of the vessel and unite in prayer. They did so again and again without any apparent good result, and Brother Evans marveled at the cause. It was such

21. *Ibid.*, pp. 73-74.
22. *Ibid.*, p. 67.

an unusual thing for him to fail to have his prayers answered, that he was surprised that it should be so in that instance, and he could only account for it by lack of union or worthiness on the part of the Elders. He therefore called the four Elders again to retire with him to the hold of the ship, and took with him a basin of clear water. When they had reached a secluded place where they were not likely to be overheard or disturbed by others, he talked to the Elders about the necessity of their being united in faith and clear of sin before God if they desired to call upon Him and receive a blessing. 'Now,' he said, 'I want each of you Elders, who feels that his conscience is clear before God, who has committed no sin to debar him from the enjoyment of the Holy Spirit, and who has faith in the Lord Jesus Christ sufficient to call upon the Almighty in His name and claim the desired blessing, to wash his hands in the basin!' Three of the Elders stepped forward and did so; the fourth could not — his conscience smote him. He was therefore asked kindly to retire, and the four others joined in earnest prayer before the Lord and rebuked the disease by which the people were afflicted. The result was that the epidemic ceased its ravages and the sick recovered from that very hour, much to the surprise of the ship's officers and others on board who knew nothing of the power by which such a happy result was accomplished.[23]

Experience has shown that the tempter is ever ready to lead priesthood bearers into unworthy thoughts or acts which would keep them from enjoying the full power of their faith when it is most needed. A state of continual worthiness and righteousness is necessary if the gift of faith to heal others is to be enjoyed in full measure.

Those Who Administer Must Follow the Will of The Lord

It is imperative that those who attempt to heal others seek and receive guidance through the Holy Spirit as they administer to the sick. It is neither their duty, their calling, nor their privilege to command a person to be made well without being guided to do so through promptings of the Spirit. If they receive no guidance as they administer they should make their administration in the form of a prayer and supplication for divine help rather than a promise and command that the person be made well. How can a person exercise his faith to heal others when

23. *Ibid.*, p. 40.

he is unsure of the goal in which his faith should be vested?
Surely his faith cannot successfully operate in opposition to the
will of God.

Consider the continuation of suffering which was brought to
Newel Knight because of the action of well-meaning but spiritually unprepared Elders. His wife wrote,

> On Monday morning, Jan. 4, 1847, Brother Knight, whose
> health had been failing for some time, did not arise as usual,
> and on going to him, he said, 'Lydia, I believe I shall go to rest
> this winter.' The next night he awoke with a severe pain in
> his right side, a fever had also set in, and he expressed himself
> to me that he did not expect to recover. From this time until
> the 10th of the month, the Elders came frequently and prayed
> for my husband. After each administration he would rally and
> be at ease for a short time and then relapse again into suffering.
> I felt at last as if I could not endure his sufferings any longer
> and that I ought not to hold him here. I knelt by his bedside,
> and with my hand upon his pale forehead asked my Heavenly
> Father to forgive my sins, and that the sufferings of my
> companion might cease, and if he was appointed unto death,
> and could not remain with us that he might be quickly eased
> from pain and fall asleep in peace. Almost immediately all
> pain left him and in a short time he sweetly fell asleep in death,
> without a struggle or a groan, at half past six on the morn-
> ing of the 11th of January, 1847.[24]

The author, while in the mission field, had occasion to learn
that the Lord's will must be followed while administering to the
sick. He was confronted with the responsibility of blessing a
choice sister whom he wished to be able to heal. He found that
he would have to give her a blessing which did not conform to
his personal wishes. The following is quoted from his Missionary
Journal:

> About a month ago our Primary President, Sister Clemencia
> Calderon, became very ill with a severe attack of rheumatism.
> She was confined to her bed and was suffering a great deal of
> pain. The other pair of missionaries went and administered to
> her. She was a little better for a few hours and then grew
> worse again. That happened twice. Finally, the day after we
> returned from the conference in Guatemala City, they came and
> asked all the missionaries to come and administer to her again.

24. Jenson, II, p. 775.

It was late in the evening and we had all been in quite a light-hearted mood. The four of us prayed at our apartment door before leaving, and we could feel that we weren't yet in tune with the Spirit. It was suggested that we kneel down and pray once again for the guidance of the Lord as to what we should do. Elder Goodman, the district president, asked me to pray, and after my prayer was finished I knew we would still have to fast and do some more praying. Elder Goodman and I went up to Sister Calderon's house and asked them to fast there as we fasted here. The next afternoon, after fasting two meals, the four of us went to her house to administer to her. Elder Goodman said he would anoint her and asked me to seal the administration. *As I began I didn't know what I was to tell her, but as I prayed I felt the Spirit within me. I found through the Spirit that I had to tell her that her rheumatism would be with her during all the remainder of her life. It was to serve as a challenge to her faith and testimony — when she would be faithful and true to the gospel she would be freed from the effects of the disease; yet it would return to afflict her later.* It was a hard thing to tell her, but that's what the Spirit prompted me to say, so I said it. It sure shakes you up to do something like that. But when you can speak by the Spirit, it is a testimony and you know what you have said is true. She found relief from our administration and was able to sleep well during the night, although her rheumatism did not completely leave her.[25]

It is important that those who are called on to administer to the sick seek guidance and aid from God through prayer. A good example may be found in the actions of Lorenzo Snow, who was attempting to open a mission for the Church in the city of Piedmont, Italy.

At the call from President Young in 1850, he had left his family in tragic conditions, trusting their welfare to neighboring Saints and the protection of God and left for Europe to start a mission in Italy. He had labored for months without any headway. The Italian people knew only one church and were taught not to listen to any other type of teachings. Elder Snow

---

25. *Missionary Journal* of Duane S. Crowther, from a letter to his family dated April 24, 1955. At this time he was serving as Branch President of the Quezaltenango, Guatemala, branch of the Central American Mission.

prayed with all of his heart for an opportunity to awaken the
people to the Restoration of Truth. On the evening of September
6th, he had visited the Grey family and witnessed the hope-
less condition of the little boy. He realized that by faith,
through the power of the Priesthood, that child could live. He
knew what this would mean to the people of Piedmont. As he
went to his room that evening, he called upon the Lord for
assistance. After praying late into the night, he retired but
was up early the next morning. Continuing to fast, he walked
out of town and up the steep slopes of the Alps which towered
skyward to the north.

As the vast importance of the circumstances bore down
upon his mind, he knelt upon the ground and humbly petitioned
his Father in Heaven for the privilege of using divine power to
heal the child. As the spirit of prayer filled his being, he poured
out his desires with all the strength of his soul. He needed to
know what the Lord wanted him to do. The answer could be
yes or it could be no, but an answer he had to have.

Have you ever prayed for one whole hour without stopping?
I don't mean to just casually offer a lot of words, but to plead
and reason with every ounce of energy you could muster, to
humble yourself to the very depth? If you have ever done that
for one hour, you will have some idea of what this man went
through when he prayed for six, long, *struggling hours*. He
wanted to know for certain whether or not he might magnify
his Priesthood to heal this child and thereby help to bring
salvation to a nation. He felt the need for this blessing so
deeply that he asked the Lord to take anything He wanted
from him, even his life, if He would only allow this to be the
means of opening the blind eyes of the people in this land to
the glorious, restored gospel.

And he meant it. His whole life shows that he meant it.
There was no hypocrisy. Just try to really pray that long
hypocritically, and you will agree. At last, at the end of six
hours, the answer came! The reply was 'Yes.' He would be
granted the privilege. Oh, the joy that must have surged
through his being when he knew that God had heard and
answered his prayer. The 'powers of the world to come' [Heb.
6:5] had been poured out upon him through this direct response
to his earnest petition. As an agent of the Almighty God,

filled with consuming joy, he walked down from the mountain side in perfect faith to save a dying child.[26]

There are many occasions when no time is available for extensive prayer and fasting before administering to the sick. In theses instances, however, the will of the Lord should still be sought, as in this experience of Orson F. Whitney:

Mrs. Frink had been confined to her room with an attack of neuralgia, which for many weeks had caused her intense pain. Her daughter had learned through Sister Frink, that faith-healing was practiced by the Latter-day Saints, and had heard me testify that the miraculous 'signs' promised by the Savior to 'follow them that believe,' were manifested now the same as in days of old. She therefore invited me to come and bless her mother, that she might be healed. Sister 'Angie' seconded the suggestion — if, indeed, she did not originate it — and again I was all but paralyzed at the prospect.

Never did I feel so helpless — or so humble. I besought the Lord with all my soul to stand by me in this critical hour, to perfect my faith, and use me, if he could consistently, as an instrument for showing forth His merciful power upon the afflicted one. I then consecrated, as best I could, some olive oil provided by Sister Frink, and went with her, and her husband to Mrs. Frink's abode. . . .

Mrs. Frink, with her head bandaged, was sitting up, but still suffering much pain. Laying my hands upon her head, which I previously had anointed, I proceeded to bless her. *Scarcely had I begun, when a power fell upon me that I had never felt before, nor have I ever felt it since in the same degree. It was a warm glow in my throat and breast — not painful, but powerful, almost preventing utterance, and it ran like liquid*

26. Max B. Skousen, *How to Pray and Stay Awake* (Salt Lake City, Utah: Bookcraft, 1949), pp. 2-4. It would be well to record the results of Elder Snow's prayer and administration:

I might add that the effect of this incident was marvelous. For the first time people gladly opened their doors and listened to his message. Within a few short months, a large branch was organized for scores of newly baptized converts. Lorenzo Snow rejoiced in thanksgiving for this blessing. It was over a year later, however, when he returned home, that he heard the other side of the story. It should be a lesson for us all, for the path of the righteous has never been easy. Those whom the Lord desires to make the greatest, He seems to test the hardest. Evidently the Lord had taken Lorenzo Snow at his word, for when he returned, he found that his wife, his childhood sweetheart, had died. She had passed away suddenly on the very day he had healed the dying child in Italy. (pp. 4-5).

flame to the very tips of my fingers. The effect was instant. 'Thank God!' said the sufferer, 'the pain has gone.' Sister Angie almost shouted, 'Glory to God!' As for me, I was so overcome by a sense of gratitude for this signal manifestation of divine favor, that I sank into a chair and burst into tears.[27]

At times the will of the Lord awaits the decision and faith of the individual who is sick, and the administering elder is left without guidance until that time when the sick person is ready to be healed. This was the case with Wilford Woodruff, who was traveling to Zion to fill his newly received call as an apostle. As he journeyed his wife was overcome with brain fever and lay upon the point of death.

> I alighted at a house and carried my wife and her bed into it, with a determination to tarry there until she either recovered her health, or passed away. This was on Sunday morning, December 2nd.
>
> After getting my wife and things into the house and wood provided to keep up a fire, I employed my time in taking care of her. It looked as though she had but a short time to live.
>
> She called me to her bedside in the evening and said she felt as though a few moments more would end her existence in this life. She manifested great confidence in the cause she had embraced, and exhorted me to have confidence in God and keep His commandments.
>
> To all appearances, she was dying. I laid hands upon her and prayed for her, and she soon revived and slept some during the night.
>
> December 3rd found my wife very low. I spent the day taking care of her, and the following day I returned to Eaton to get some things for her. She seemed to be gradually sinking, and in the evening her spirit apparently left her body, and she was dead.
>
> The sisters gathered around her body, weeping, while I stood looking at her in sorrow. *The spirit and power of God began to rest upon me until, for the first time during her sickness, faith filled my soul, although she lay before me as one dead.*
>
> I had some oil that was consecrated for my anointing while in Kirtland. I took it and consecrated it again before the Lord for anointing the sick. I then bowed down before the Lord and prayed for the life of my companion, and I anointed her body

---

27. Hinckley, *Faith of our Pioneer Fathers*, pp. 213-215.

with the oil in the name of the Lord. I laid my hands upon her, and in the name of Jesus Christ, I rebuked the power of death and the destroyer, and commanded the same to depart from her, and the spirit of life to enter her body.

Her spirit returned to her body, and from that hour she was made whole; and we all felt to praise the name of God, and to trust in Him and to keep His commandments.

While this operation was going on with me (as my wife related afterwards) her spirit left her body, and she saw her body lying upon the bed, and the sisters weeping. She looked at them and at me, and upon her babe, and while gazing upon this scene, two personages came into the room carrying a coffin, and told her they had come for her body. *One of these messengers informed her that she could have her choice: she might go to rest in the spirit world, or, on one condition she could have the privilege of returning to her tabernacle and continuing her labors upon the earth. The condition was, if she felt that she could stand by her husband, and with him pass through all the cares, trials, tribulations and afflictions of life which he would be called to pass through for the gospel's sake unto the end.* When she looked at the situation of her husband and child she said: 'Yes, I will do it!'

At the moment that decision was made the power of faith rested upon me, and when I administered unto her, her spirit entered her tabernacle, and she saw the messengers carry the coffin out at the door.[28]

Seeking the will of God in connection with administering to the sick often allows the person administering to receive special revelation concerning the sick person. In this way Elder G. W. Hill was able to bless a dying Indian child to get well because he was allowed to "see the child at different stages until it was grown."[29] Through the same gift Elder David W. Patten was able to raise up a woman from the bed where she had lain ill for a year, heal her, and promise her that "in less than one year she should have a son,"[30] and this in spite of the fact that her marriage had been childless for twelve years.

28. *Leaves from My Journal,* pp. 54-55.
29. *A String of Pearls* (Salt Lake City, Utah: Juvenile Instructor Office, 1880) p. 85.
30. Jenson, I, p. 77.

Summary

1. Faith sufficient to heal others comes to man as a gift of the Spirit.

2. Christ had the power to heal others. He promised that his followers would be able to imitate his miraculous feats and perform even greater works.

3. Four factors which influence the gift of healing are
    A. the faith of those who attempt to heal others;
    B. the Priesthood, or authorization to perform deeds in the name of Christ;
    C. the sick person's faith to be healed; and
    D. the will of God that the individual be healed.

4. Man acting as God's instrument may bring to pass miracles by restoring life and good health to individuals even when they are far beyond the reach of medical technology. Those who scoff at this premise forfeit their claim to this gift for it is based on true belief and faith.

5. To enjoy the gift of faith to heal others one must be worthy.

6. Those who administer to others must not command nor promise blessings without knowing the will of the Lord. If no inspiration is given, the administration should take the form of a prayer of supplication.

7. A few individuals have lived close enough to the Lord to receive the promise that their commands would be binding upon the powers of heaven since their will had become synonymous with God's.

8. At times the administering elder is not given guidance because the faith and intent of the sick person has not yet come into focus.

9. Revelation pertaining to matters other than the immediate condition of the patient may come to persons seeking the will of the Lord in connection with the gift of healing.

CHAPTER IX
Faith To Be Healed

Man Healed Through His Own Faith

The gift of faith to be healed[1] is amply demonstrated in the scriptures. The theme of personal faith as being the cause for one's being miraculously healed is often found in the histories of the Savior's work. The leper was cured when he sought the Lord's aid by saying, "Lord, if thou wilt, thou canst make me clean."[2] The man who was lowered on a bed through the ceiling was healed by the Savior because the Master recognized the faith of the man and of those who brought him.[3] The servant was healed when the centurion professed his faith in the Christ with the words, "Lord, I am not worthy that thou shouldest come under my roof: but speak the word only, and my servant shall be healed."[4] Jesus' reply was a recognition of that faith:

> Verily I say unto you, I have not found so great faith, no, not in Israel. . . .
>
> And Jesus said unto the centurion, Go thy way; and *as thou hast believed, so be it done unto thee.* And his servant was healed in the selfsame hour.[5]

It was because of their faith that the two blind men regained their sight, through the power of the Savior:

> And when he was come into the house, the blind men came to him: and Jesus saith unto them, Believe ye that I am able to do this? They said unto him, Yea, Lord.
>
> Then touched he their eyes, saying, *According to your faith be it unto you.*
>
> And their eyes were opened; and Jesus straitly charged them, saying, See that no man know it.[6]

---

1. D & C 46:19.
2. Mt. 8:2.
3. Lk. 5:20.
4. Mt. 8:8.
5. Mt. 8:10, 13.
6. Mt. 9:28-30.

In the last days the gift of faith to be healed has often been manifested, and revelation in the Doctrine and Covenants gives clear promise of its continuing availability. The Lord assures His people that

> He who hath faith to see shall see.
>
> He who haith faith to hear shall hear.
>
> The lame who hath faith to leap shall leap.
>
> And they who have not faith to do these things, but believe in me, have power to become my sons; and inasmuch as they break not my laws thou shall bear their infirmities.[7]

Provision is also made for those who are lacking the gift of faith to be healed, for the Lord has said that "whosoever among you are sick, and have not faith to be healed, but believe, shall be nourished with all tenderness, with herbs and mild food, and that not by the hand of an enemy."[8]

The Nature of Faith to be Healed

In what must the faith to be healed be centered? Examples from the history of the Church show that this faith falls into several categories. First, the faith to be healed must constitute an overpowering belief that the sickness or injury one possesses can be overcome and healed through the power of Jesus Christ and that life can be sustained. Such a faith is what brought the wife of John Johnson to the prophet Joseph. While she was initially hesitant to accept Joseph as a servant of the Lord, she did have an abiding faith that God would heal her arm:

> When Joseph came to Kirtland his fame spread far and wide. There was a woman living in the town of Hiram, forty miles from Kirtland, who had a crooked arm, which she had not been able to use for a long period. She persuaded her husband, whose name was Johnson, to take her to Kirtland to get her arm healed.
>
> I saw them as they passed my house on their way. She went to Joseph and requested him to heal her. Joseph asked her if she believed the Lord was able to make him an instrument in healing her arm. *She said she believed the Lord was able to heal her arm.*

7. D & C 42:49-52.
8. D & C 42:43.

Joseph put her off till the next morning, when he met her at Brother Whitney's house. There were eight persons present, one a Methodist preacher, and one a doctor. Joseph took her by the hand, prayed in silence a moment, pronounced her arm whole, in the name of Jesus Christ, and turned and left the room.

The preacher asked her if her arm was whole, and she straightened it out and replied: 'It is as good as the other.' The question was then asked if it would remain whole. Joseph hearing this, answered and said: It is as good as the other, and as liable to accident as the other.'

The doctor who witnessed this miracle came to my house the next morning and related the circumstance to me. He attempted to account for it by his false philosophy, saying that Joseph took her by the hand, and seemed to be in prayer, and pronounced her arm whole in the name of Jesus Christ, which excited her and started perspiration, and that relaxed the cords of her arm.[9]

Faith to be healed also centers in a belief in the divinity of Jesus Christ. At times individuals may be physically so weak as to lose their confidence in the possibility that they may be healed, but they retain an unshakable testimony of the divinity of the Savior and this suffices to restore them to health. The case of Elijah Fordham, who lay near death on the banks of the Mississippi on July 22, 1839, may be cited as an example. Just as they healed hundreds of others on that fateful day, the prophet Joseph and his followers sought to do the same with Brother Fordham, who

Had been dying for an hour, and we expected each minute would be his last. I felt the spirit of God that was overpowering His Prophet. When we entered the house, Brother Joseph walked up to Brother Fordham and took him by the right hand, his left hand holding his hat. He saw that Brother Fordham's eyes were glazed, and that he was speechless and unconscious.

After taking his hand, he looked down into the dying man's face and said: "Brother Fordham, do you not know me?" At first there was no reply, but we could see the effect of the spirit of God resting on the afflicted man. Joseph again spoke. "Elijah, do you not know me?" With a low whisper Brother Fordham answered "Yes." The Prophet then said: "Have you

9. *Early Scenes In Church History,* p. 79.

not faith to be healed?" The answer, which was a little plainer
than before, was: "*I am afraid it is too late; if you had come
sooner, I think I might have been.*" He had the appearance of
a man waking from sleep; it was the sleep of death. Joseph
then said: "*Do you believe that Jesus is the Christ?*" "*I do,
Brother Joseph,*" was the response. Then the Prophet of God
spoke with a loud voice, as in the majesty of Jehovah: "Elijah,
I command you, in the name of Jesus of Nazareth, to arise and
be made whole."

The words of the Prophet were not like the words of man,
but like the voice of God. It seemed to me that the house shook
on its foundation. Elijah Fordham leaped from his bed like a
man raised from the dead. A healthy color came to his face,
and life was manifested in every act. His feet had been done
up in Indian meal poultices; he kicked these off his feet, scattered the contents, then called for his clothes and put them on.
He asked for a bowl of bread and milk, and ate it. He then
put on his hat and followed us into the street, to visit others
who were sick.[10]

Faith in Christ has served as the criterion upon which the
healing of man has been effected. Typical is this instance
recorded by a missionary companion of Elder David W. Patten:

I think Elder David W. Patten possessed the gift of healing to
a greater degree than any man I ever associated with. I
remember on one occasion when I was laboring with him as a
missionary in Tennessee, he was sent for to administer to a
woman who had been sick for five years and bed-ridden for one
year and not able to help herself. Brother Patten stepped to
her bedside and *asked her if she believed in the Lord Jesus
Christ. She replied that she did.* He then took her by the hand
and said, 'In the name of Jesus Christ, arise!'

10. Matthias F. Cowley, *Wilford Woodruff: History of His Life and Labors*
(Salt Lake City: Bookcraft, 1964), pp. 104-05. After recording this incident, Wilford Woodruff made this commentary:
The unbeliever may ask, "Was there not deception in this?" If
there is any deception in the mind of the unbeliever, there was certainly none with Elijah Fordham, the dying man, or with those who
were present with him; for in a few minutes he would have been in the
spirit world, if he had not been rescued. Through the blessing of
God he lived up till 1880, when he died in Utah; while all who were
with him on that occasion, with the exception of one (myself), are in
the spirit world. Among the number present were Joseph and Hyrum
Smith, Sidney Rigdon, Brigham Young, Heber C. Kimball, George
A. Smith, Parley P. Pratt, Orson Pratt, and Wilford Woodruff.
(p. 105).

She immediately sat up in bed, when he placed his hands upon her head and rebuked her disease, pronounced blessings upon her head and promised that she should bear children. She had been married for several years and had never had any children, and this promise seemed very unlikely ever to be fulfilled. But she arose from her bed immediately, walked half a mile to be baptized and back again in her wet clothes. She was healed from that time, and within one year became a mother, and afterwards bore several children.[11]

At times the Lord sees fit to create special faith in particular individuals so that healings can be accomplished. This is done with special promptings, visions or dreams. By means of a dream, Elder Abel Evans had the way prepared for his administration during a mission to England.

Near the same time and in the same region a sister in the Church, named Morgan, was taken very sick. Her friends did all they could for her, but she continued growing worse. When she had grown so bad that the persons waiting upon her expected her to die almost hourly, she fell asleep and *dreamed that Elder Evans came and laid his hands upon her and she recovered immediately.* On relating the dream to her friends, they tried to find out where Brother Evans was, and sent to different parts of the country in search of him, without finding him, however; but during the day Elder Evans happened to call at the house where the sick woman was. She saw him as he passed the window before he entered the door and *she declared afterwards that the sight of him caused her pain to vanish, and when he laid his hands upon her head she was healed instantly,* and arose and ate her supper.[12]

A similar experience was recorded by Newel Knight, whose aunt was given a dream that Newel would heal her:

Soon after I left, my aunt, Electa Peck fell and broke her shoulder in a most shocking manner; a surgeon was called to relieve her sufferings, which were very great. *My aunt dreamed that I returned and laid my hands upon her, prayed for her, and she was made whole, and pursued her journey with the company.* She related this dream to the surgeon who replied, 'If you are able to travel in many weeks it will be a miracle, and I will be a Mormon too.'

11. *Early Scenes In Church History,* p. 29.
12. *Ibid.,* p. 60.

I arrived at the place, where the company had stopped, late in the evening but, on learning of the accident, I went to see my aunt, and immediately on my entering the room she said, 'O, Brother Newel, if you will lay your hands upon me, I shall be well and able to go on the journey with you.' I stepped up to the bed, and in the name of the Lord Jesus Christ, rebuked the pain with which she was suffering, and commanded her to be made whole; and it was done; for the next morning she arose, dressed herself, and pursued the journey with us.[13]

Faith to be healed, then, involves the firm belief that a healing can be effected through the healing power of the divine Savior, Jesus Christ.

Those Who Possess Faith Healed in Many Ways

What healing found in the scriptures is better known than that of the woman with the issue of blood, who followed behind the Master and said to herself, "If I may but touch his garment, I shall be whole."[14] The Savior told her, "Daughter, be of good comfort; *thy faith* hath made thee whole."[15]

In the latter days the faith to be healed possessed by many individuals has been manifested in various ways. Many were healed as they were being baptized into the Church. Brother Carl Jensen, for instance, was completely cured of rheumatism at the time of his baptism on December 20, 1874, in Jutland:

At the time of his baptism, he was badly crippled with rheumatism, his lower limbs being almost useless. A hole was cut in the ice, which at the time was very thick, and he was taken out of bed to be baptized. When he came out of the water he was perfectly well, and able to walk home unassisted, the distance to walk being over a mile.[16]

Brother Abraham O. Smoot recorded the healing effects of a baptism he performed at Winter Quarters:

During the winter of 1846-47 while the Saints were encamped on the banks of the Missouri there was a great deal of sickness among them, and many died. Among others who were afflicted was a man by the name of Collins, who had

13. *Scraps of Biography,* p. 69.
14. Mt. 9:21.
15. Mt. 9:22.
16. Jenson, II, p. 435.

followed up the Church for some time on account of his wife being a member, but who never felt quite satisfied to embrace the gospel, although he never opposed the work. When he was taken sick it was not thought by his friends that he could recover, as he had appeared to be sinking rapidly under the effects of the disease, and for some time he lay in a semi-conscious state, from which it was feared he would never rally.

However, he finally regained consciousness and looked around, when I asked him if he had any message to leave before he died. He immediately replied that it would not do for him to die then, as he had not been baptized, and urged very strongly to be taken right down to the river to receive this ordinance.

Yielding to his solicitations, some of the brethren brought the running gear of a wagon with a few boards on it, up to the door of the cabin in which he was living, and his bed, with him lying upon it, was carried out and placed on the wagon. When we had proceeded part way down to the river the wagon tire commenced running off one of the wheels and a halt was made to hammer it on again. On noticing the wagon stop and hearing the hammering, he inquired what was the matter, and when he was informed that the tire was running off, he replied impatiently, 'Oh, never mind the tire; go on, or I'll die and go to hell yet before I'm baptized!'

We proceeded on with him till we reached the river, which at that time was frozen over, but the ice had been cut away near the shore in order that our animals might drink. There he was lifted from his bed, carried into the water and I baptized him for the remission of his sins and his restoration to health. After being taken out of the water a blanket was wrapped around him and he was seated for a moment to rest upon a block of ice upon the shore. Seeing the brethren turning the wagon around, he inquired what they were going to do. They replied that they were going to put him on the bed and haul him back home, *when he arose to his feet and assured them that they need not go to that trouble, for he could walk back, and he did so, and from that time became a healthy man.*[17]

At times individuals have possessed sufficient faith to be healed that they were able to be made well just by coming in contact with one of the Lord's servants. An example may be found in the faith of a sister in Montevideo, Uruguay in 1955, when she was cured of bone cancer by shaking hands with Presi-

---

17. *Early Scenes In Church History,* pp. 30-1.

dent David O. McKay. For more than a year she had suffered
with a swelling in her right hand:

> A swelling had developed there which made a lump nearly as
> big as a golf ball. She went to several of the principal doctors
> of the city and also to the clinics and hospitals of the city,
> seeking every type of relief. All of the doctors diagnosed it as
> cancer of the bone. There was no question about the diagnosis
> as the doctors agreed with each other. . . . The doctors told
> her that there was no cure for this cancerous condition. The
> only thing would be amputation of the arm. She did not wish
> to have an operation of that kind. When she heard that Presi-
> dent McKay was coming, the thought occurred to her that if
> she could just shake hands with him her hand would be healed.
>
> With this in mind she stood in line when President McKay
> was shaking hands with the people following the meetings he
> attended there in Montevideo. When it came her turn to shake
> hands, she merely did so and expressed her pleasure at his
> coming to the conference. She said nothing about her sore hand
> and said nothing about her hope that she would be healed by
> shaking the President's hand. She merely shook hands, ex-
> pressed a few pleasantries, and went on her way.
>
> She told me there in Montevideo that within three days
> the cancer was gone from her hand. She said further that there
> had been no recurrence in the past year. I examined her hand
> again, and it was perfectly free from any kind of sores but
> merely had a well-healed scar in the palm as I have described.[18]

Another sister was reportedly cured of arthritis in 1954 by shaking hands with President McKay following his performance of a
temple marriage in the Salt Lake Temple. The woman healed,
Sister Nina Penrod, was among a group of about thirty who
greeted President McKay on this occasion:

> As President McKay shook Sister Penrod's hand, she asked
> him if he remembered her mother, a Sister Graham from Ogden
> Valley. He answered: 'Why, of course I do,' and placed his left
> hand on top of her hand as he clasped it in his right. At the
> moment of the handshake I saw Sister Penrod's face flush.
> She said she became overwhelmed and humble, more because
> as both of President McKay's hands were on her right hand,
> she felt a shock, and she wondered if others might have heard
> the sound that accompanied the shock which had seemed very

---

18. Middlemiss, *op. cit.*, pp. 159-60. See accompanying details for further
    substantiation.

loud to her. She said a weakness came over her. And this is odd, as President McKay held her right hand with his left hand, he shook hands with many others with his right hand. Sister Penrod said it was very humbling in the extreme to her, yet she felt elated because something wonderful had happened to her, for her arthritis pains were all gone. . . . Sister Penrod tried to leave with the others but had to be assisted as she was too weak to go alone. They proceeded slowly, and in descending the stairs she cried out, sinking down. She was helped to bed in the dressing room where after a short time her strength returned, and she stood up, turned her back to those with her, and reached each arm up her back touching her shoulder blades, saying, 'I haven't been able to do this for years.'[19]

Thus it can be seen that a mere handshake, a touch of a revered person's clothing, or other contact can become a source of healing strength when coupled with one's faith to be healed.

Faith to be Healed and the Forgiveness of Sins

Several scriptural passages seem to link sickness and its subsequent healing with worthiness and cleansing from sin. Paul warned of the dangers of partaking of the Sacrament unworthily, saying:

He that eateth and drinketh unworthily, eateth and drinketh damnation to himself, not discerning the Lord's body.

For this cause many are weak and sickly among you, and many sleep.[20]

James wrote of the power of anointing for the benefit of the infirm and said:

The prayer of faith shall save the sick, and the Lord shall raise him up; and *if he have committed sins, they shall be forgiven him.*

Confess your faults one to another, and pray one for another, that ye may be healed. The effectual fervent prayer of a righteous man availeth much.[21]

When Jesus spoke with the impotent man he had healed at the pool of Bethesda He told him, "Behold, thou art made whole:

---

19. *Ibid.,* pp. 156-7.
20. I Cor. 11:29-30.
21. Jas. 5:15-16.

sin no more, lest a worse thing come unto thee.[22] **In curing the man** with palsy who was carried to Jesus on a bed, the Savior forgave his sins:

> And, behold, they brought to him a man sick of the palsy, lying on a bed: and Jesus seeing their faith said unto the sick of the palsy; Son, be of good cheer; *thy sins be forgiven thee.*
>
> And, behold, certain of the scribes said within themselves, This man blasphemeth.
>
> And Jesus knowing their thoughts said, Wherefore think ye evil in your hearts?
>
> For whether is easier, to say, thy sins be forgiven thee; or to say, Arise, and walk?
>
> *But that ye may know that the Son of man hath power on earth to forgive sins,* (then saith he to the sick of the palsy), Arise, take up thy bed, and go unto thine house.[23]

With these instances in mind, perhaps Jesus' comment in regard to his role as a physician takes on new meaning:

> They that be whole need not a physician, but they that are sick.
>
> But go ye and learn what that meaneth, *I will have mercy, and not sacrifice: for I am not come to call the righteous, but sinners to repentance.*[24]

Instances in the latter days also show the close relationship between sickness and sin. Elder George Q. Cannon, while recounting the experiences of his mission to the Hawaiian Islands, told of this incident:

> Another instance which happened about the same time was that of a woman who was a member of the Presbyterian church. She was afflicted with dropsy, or something very like that disease. She had tried various remedies, but obtained no relief. She had heard about the gifts in the Church, and she called upon Brothers Napela and Uaua to administer to her, saying she was willing to covenant and forsake her sins. They administered to her and she was healed; all the swelling left her and she was baptized. On Sunday she attended meeting, and *afterwards made some remarks derogatory to the work, indulging in a*

---

22. Jn. 5:14.
23. Mt. 9:2-6.
24. Mt. 9:12-13.

*spirit of apostasy; her disease returned immediately, and she
was as bad as ever.*[25]

Incidents of a similar nature are often recounted in the personal histories of L.D.S. missionaries. Typical is the experience
of David W. Patten and Wilford Woodruff as they labored in
Tennessee.

Elders Patten and Woodruff laid hands on a woman by the
name of Margaret Tittle, who was laying at the point of death,
and she was instantly healed through the power of God.
Bro. Patten had preached faith, repentance and baptism to
her, and she covenanted to be baptized. But *after she was
healed, she refused to attend to that ordinance.* Elder Patten
told her that she was acting a dangerous part, and she would
again be afflicted, if she did not repent. The brethren pursued
their journey, and *on their return found her very low with the
same fever.* She begged them to lay hands upon her and heal
her, and she would obey the gospel. They complied with her
request, and she was healed, after which Wilford Woodruff
baptized her.[26]

Resisting the truth can also open the door to afflictions
caused by the entering in of evil spirits, as was discovered by
two missionaries, Amasa Lyman and Zerubbabel Snow, in 1832:

The following Sabbath evening they met in prayer meeting
with a few Saints in Chippewa township. A few non-members
also attended, among whom was a Miss Smith, who reclined on
a bed in the corner of the room. The brethren sang a hymn and
prayed, and Elder Snow proceeded to make some remarks, when,
in an instant, a cry of alarm from the bed attracted the attention of all. On stepping to the bedside the Elders discovered
that Miss Smith's face and her entire form were distorted in
the most shocking manner, her eyes were glaring wildly, but
apparently sightless, her respiration was very difficult and her
limbs were rigid as iron. The common restoratives were used
without effect. The Elders laid their hands upon her and
rebuked the devil, when she was instantly relieved, but in
another moment she was bound as before: they now kneeled
down by her bed and prayed, when she was again released,
and asked for baptism, *stating that she had been acting against
her convictions of right in some conversations the missionaries*

25. *My First Mission*, p. 64.
26. Jenson, I p. 78.

had held with her during the day. They repaired to the water
and there under the mantle of night introduced the first soul
into the Church as the fruits of their labors.[27]

Another sister chose to rebuke the Elders and in so doing allowed
evil spirits to possess her body. Elder Benjamin Brown, who
labored with her, told of the call which he and two other missionaries made upon her:

> Directly we entered her room, she called out, 'Take your shoes
> from off your feet; this is holy ground, the Prophet Elijah is
> here.'
>
> I saw the spirit by which she was influenced, so I walked
> up to her and said, 'I am a servant of the Lord, I obey no com-
> mand of the devil.'
>
> She became uproarious directly, for all who had gone in
> previously had complied with her directions. As soon as we
> attempted to rebuke the evil spirit in the name of the Lord,
> she arose up from the bed on her feet, without apparently
> bending a joint in her body, as stiff as a rod of iron.
>
> From this we saw the power with which we had to contend;
> and, failing at first to eject the spirit, we bowed ourselves in
> prayer before the Lord, and asked him to assist us.
>
> The evil spirit then came out full of fury, and, as he passed
> by one of the brethren, seized him by both arms and gripped
> them violently. Passing towards me, something, which by the
> feel appeared like a man's hand, grasped me by both sides of
> the face, and attempted to pull me sideways to the ground, but
> the hold appearing to slip, I recovered my balance immediately.
>
> My face was sore for some days after this. The other
> brother that was seized was lame for a week afterwards.
>
> As soon as this was done, the sister partly recovered, so
> much so that she obeyed everything I chose to tell her to do,
> whereas, before, she was perfectly ungovernable.
>
> Still she seemed to be surrounded by some evil influence.
> This puzzled us, for we knew the spirit was cast out, but we
> learned the cause afterwards. Just then it was revealed to us
> that if we went to sleep the devil would enter one of the
> brethren.
>
> My nephew, Melvin Brown, neglected the warning, and com-
> posed himself to sleep in an arm chair, while we were still

27. *Ibid.,* p. 97.

watching with the sister. Directly he did so the devil entered into him, and he became black in the face, and nearly suffocated.

He awoke immediately, and motioned for us to lay hands on him, for he could not speak. We did so, and the evil spirit then left him, and he recovered at once.

About a week afterwards the same spirit re-entered the sister, and this time fully confessed his character. In answer to our enquiries, he said his name was 'Legion.' This explained how it was that the woman, after we had cast out an evil spirit, was under an evil influence, for there must have been many spirits.

He also reviled our priesthood, but he had to submit to it at last, saying to us, 'O! you have the priesthood have you? Well, then, cast me out, command me to come out,' trying to shake our faith, and thus incapacitate us to rebuke him successfully.

Failing in this, he tried another method by entering me. I felt seized by a strange influence, and to every question put to the woman I knew the answer she was going to give, for I was possessed by a similar spirit. This broke the chain of our union and strength, consequently I requested the Elders to rebuke the evil spirit from me, after which, at our united rebuke, he left the woman.

Previous to this the sister had been a very faithful Saint, and she ever afterwards was, but *she had given the devil ground by encouraging a spirit contrary to the order of the Church, taking herself to rebuke the Elders*, and he claimed his right by virtue of her transgression.[28]

Even though a close relationship between sin and physical affliction clearly can be demonstrated, it must not be assumed, by any means, that all sickness is the result of evil doing. As the prophet Joseph Smith taught,

It is a false idea that the Saints will escape all the judgments, whilst the wicked suffer; for all flesh is subject to suffer, and 'the righteous shall hardly escape;' still many of the Saints will escape, for the just shall live by faith; yet many of the righteous shall fall a prey to disease, to pestilence, etc., by reason of the weakness of the flesh, and yet be saved in the Kingdom of God. So that *it is an unhallowed principle to say that such and such have transgressed because they have been preyed upon by disease*

28. *Gems For The Young Folks*, pp. 71-3.

or death, for all flesh is subject to death; and the Saviour has said, 'Judge not, lest ye be judged.'[29]

The Savior's teaching to his disciples also stresses that sickness must not always be considered the result of sin:

And as Jesus passed by, he saw a man which was blind from his birth.

And his disciples asked him, saying, Master, who did sin, this man or his parents, that he was born blind?

Jesus answered, Neither hath this man sinned, nor his parents: but that the works of God should be made manifest in him.[30]

Sickness also Caused by Satan

It appears that sickness can also be sent by the devil to retard the righteous efforts of good men. Such was the observation of Apostle Wilford Woodruff, who told of the difficulty experienced by the Twelve as they attempted to fulfill their missionary callings in 1839:

Inasmuch as the devil had been in a measure thwarted by the Twelve going to Far West, and returning without harm, it seemed as though the destroyer was determined to make some other attempt upon us to hinder us from performing our mission; for it seemed that *as soon as any one of the Apostles began to prepare for starting, he was smitten with chills and fever or sickness of some kind.*

Nearly all of the quorum of the Twelve or their families began to be sick, so it still required the exercise of a good deal of faith and perseverence to start off on a mission.[31]

No doubt the ability to bring sickness upon the servants of the Lord is a tool which Lucifer has attempted to use in his efforts to thwart the work of God's servants. It can be seen that if Satan is going to use such powers, Church members should be more than willing to lay claim to the gift of faith to be healed and to the healing powers of the priesthood.

Summary

1. In Jesus' day many individuals were granted the gift of faith to be healed. This same gift is promised to the people who live in the last days.

---

29. HC, IV, p. 11.
30. Jn. 9:1-3.
31. *Leaves From My Journal*, p. 68.

2. Those who believe but lack the gift of faith to be healed are to be nourished and cared for with medicine and tender care.

3. The gift of faith to be healed involves a movitating belief
   A. that the sickness or injury can be healed through the power of Jesus,
   B. that Christ is divine,
   C. that the individual who is administering possesses the the authority to heal the sick through divine power.

4. At times the Lord grants special visions, dreams, or promptings to create stronger faith to be healed in an individual.

5. The healing of those who possess the faith to be healed can take place in more than one way. While the normal method for healing involves the ordinance of administration, some have been healed at the time of baptism, through coming in contact with certain servants of the Lord, etc.

6. While sin is certainly not the cause of all sickness, some people become sick because of their unworthiness and sinfulness.

7. It appears that Satan possesses the power to bring sickness upon mortal beings.

CHAPTER X

Miracles

Miracles a Sign of the Faithful

It was to Nephi that the Lord proclaimed "Behold, *I am God; and I am a God of miracles;* and I will show unto the world that I am the same yesterday, today, and forever."[1] "*With God nothing shall be impossible.*"[2]

The power to perform miracles has been granted unto some by God, as a gift of the Spirit.[3] Indeed, the Savior revealed that "*unto as many as received me gave I power to do many miracles, and to become the sons of God.*"[4] While talking to His disciples, the Master taught, "Verily, verily, I say unto you, He that believeth on me, *the works that I do shall he do also; and greater works than these shall he do. . . .*"[5]

According to the teachings of Mormon, miracles will continue on the earth as long as man manifests faith in Christ, and they will be a characteristic of the true followers of the Lord.

> Christ hath said: *If ye will have faith in me ye shall have power to do whatsoever thing is expedient in me. . . .*
>
> And now, my beloved brethren, if this be the case that these things are true which I have spoken unto you, and God will show unto you, with power and great glory at the last day, that they are true, and if they are true *has the day of miracles ceased?*
>
> Or have angels ceased to appear unto the children of men? Or has he withheld the power of the Holy Ghost from them? Or will he, so long as time shall last, or the earth shall stand, or there shall be one man upon the face thereof to be saved?
>
> Behold, I say unto you, Nay; for *it is by faith that miracles are wrought;* and it is by faith that angels appear and minister

---

1. 2 Ne. 27:23.
2. Lk. 1:37; Mt. 19:26.
3. See I Cor. 12:10; D & C 46:21; Moro. 10:12.
4. D & C 45:8.
5. Jn. 14:12.

unto men; wherefore, if these things have ceased wo be unto
the children of men, for it is because of unbelief, and all is vain.

For no man can be saved, according to the words of Christ,
save they shall have faith in his name; wherefore, if these things
have ceased, then has faith ceased also; and awful is the state
of man, for they are as though there had been no redemption
made.[6]

The word of prophecy, however, indicates that the churches of
men which will exist in the last days will deny and reject the gift
of miracles and will not enjoy this power:

They deny the power of God, the Holy One of Israel; and
they say unto the people: Hearken unto us, and hear ye our
precept; for behold there is no God today, for the Lord and the
Redeemer hath done his work, and he hath given his power
unto men;

Behold, hearken ye unto my precept; *if they shall say there
is a miracle wrought by the hand of the Lord, believe it not;
for this day he is not a God of miracles; he hath done his work.*[7]

Miraculous Powers Granted to Man

Through the gift of the Spirit, God grants unto His servants
the power to perform miracles. Such was the great promise which
God made to the prophet Nephi:

Behold, thou art Nephi, and I am God. Behold, I declare
it unto thee in the presence of mine angels, that ye shall have
power over this people, and shall smite the earth with famine,
and with pestilence, and destruction, according to the wickedness of this people.

Behold, I give unto you power, that whatsoever ye shall
seal on earth shall be sealed in heaven; and whatsoever ye shall
loose on earth shall be loosed in heaven; and thus shall ye have
power among this people.

And thus, if ye shall say unto this temple it shall be rent
in twain, it shall be done.

And if ye shall say unto this mountain, Be thou cast down
and become smooth, it shall be done.

And behold, if ye shall say that God shall smite this people,
it shall come to pass.[8]

---

6. Moro. 7:33, 35-38.
7. 2 Ne. 28:5-6.
8. Hel. 10:6-10. For fulfillment of the promise, see Hel. 10:15-11:18.

Enoch had enjoyed a similar blessing, for God had promised him: "Behold my Spirit is upon you, wherefore *all thy words will I justify; and the mountains shall flee before you, and the rivers shall turn from their course;* and thou shalt abide in me, and I in you; therefore walk with me."[9] Leading the Israelites out of bondage, Moses had been promised the power to perform miracles:

Blessed art thou Moses, for I, the Almighty, have chosen thee, and *thou shalt be made stronger than many waters; for they shall obey thy command as if thou wert God.*

And lo, I am with thee, even unto the end of thy days; for thou shalt deliver my people from bondage, even Israel my chosen.[10]

The scriptures give man instruction as to the methods by which the gift of miracles should be controlled. First of all, the power should be used sparingly and with great discretion:

Require not miracles, except I shall command you, except casting out devils, healing the sick, and against poisonous serpents, and against deadly poisons;

And these things ye shall not do, except it be required of you by them who desire it, that the scriptures might be fulfilled; for ye shall do according to that which is written.[11]

Man must never assume the glory and honor for performing these deeds through the power of the Spirit, for without God's help and direction, man is impotent and useless. The power to perform miracles should be regarded as a gift from God and the glory be given to Him, as Ammon did:

Yea, I know that I am nothing; as to my strength I am weak; therefore I will not boast of myself, but *I will boast of my God, for in his strength, I can do all things; yea, behold, many mighty miracles we have wrought in this land,* for which we will praise his name forever.[12]

The power to perform miracles is not granted by God to the unrighteous. As Nephi wrote,

Now it came to pass that according to our record, and we know our record to be true, for behold, it was a just man who did

---

9. Moses 6:34. For fulfillment of the promise, see Moses 7:13.
10. Moses 1:25-26.
11. D & C 24:13-14.
12. Al. 26:12.

keep the record—for he truly did many miracles in the name of Jesus; and *there was not any man who could do a miracle in the name of Jesus save he were cleansed every whit from his iniquity.*[13]

Being able to perform miracles in the name of the Lord also is dependent upon faith. Jesus' well-known admonition should be reconsidered in this context: "If ye have faith as a grain of mustard seed, ye shall say unto this mountain, Remove hence to yonder place: and it shall remove; and nothing shall be impossible unto you."[14]

Many Types of Miracles

The dictionary defines the term miracle as "a wonderful happening that is contrary to or independent of the known laws of nature." The gift of working miracles has been manifested throughout history in many ways. For example, physical needs have been supplied by the operation of this gift. Elijah used it to increase the meal and oil of the widow of Zarephath.[15] The gift of miracles was granted to Elisha, who multiplied the widow's oil so that her creditors would not seize her home.[16] He also fed one hundred men with twenty small barley loaves.[17] Moses was the instrument for the working of miracles when the bitter waters of Marah where made sweet,[18] when water was drawn from rocks at Rephidim[19] and Meribah;[20] similarly with Elisha when the waters of Jericho were healed with salt,[21] and when water was supplied for the army of Jehoshaphat.[22] The same power was manifested by Jesus when He miraculously provided the tribute money,[23] changed the water to wine at Cana,[24] helped

---

13. 3 Ne. 8:1.
14. Mt. 17:20.
15. I Kin. 17:14-16.
16. II Kin. 4:1-7.
17. II Kin. 4:42-44.
18. Exo. 15:23-25.
19. Exo. 17:5-7.
20. Num. 20:7-11.
21. II Kin. 2:19-22.
22. II King. 3:16-20.
23. Mt. 17:24-27.
24. Jn. 2:1-11.

his disciples catch a huge drought of fishes,[25] and multiplied the food to feed groups of four[26] and five thousand.[27]

Some of the most spectacular examples of the gift of working miracles are in the area of restorations to life. Through this gift Elijah restored the widow's son to life.[28] It was manifest when Elisha restored the Shunammite woman's son to life.[29] Jesus restored life to the son of the widow of Nain,[30] and to the daughter of Jairus.[31] The Book of Mormon tells of Nephi's raising his brother from the dead.[32]

The raising of people from the dead is not unheard of in the restored Church. An example is the raising of Brother Henager from the dead, as told by himself in a testimony meeting held in Pueblo, Colorado, in 1910:

> My father's family lived in a mountainous region in Virginia, and during the period that President John Morgan was in charge of the Southern States Mission, he came into our country to hold a series of meetings; one of which was about thirty miles distant from our home.
>
> Apparently he had known our family and when the evening meeting was finished, he made inquiry concerning my father and mother. One member of our family who had gone to the meeting told President Morgan that his folks were unable to attend because of the serious illness of his brother. 'Well,' replied President Morgan, 'I have a message for them, and we must get it to them immediately.'
>
> He arrived at our home about 3:00 o'clock the following morning. In the meantime the boy who was sick had died several hours previously. *President Morgan went into the room where the boy of ten years lay and prayed for him; blessed him and raised him to life.*
>
> The boy went to school the following morning and when the school teacher arrived, he was sitting on the fence in front of the school. She thought he was an apparition since the word had traveled around the neighborhood that he had died the night

25. Jn. 21:1-8.
26. Mt. 15:32.
27. Mt. 14:15.
28. I Kin. 17:17-24.
29. II Kin. 4:29-37.
30. Lk. 7:11-17.
31. Mk. 5:22-43. He also called Lazarus back to life (Jn. 11:1-46).
32. 3 Ne. 7:19-20; 19:4.

before, and she wouldn't believe otherwise until she looked for
and found a scar that he had upon his wrist—' Then he continued: 'I was that boy.'[33]

Le Roi C. Snow, son of President Lorenzo Snow, recounted
an instance in which his father called back a twenty-year-old
woman from the dead:

> *'The dead shall rise and come forth at thy bidding'* — *was
> the promise made to Lorenzo Snow, when he was a young man
> twenty-two years of age, by the first Patriarch of the Church,
> Joseph Smith, Sr. . . .*
>
> For several weeks Ella Jensen had lingered between life and
> death with scarlet fever. On one particular night, a close girl
> friend, Lea Reese, now Mrs. Wilford Reeder of Brigham City,
> was staying with her to relieve Ella's over-weary parents of the
> night vigil. She relates: 'About three o'clock in the morning
> I was suddenly awakened by Ella calling me. She was excited.
> She said: 'They are coming to get me at ten o'clock in the morn-
> ing. I am going to die and they are coming at ten o'clock to take
> me away. I must get ready. Will you help me?' She asked me to
> call her parents. I explained to her that they were tired and
> asleep and it would be better not to disturb them. 'You must
> call them,' she said. 'I want to tell them now.' The parents
> were called, and she explained that *her Uncle Hance, who was
> dead, had appeared to her while she was awake, her eyes open,
> and told her that the messengers were to be there at ten o'clock
> to conduct her into the spirit world.* The parents thought that
> she was delirious and tried to get her to quiet down and go to
> sleep but she insisted that she was going to die and that they
> were coming for her. She wanted to see the members of the
> family and bid them goodby. As ten o'clock approached while
> her father was holding her hand, he felt the pulse become very
> weak. A few moments later it stopped; he turned to his wife
> and said: 'She has gone; her pulse has stopped.' The grief-
> stricken parents concluded to send for President Lorenzo Snow,
> the girl's uncle, and advise with him.
>
> President Snow, upon receiving the word, left a meeting in
> the Tabernacle and invited Rudger Clawson, who was then
> President of the Box Elder Stake of Zion, to accompany him to
> the Jensen home. President Snow was Brother Jensen's brother-
> in-law. When they arrived at the home they found the family
> almost hysterical with grief. . . .

---

33. Hinckley, *Faith of Pioneer Fathers,* p. 256.

President Clawson relates: 'As we entered the home, we met Sister Jensen who was very much alarmed. We went to Ella's bedside. We were impressed by the thought that her spirit had passed out of the body and gone beyond. Turning to me, President Snow said; 'Brother Clawson, will you anoint her?' which I did. We then laid our hands upon her head and the anointing was confirmed by President Snow. He blessed her, and among other things, used this very extraordinary expression in a commanding voice: 'Come back Ella, come back. Your work upon the earth is not completed. Come back.' Shortly thereafter, we left the home. President Snow said to the parents: 'Now do not mourn or grieve any more, it will be all right. Brother Clawson and I are busy and must go. We cannot stay but you must be patient and wait and do not mourn because it will be all right.'

Her father said that she remained in this condition for an hour and a half after President Snow left the house. Three hours from the time she first passed away, her parents remained sitting by her bedside watching, waiting, when all at once, she opened her eyes. She looked about the room, saw us sitting there and still looked for someone else. First thing she said was: *'Where is he?* We asked: 'Who, where is who?' 'Brother Snow,' she replied. *'He called me back.'* They told her he had gone. She said *'Why did he call me back? I was happy. I did not want to come back.'*[34]

---

34. *Ibid.,* p. 45-47. "Regarding the more than three and one half hours that Ella spent in the spirit world, she says: 'At ten o'clock, my spirit left my body. It took me some time to make up my mind to go as I could hear and see the folks crying and mourning over me. It was very hard for me to leave them. As soon as I had a glimpse of the other world I was anxious to go, and all the cares of the world left me. *I entered a large hall. It was so long that I could not see the end of it, and it was filled with people.* As I went through this hall, the first person I recognized was my grandpa, H. P. Jensen, who was sitting in one end of the room writing. He looked up somewhat surprised to see me and said: 'Why, there is my granddaughter Ella'. He was very much pleased, greeted me and as he continued with his writing, I passed on through the room and met many of my relatives and friends. It was like going along the crowded streets of a city where you meet many people, only a very few of whom you recognize. People seemed to be in family groups. Some inquired about their friends and relatives on the earth. Among this number was my cousin. *The people were all dressed in white,* excepting Uncle Hance Jensen who had on his dark clothes, long rubber boots, the things he wore when he drowned in the Snake River in Idaho. *Everybody appeared to be perfectly happy.* I was having a very pleasant visit with each one that I knew. When I reached the end of the long room,

Among the best known treatments of the subject of the working of miracles was one given in a Brigham Young University assembly in 1953 by Elder Matthew Cowley. This apostle, who himself enjoyed the gift to a great degree, drew from his memories of his labors in New Zealand the following instance of raising the dead:

I was called to a home in a little village in New Zealand one day. There the Relief Society sisters were preparing the body of one of our saints. They had placed his body in front of the big house, as they call it, the house where the people came to wail and weep and mourn over the dead, when in rushed the dead man's brother.

He said, 'Administer to him.'

And the young natives said, 'Why, you shouldn't do that; he's dead.'

'You do it!'

This same old man that I had with me when his niece was so ill, was there. The younger native got down on his knees and he anointed this man. Then this great old sage got down and blessed him and commanded him to arise. You should have seen the Relief Society sisters scatter. And he sat up and he

---

I opened the door and went into another room filled with children. They were all arranged in perfect order, the smallest one first, the larger ones according to age and size in the back rows all around the room. *They seemed to be convened in a sort of a Primary or a Sunday School,* presided over by Aunt Eliza R. Snow. There were hundreds of small children.

"It was while she was listening to the children sing that she heard President Snow's voice. He said: 'Sister Ella, you must come back as your mission is not finished here on earth.' Ella relates: 'So I just spoke to Aunt Eliza and told her that I must go back.' She obeyed this call although it was very much against her desire, such perfect peace and happiness prevailed there. *There was no suffering, no sorrow.* This was always a source of comfort to her. She learned by this experience that we should not grieve too much for our departed loved ones, especially at the time they leave us.

"'As I was leaving,' relates Ella, 'the only regret that I had was that the folks were grieving so much for me, but I soon forgot all about this world in my delight with the other. For more than three hours my spirit was gone from my body. As I returned, I could see my body lying on the bed and the folks gathering about in the room. I hesitated for a moment, then thought. 'Yes, I will go back for a little while.' I told the folks I would stay only a short time to comfort them."

She described that there was practically no pain on leaving the body in death but the pain was intense in coming back to life. (pp. 47-48).

said, *'Send for the elders; I don't feel very well.'* Now, of course, all of that was just psychological effect on that dead man. Wonderful, isn't it — this psychological effect business? Well, we told him he had just been administered to, and he said, 'Ho, that was it.' He said, 'I was dead. *I could feel life coming back into me just like a blanket unrolling.'* Now he outlived the brother that came in and told us to administer to him.[35]

Several instances of miraculous healings are recorded in chapters VIII and IX; examples of this type of miracle will therefore he omitted here.

Some of the greatest examples of the gift of working miracles center around the control of the elements. One may recall, for instance, how Moses parted the waters of the Red Sea so that the Israelites could flee from the Egyptians.[36] Israel also crossed the River Jordan on dry ground when a similar miracle was performed under Joshua's direction.[37] A similar feat was performed twice again on the River Jordan by Elijah and Elisha.[38]

The rotation of the earth was, apparently, altered through the operation of this gift. Joshua commanded the sun to stand still:

> And the sun stood still, and the moon stayed, until the people had avenged themselves upon their enemies. Is not this written in the book of Jasher? *So the sun stood still in the midst of heaven, and hasted not to go down about a whole day.*
> And there was no day like that before it or after it, that the Lord hearkened unto the voice of a man: for the Lord fought for Israel.[39]

The control of the elements through this gift of working miracles has similarly been experienced in modern times. There are many accounts of terrible storms at sea being instantly calmed through the prayers of missionaries and other Latter-day Saints who were in passage. Elder John Tanner wrote of one such experience:

> At the Spring conference, in 1853, I was called on a mission to Europe, with a number of others. While crossing the ocean,

---

35. Matthew Cowley, *Miracles* (A talk given Wednesday, Feb. 18, 1953, at Brigham Young University. Published by BYU Extension Services), p. 9.
36. Exo. 14:21-31.
37. Josh. 3:13-17.
38. II Kin. 2:7-8, 14.
39. Josh. 10:13-14.

when about two hundred miles from Liverpool, we encountered, what the captain said, was the severest storm he had experienced during thirty years of sea-faring life. There were seven Elders on board the English Sailing ship, *Asburton*. When the storm became the most severe only four could be got together. We had taken second cabin passage, and, of coure, had a room with bunks in which to sleep. To this room Elders Charles R. Dana, Israel Barlow and myself repaired, leaving Brother Thomas Colburn outside to watch and tend the door while we prayed and rebuked the raging wind and boisterous sea. We had but just commenced to pray when the door of the ventilator of our room flew open and let a large stream of water upon us. Brother Barlow sprang upon one of the upper bunks and closed the door and held it to its place while Brother Dana and myself continued the prayer. By this time the ship had come so near capsizing that a bottle of ink being open, and standing over one door-post, which was about six feet high, emptied its contens upon the opposite post about one and a half feet from the door sill, making an angle, by actual measurement, of over fifty degrees, which was just about as far as she could go without capsizing. *Just at this juncture the wind was rebuked by the servants of the Lord, and so sudden was the reaction that the ship creaked from stem to stern and we did not know but what she might fall to pieces.* But the main damage done was to lose her sails and cause the yard-arm to fall and break the ship-carpenter's leg. The cargo was shipped to one side so that she could not run level during the remainder of the voyage. We had on board, among other passengers, a Presbyterian temperance lecturer, with whom we had had many arguments on the use of the spiritual gifts, he taking the view that they were done away because no longer needed. His berth was on the opposite side of the ship. Before the prayer was closed and the door opened, he stood trembling with excitement outside. No sooner was the door opened than he exclaimed hastily and in an excited manner, '*Haven't you been praying? haven't you been praying?* On Elder Dana inquiring why he asked that question, he nervously answered, '*I thought you had; the wind stopped blowing so suddenly.*'

During the remainder of the journey, whenever there was more than a gentle breeze of wind, this man and his friends were sure to find their way to our cabin, as though they thought, if all the balance of the ship sank, our side would float all right.[40]

---

40. *Scraps of Biography,* pp. 38-39.

Miracles Performed Other Than By Divine Power

Possession of the gift of miracles should not be regarded as the only identifying characteristic of Christ's church. While it is a necessary sign, and must be possessed by any church which would claim to be Christ's true church, an individual's belief in miracles is a fertile field for deception by the Evil One. The instance of Moses and Aaron before Pharaoh demonstrates this ability to duplicate miracles which Satan possesses. When challenged to perform a miracle, Moses told Aaron to throw down his rod; Aaron obeyed and the rod became a serpent. The evil magicians of Egypt then proceeded to duplicate the feat:

> Then Pharaoh also called the wise men and the sorcerers: now the magicians of Egypt, they also did in like manner with their enchantments.
>
> For *they cast down every man his rod, and they became serpents.*[41]

Jesus also taught that some people may perform miracles through other than divine power. His teaching leaves unanswered the question of whether these people are intentional tools of Satan or whether they are themselves deceived.

> Many will say to me in that day, Lord, Lord, have we not prophesied in thy name? and in thy name have cast out devils? and in thy name done many wonderful works?
>
> And then will I profess unto them, I never knew you: depart from me, ye that work iniquity.[42]

Miracles Not Shown to Unbelievers

Just as lack of faith may prevent man from performing miracles, it may also prevent others from doing them in his presence, "for if there be no faith among the children of men, God can do no miracle among them."[43] When Jesus visited Galilee He "did not many mighty works there because of their unbelief."[44] Other people may be without the spirit of discernment and be frightened by the works of God and His servants. They may reject the doers of righteousness and cast them from

41. Exo. 7:11-12.
42. Mt. 7:22-23. See 2 Ne. 28:14.
43. Eth. 12:12.
44. Mt. 13:58.

their midst because of fear. This was the case with the Gadarenes, who rejected the Master because He cast evil spirits from a man, a manifestation which frightened them.[45]

Some people are blinded and will not accept the miracles which may be manifested to them, as was prophesied by Isaiah, "He hath blinded their eyes, and hardened their heart; that they should not see with their eyes, nor understand with their heart, and be converted."[46]

To all those who reject the miracles of God or who lack the faith to witness them, the warning of Nephi should be repeated: "Wo be unto him that hearkeneth unto the precepts of men, and denieth the power of God, and the gift of the Holy Ghost!"[47] Such individuals are like the Sadduccees, to whom Jesus said, "Ye do err, not knowing the scriptures, nor the power of God."[48]

Summary

1. The Lord is a God of miracles. He had granted unto his true followers the ability to perform miracles just as he performed while upon the earth.

2. The ability to perform miracles is another of the gifts granted through the Holy Spirit.

3. Miracles are a characteristic of the true Church of Jesus Christ. Unauthorized churches tend to reject them.

4. Satan also has the power to perform miracles and may do so to deceive those who would follow Christ.

5. Some may perform miracles and claim to do so in the name of Christ. Yet, if they are not authorized their miraculous works will not serve to bring them closer to salvation.

6. Some of the different types of miracles were discussed.

7. Miracles should not be required or performed unless prompted or commanded of the Lord.

8. Man must not glory and assume honor because he possesses the gift of miracles. The power stems from God; without it, man can do no miracles.

9. The lack of faith of unbelievers can sometimes hinder the power to perform miracles which others may possess and thus prevents the unbeliever from having the opportunity to witness miracles.

---

45. Lk. 8:37.
46. Jn. 12:40.
47. 2 Ne. 28:26.
48. Mt. 22:29.

CHAPTER XI

Helps and Governments

The gift of helps and governments[1] seems to refer to those items of counsel which are revealed by the Spirit to aid individuals in conducting their personal affairs. It consists of help in solving personal problems and aid in governing and controlling one's actions. It includes advice on personal morality, family living, earning a living, getting along with others, respecting civil authority, handling arguments, developing one's talents, and numerous other subjects. The important characteristic of this gift is that it is variable in its nature; it is the manifestation of the Spirit in the assisting of every person who seeks Him with his own particular problems.

Preparation for Church Callings

It is through this gift that the Holy Ghost prepares men for callings within the Church. Rulon S. Wells, for instance, was led by the Spirit to kneel in prayer, though he did not understand why until the following day:

> I was measuring lumber as it came from the mill and was being stacked near by, when *I was seized with a peculiar feeling over which I had no control*, and which impelled me to descend from the pile of lumber and go to the office, a little board shanty which served the purpose of office, store, and bed-room combined. It was situated about 300 or 400 feet from where I was working. After entering the door and locking it, *I knelt down and prayed to the Lord "to send me where He wanted me to go." This was the whole burden of my prayer which lasted only about one minute. The whole proceeding was to me a very strange one, for I did not understand the meaning of it*, and it was so unusual and out of the ordinary. On this very day, and probably at the same moment, my name was being called in the Tabernacle at Salt Lake City, where the conference was then being held, for a mission. The first intimation I had of this call was when my mother, then fifty-one years old, rode on horseback,

---

1. I Cor. 12:28.

in company with Archibald Livingstone, who was superintendent
of the mills, on the following day to mill F and apprised me of
this fact.[2]

Wilford Woodruff received preparation for responsibility and
the answer to his prayer as a manifestation of this gift.

> He wanted to go on a mission, but felt that he should be
> called, and yet he sincerely believed that the Lord would prompt
> those whose duty it was to bestow upon him such an honor, such
> a privilege. He retired to the woods in prayer. There upon his
> knees in humility and childlike simplicity, he told the Lord
> his wishes and his hopes. He asked Him, if it was within His
> holy will, that the way might be opened for him to preach the
> gospel in the world. 'Before I arose from my knees,' he says,
> *'the spirit of the Lord rested upon me and bore witness that my
> prayer was heard and should be answered upon my head.* I arose
> very happy and walked through thick woods about forty rods
> into an open road. As I entered the roadway, I met Judge Elias
> Higbee. Brother Hibgee [sic] was a high priest and a very
> faithful man, one of the noblest men of God in the last days.
> I had associated with him daily, but never mentioned to him
> my desire to preach the gospel. To my surprise, as soon as I
> approached him he said: "Brother Wilford, *the spirit of the Lord
> tells me that you should be ordained to go and preach the
> gospel."* '[3]

In another manifestation of this gift, Elder Woodruff was
prepared for his call to the apostleship by revelation several weeks
before he was appointed to that position by the prophet. At this
time he was serving as a missionary in the Fox Islands.

> While holding meeting with the Saints at North Vinal
> Haven on the 9th of August, I received a letter from Thomas B.
> Marsh, who was then President of the Twelve Apostles, in-
> forming me that Joseph Smith, the Prophet, had received a
> revelation, naming as persons to be chosen to fill the places
> of those who had fallen: John E. Page, John Taylor, Wilford
> Woodruff and Willard Richards.

> President Marsh, added, in his letter, 'Know then, Brother
> Woodruff, by this, that you are appointed to fill the place of
> one of the Twelve Apostles, and that it is agreeable to the word
> of the Lord, given very lately, that you should come speedily

2. Jenson, I, p. 213.
3. Cowley, *Wilford Woodruff,* pp. 46-7.

to Far West, and, on the 26th of April next, take your leave
of the Saints here and depart for other climes across the mighty
deep.'

> *The substance of this letter had been revealed to me several*
> *weeks before, but I had not named it to any person.*[4]

Others were prepared by previous revelations to assume callings in the Church. One such individual was Heber J. Grant, for
"in his youth, Sister Eliza R. Snow, *in the gift of tongues, prom-*
ised him that he should be one of the leading men in the Church,
the interpretation being given by Zina D. Young."[5] His calling
was also prophesied by Heber C. Kimball, although Brother Grant
apparently did not know about it until he was actually called.
When he was named to the apostleship, President Grant's mother
asked her son,

> "Do you remember Heber C. Kimball picking you up when
> you were a young boy and putting you on a table and talking
> to you at a great dinner he was having for a lot of his friends?"
> "Yes." "Do you remember anything that he said?" "No, I only
> remember that he had the blackest eyes I have ever looked
> into. I was frightened. That is all I can remember." *"He*
> *prophesied in the name of the Lord, Jesus Christ that you would*
> *become an Apostle of the Lord Jesus Christ and become a*
> *greater man in the Church than your own father,* and your
> father, as you know, became one of the counselors to President
> Brigham Young. That is why I have told you to behave."[6]

After his calling to the apostleship, Elder Grant for a time was
constantly troubled with a feeling of unworthiness and a feeling
of incapability about fulfilling this important responsibility.
While on a stake conference assignment, Elder Grant received
this revelation which helped him to understand the reason for his
calling:

> In the kind providence of the Lord, it was manifested to me
> perfectly so far as my intelligence is concerned — I did not
> see heaven — I did not see a council held there, but like Lehi
> of old *I seemed to see, and my very being was so saturated with*
> *the information that I received as I stopped my animal and*
> *sat there and communed with heaven, that I am as absolutely*

---

4. *Leaves From My Journal,* p. 51.
5. Jenson, I, p. 150.
6. Hinckley, *Faith of Our Pioneer Fathers,* pp. 69-70.

*convinced of the information that came to me upon that oc-
casion as though the voice of God had spoken the words to me.*

It was manifested to me there and then that it was not because of any particular intelligence that I possessed, that it was
not because of any knowledge that I possessed more than a testimony of the Gospel, that it was not because of my wisdom, that
I had been called to be one of the Apostles of the Lord Jesus
Christ in this last dispensation, but *it was because the Prophet
of God, the man who was the chosen instrument in the hands
of the living God of establishing again upon the earth the plan
of life and salvation, Joseph Smith, desired that I be called, and
that my father, Jedediah M. Grant, who gave his life for the
Gospel, and who had been dead for nearly twenty-six years,
desired that his son should be a member of the Council of the
Twelve.* It was manifested to me that the Prophet and my
father were able to bestow upon me the apostleship because of
their faithfulness, inasmuch as I had lived a clean life, but *now
it remained for me to make a success or a failure of that calling.*[7]

Elder Matthias F. Cowley was lead to anticipate his call to
the apostleship by a prophecy sent to him in a letter by John W.
Taylor. The prophecy was made to him fifteen years before he
was named to the Quorum of the Twelve. Elder Taylor's letter
said,

> *I believe I speak by the spirit of prophecy when I say, if
> you are faithful you will yet become one of the Twelve Apostles
> of the Church of Jesus Christ* in all the world, and by the
> power of God and the eternal Priesthood will become great in
> wisdom and knowledge. Amen.[8]

Elder Alonzo A. Hinckley was promised a call to the apostleship in his patriarchal blessing, thirty years before his ordination.
Patriarch John Ashman told him, on October 21, 1903,

> Your spirit is a noble spirit of the House of Abraham, and
> Prince of the Tribe of Ephraim. If you continue faithful in this
> calling, wherein you are called to labor, you will accomplish
> much good in your day and generation. You already have done
> a great work. And if you continue to labor with the zeal with
> which you have started, *you will be numbered with the Twelve
> Apostles of the Church of Jesus Christ of Latter-day Saints.*[9]

---

7. *Ibid.,* pp. 79-80.
8. Jenson, I, p. 154.
9. Hinckley, *Faith of Our Pioneer Fathers,* pp. 234-5.

The call to the Twelve of Elder Matthew Cowley was
prophesied by a New Zealand Saint who was preaching a mem-
orial sermon:

> After President Hardy died we had a memorial service for
> him. I'll never forget the native who was up speaking, saying
> what a calamity it was to the mission to lose this great New
> Zealand missionary who could do so much for them as one of
> the Authorities of the Church. He was talking along that line,
> and all of a sudden he stopped and he looked around at me and
> said, 'Wait a minute. There's nothing to worry about. Not a
> thing to worry about. *When President Cowley gets home he'll
> fill the first vacancy in the Council of the Twelve Apostles, and
> we'll still have a representative among the Authorities of the
> Church.*' Then he went on talking about President Hardy.
> When I arrived home the following September I filled the first
> vacancy in the Quorum of the Twelve. Now did that just hap-
> pen by chance? Oh, I might have thought so if it had been one
> of you white Gentiles that had prophesied that, but not from
> the blood of Israel. Oh no, I could not deny, I couldn't doubt
> it.[10]

That David O. McKay would sit in the leading councils of
the Church was prophesied by a member of his mission presidency in 1899 in a missionary testimony meeting:

> During the progress of the meeting, an elder on his own
> initiative arose and said, 'Brethren, there are angels in this
> room.' Strange as it may seem, the announcement was not
> startling; indeed, it seemed wholly proper; though it had not
> occurred to me there were divine beings present. I only knew
> that I was overflowing with gratitude for the presence of the
> Holy Spirit. I was profoundly impressed, however, when Presi-
> dent James L. McMurrin arose and confirmed that statement
> by pointing to one brother sitting just in front of me saying,
> 'Yes, brethren, there are angels in this room, and one of them is
> the guardian angel of that young man sitting there.' and he
> designated one who today is a patriarch of the Church.
> Pointing to another elder, he said, 'And one is the guardian
> angel of that young man there,' and singled out one whom I
> had known from childhood. Tears were rolling down the cheeks
> of both of these missionaries, not in sorrow or grief, but as an
> expression of the overflowing Spirit; indeed, we were all weeping.
> Such was the setting in which James L. McMurrin gave
> what has since proved to be a prophecy. I had learned by inti-

10. Cowley, *Miracles*, p. 7.

mate association with him that James McMurrin was pure gold; his faith in the gospel implicit; that no truer man, no more loyal man to what he thought was right ever lived; so when he turned to me and gave what I thought then was more of a caution than a promise, his words made an indelible impression upon me. Paraphrasing the words of the Savior to Peter, he said: 'Let me say to you Brother David, *Satan hath desired you that he may sift you as wheat, but God is mindful of you.*' Then he added, '*If you will keep the faith, you will yet sit in the leading councils of the Church.*' At that moment there flashed in my mind temptations that had beset my path, and I realized even better than President McMurrin, or any other man, how truly he had spoken when he said, 'Satan hath desired thee.' With the resolve then and there to keep the faith, there was born a desire to be of service to my fellow men, and with a realization, a glimpse at least, of what I owed to the elder who first carried the message of the Restored Gospel to my grandfather and grandmother who had accepted the message years before in the north of Scotland, and in South Wales.[11]

This pattern of preparation by the Spirit has undoubtedly been followed in other cases, as men have been led to prepare for greater responsibilities in the Lord's kingdom.

The author had occasion to experience special guidance of the Spirit in preparation for a Church assignment while he was a sophomore student at Brigham Young University. It is related here because of the lasting impression it made upon him and the molding influence it had upon his life.

In January, 1954, I received a manifestation from the Holy Ghost which taught me to recognize the nature of spiritual guidance. The manifestation concerned a calling to serve in the Church — a common occurrence which might make it seem insignificant to others. Yet to me it was a turning point in my life because it taught me of the actuality of the promptings of the Spirit. Although my prayers had often been answered in small ways before, this instance was the first time that I knew, without doubt, that I had received a communication from God as a direct manifestation of His will unto me.

I was a sophomore student at Brigham Young University and a member of the Campus Branch of the Church. This branch served as the L.D.S. Church unit for many of the BYU students who were not affiliated with the local wards in Provo. It was

11. Middlemiss, *op. cit.*, pp. 13-14.

large — three or four times the size of a normal ward — and one could easily feel "lost in the crowd" within it. One Sunday evening, as I attended Sacrament Meeting in Campus Branch, the branch officials chose to release various members from their Church assignments. This was a matter of course and left little impression upon me until suddenly they released one of the members from position of MIA Superintendent. *Immediately I received an undeniable impression that I was to be called as a member of the new YMMIA Superintendency. I heard no voice, I saw no vision, but I knew without a doubt that the calling was to come to me and that I was to prepare for it. I clearly remember the overwhelming feeling of certainty that accompanied the impression. There was no doubt.* I did not know when the calling would come, nor to what position in the Superintendency I would be called, but I knew, positively and emphatically, that such a calling would come.

During the next several days I tried to reason why the calling was to be given to me. I didn't even know any of the Branch Presidency personally. I was sure that I was just another of the unknown among the fifteen hundred or more members of the Branch. I was even new to Campus Branch, and had attended there for only a few weeks previous. My only previous activity in the Branch was the directing of an MIA chorus for about ten days before Christmas to help in a Christmas festival. Yet I had no doubt that the calling would soon come to me. I even told my roommates about it. I had registered for a heavier course load than I would be able to carry with the MIA responsibility and so I went and canceled a class. But most important, I attempted to make myself ready and worthy through fasting and prayer.

The following Sunday in Sacrament Meeting the Branch Presidency sustained Brother Robert Blair as MIA Superintendent and Brother Gene Dalton as Manual Assistant. By reason I assumed that I was to be called as Activity Assistant, although nothing was said to indicate that was to be my calling. The position was merely left vacant.

The next week was Branch Conference. President Ariel Ballif, the Stake President, was present at Sacrament Meeting and presided over the meeting. Following the opening business, President Ballif took the stand and said, "We haven't notified any speakers for tonight's service in advance, but would like to begin the meeting by calling three speakers from the audience." *As he said this I immediately knew that I was to be one of the speakers. Again there was no doubt, but a complete feeling of sureness. With this feeling I could also feel the burnings of*

*the Spirit within me, and I remember feeling like I was almost
on fire it was so strong.*

My roommate had borrowed a notebook of thoughts and
scriptural references which I had been preparing and had it
with him in the meeting. I reached over, took it from him, and
flipped the pages. *All the words were an indistinguishable blur
until suddenly one word leaped from the page at me in large
black letters as if it had been fired at me through a gun, and I
knew that was the subject upon which I was to speak.* When my
turn came I went to the stand and spoke by the power of the
Spirit. I could feel the words flowing from me and I knew
that it was not I who was formulating the thoughts being
expressed. The word I had seen was *chastity* and my talk was
a specific warning to some who were present that they were
to be ready to resist strong temptations which would confront
them within the next few days. I remember my telling the
congregation that I was speaking by the power of the Spirit,
that it was the second time I had felt His promptings within
the past few days, and that they would do well to heed my
words because they were the words of God. Suddenly the message was over and the Spirit left me. My mind was blank; I
announced that I had felt the Spirit leave me, closed in the
name of Jesus Christ, and sat down. The Stake President stood
and bore his testimony that I had spoken by the Spirit and
that my words were true.

The next afternoon on campus I passed Norene Dance, a
secretary to the Branch Presidency. She stopped me and said
that the Presidency was in a meeting in their office and that
they wanted to see me. I went to their office and, when it came
my turn, met with them. After greeting me, they said, "Brother
Crowther, you know what you're here for, don't you?" I answered, "Yes, you are going to call me into the Mutual Superintendency." There was no doubt, nor fear that I was mistaken.
I knew that was the Lord's will. They told me that normally
they conducted an extensive interview, but they could see that
in this instance I had been prepared by the Spirit and no further counsel was necessary on their part.

Although I have since been called to positions of greater
importance and responsibility, and on occasions have received
premonitions of those callings through the Spirit, yet this incident remains one of the treasured moments of my life and more
valued than any other calling. Through this experience I learned
the nature of absolute knowledge through the Holy Ghost. I
came to understand the manner in which one can testify that

he *knows* the gospel is true, and this knowledge is something valued above price with me.[12]

Guidance in Travels

Men have often been helped in their travels by the Spirit in manifestations of the gift of helps and governments. It was the guidance of the Spirit, for instance, that caused Marriner W. Merrill to settle in Richmond, Utah:

> During the winter of 1859 and 1860 Elders Benson and Hyde called at the home of Bro. Merrill and advised him to move to Cache valley, where there was more land and were better prospects financially, and a good opening for the Saints. He made preparation, and in February, 1860, went to Richmond, but did not remain long. In March, of the same year, he made the journey again and found the snow still very deep. At this time there were but few people in Logan or Cache valley, the first settlers having come to that place in 1859. Journeying farther north, Elder Merrill made his way to Richmond, in company with others, and encamped for some time where the dairy north of the town now stands, and they were about tu continue in a northerly direction their travels, when *a voice came to Brother Merrill, saying, 'Turn around and go south.' The words were repeated*, and without saying anything to his companions, Elder Merrill started southward and stopped when he reached the point where Richmond now stands, and there began work.[13]

This same gift was manifested to Joseph W. McMurrin, who became lost in a forest in Arizona:

> On one occasion, while upon the mountains in the midst of a dense forest, he lost his bearings and was unable to return to the camp where his companions were located. He searched for hours for the camp, but all in vain. His feelings at this time were most distressing, as he knew there was little hope of finding any human beings or habitation within a hundred miles if he missed his companions. As the shades of night approached he knelt down and sought the Lord in prayer, asking that he might be directed back to the camp. *Immediately on arising from his knees he felt strongly impressed to go in a direction exactly opposite to the one he had previously supposed was the one to*

---

12. Personal file of Duane S. Crowther.
13. Jenson, I, p. 159.

take. He followed this impression and to his great joy was led in a direct line to the camp.[14]

The guidance of the Spirit often has been granted to individuals to aid them in their travels. Members of the Church serving in the mission fields have been especially blessed with this type of manifestation of the Holy Ghost.

Assistance in Meeting Temporal Needs

The gift of helps and governments has often been manifested in helping people to meet their temporal needs. Elder Amasa Potter received the fruits of this gift in answer to his prayer that fare for a river ferry would be provided.

> We had a large river to cross on the way, and we were informed that the bridge had been carried off and there was a ferry established across the river which charged five shillings each passenger. We did not have any money with which to pay this charge, and my companion was anxious to know what we should do for money to pay the ferriage with. We were then about three miles from the ferry, and were passing through timber. I told him that we would go into the woods and pray to God to open the heart of some one to give it to us. We did so, and we had traveled but a short distance through a lane between two fields, when we looked ahead of us a little way and saw an old man coming across the field. He came into the road ahead of us, and as he came to meet us he had a smile on his countenance. *He reached out his hand to me, as if to shake hands, and left a crown, or five shilling piece, in my hand and went to my companion and did the same; but spoke not a word.* I cannot describe the feeling that we had when the man took hold of our hands; *we felt our hearts burn within us,* and it did not seem that we had power to ask him his name or where he was from, as we usually did when a person gave us any article of clothing or money. He was a man about six feet high, well proportioned, and wore a suit of light gray clothes and a broad brimmed hat, and his hair and beard were about eighteen inches long and as white as snow. We passed on and came to the ferry, and the money that we had was just enough to pay our ferriage.[15]

---

14. *Ibid.,* p. 216.
15. *Labors In The Vineyard,* p. 81.

Elder Thomas Phillips recorded how this gift was manifested in his behalf in providing him with a new hat:

I was traveling in the towns and villages in a part of the county of Surrey, England, preaching the gospel as revealed from the heavens through the ministry of holy beings. Under these circumstances, food and raiment were sometimes hard to obtain; consequently, at one time I had a hat that was very much the worse for wear.

In a village called Hersham, in that county, lived a brother by the name of William Hobbs, whose house I sometimes visited and received food and lodgings.

One night Brother Hobbs dreamt that a personage came to him and told him that Brother Phillips would be at his house on a certain day, naming the time, which I think was four or five days from the time he dreamt. He was further told, that he must get a new hat for Brother Phillips; for the one he wore was very shabby.

This dream was very much impressed on the mind of Brother Hobbs and troubled him sorely, for it found him without money and some miles from any town where he could buy a hat.

Brother Hobbs was the overseer of a small number of men, whose work was to keep some miles of railroad in repair for the safety of the trains.

When the day came that I was to be at his house in the evening, he went to his work very low-spirited, not having obtained the hat. While at work on the track, a long train of cars came along, and when passing the place where Brother Hobbs and his hands were at work, *a hat, suitable for the finest gentleman in the land, flew out of one of the windows.*

Brother Hobbs shouted 'That's the hat for Brother Phillips! Thank god!'

When Brother Hobbs came home in the evening, I was there, it being the time specified in the dream.

He walked up to me and said:

'Brother Phillips, I was to give you a hat, and here it is.'

To our surprise, it fitted me well.

As a matter of course I was anxious to know who was so thoughtful of an Elder of the Church of Jesus Christ of Latter-day Saints; and in answer to my questions, Brother Hobbs told me the dream.

Then I knew, and I still know, that the providences of our Heavenly Father were, and are, working in favor of the servants and Saints of the Most High.[16]

George Q. Cannon told of the answer to his prayer that he might be able to enjoy the common food of the Hawaiian Islands:

Before leaving Lahaina, I had tasted a teaspoonful of 'poi,' but the smell of it and the calabash in which it was contained was so much like that of a book-binder's old, sour, paste-pot that when I put it to my mouth I gagged at it, and would have vomited had I swallowed it. But in traveling among the people I soon learned that if I did not eat 'poi' I would put them to great inconvenience; for they would have to cook separate food for me every meal. This would make me burdensome to them, and might interfere with my success. I, therefore, determined to learn to live on their food, and, that I might do so, *I asked the Lord to make it sweet to me. My prayer was heard and answered; the next time I tasted it, I ate a bowlful, and I positively liked it.* It was my food, whenever I could get it from that time as long as I remained on the islands.[17]

An incident experienced by Alice McCracken in 1957 illustrates the willingness of the Spirit to help people with small problems. Sister McCracken found it necessary to drive by herself on a three thousand mile journey. She wrote of her experiences on the trip and told of this incident.

Blinded by the sun driving steadily westward in late afternoon I finally had to pull off the road. Never had my need for sun glasses been so great and I had no idea where they were. My packing of necessity had been hurried. Before taking a short nap I prayed that my Father in Heaven would help me find them. *When I awakened a voice said, 'Your sun glasses are in your brief case.'* Surely enough, they were there, though I hadn't used my brief case for three months.[18]

These are but a few of the hundreds of examples, in a multitude of categories, which can be cited to demonstrate the gift of helps and governments. This is the "miscellaneous" gift. It deals with any occasion in which man is granted special help or assistance in governing himself by the Holy Spirit. These helps can be manifested through dreams, visions, appearances, signs, in fact,

---

16. *A String of Pearls*, pp. 64-5.
17. *My First Mission*, pp. 33-4.
18. Hackworth, *op. cit.*, p. 269.

any means of communication can be used to convey the gifts. These are the common, every-day answers to prayer. They are the instances of spiritual phenomena best known to the average Latter-day Saint.

Summary

1. The gift of helps and governments includes any manifestation of the Spirit which helps man in the conduct of his personal affairs. This is the "miscellaneous" of the spiritual gifts.

2. A large portion of Latter-day Saint scripture is comprised of counsel which would fit into this category.

3. Many instances are on record of aid being given so individuals will prepare for new assignments in the Church.

4. This gift is often manifested in guidance to members of the Church in their travels.

5. The help which man receives in providing for his temporal needs often falls into this category.

Part IV

GIFTS OF
COMMUNICATION

CHAPTER XII

Revelation

Revelation Necessary for the Progress of Man

A great truth was spoken by John the Baptist, who bore witness that *"a man can receive nothing, except it be given him from heaven."*[1] All knowledge, all wisdom, all understanding, all truth which pertains to the things of God has had to be revealed to man by the Divine. The only avenue of growth in spiritual matters is revelation from God, and *"where there is no vision, the people perish."*[2]

Revelation, in the scriptural sense, is communication from God to man. The privilege of receiving such communication is another of the gifts of the Spirit, for man cannot know the will of God unless He chooses to reveal it. Without revelation, man could receive no direct answer to prayer. If there were no revelation there could be no church on the earth led and guided by God, and all religious activities would be functions of men, without guidance and approbation from on high.

Revelation Given in Many Ways

God communicates with man in numerous manners.

1. *Personal Appearance of Deity.* Direct face-to-face communication is one of the methods God has used to manifest His will unto man. A previous chapter[3] has enumerated a number of cases in which the Savior has made such personal appearances to communicate with men.

2. *The Voice of God.* There have been many times in which the voice of a member of the Godhead has spoken to reveal the will of Deity to man. Many of the revelations in the Doctrine and Covenants, for instance, begin with words such as "Listen to

---

1. Jn. 3:27.
2. Pro. 29:18.
3. Chapter III.

the voice of Jesus Christ, your God, and your Redeemer, whose word is quick and powerful."[4]

There are occasions wherein other messengers carry revelations from the Lord and yet actually speak as if they are the Savior as they deliver their message. The Holy Ghost may apparently speak for Christ in the first person as if He were the Savior, thus giving a revelation from the Savior with the voice of the Holy Ghost rather than with the Savior's voice. It seems that Section 97 of the Doctrine and Covenants is a case in point, for it begins with the words, "Verily I say unto you my friends, I speak unto you with my voice, *even the voice of my Spirit*, that I may show you my will."[5]

John the Revelator received a visitation from an angel who similarly spoke as though he were the Lord himself.[6]

3. *The Ministering of Angels.* Accounts of the coming of angels (representatives of God in either spirit or resurrected form) show that this is one of the methods which God has used in communicating with man. Perhaps the best known scriptural instance of revelation through this medium is the appearance of the angels to the shepherds at the time of Jesus' birth.[7]

An appearance of an angel is an actual experience and leaves a vivid impression of the visitation. The clarity of Joseph Smith's description of the Angel Moroni who visited him in his room in 1823 demonstrates the vividness of this occurrence:

> While I was thus in the act of calling upon God, I discovered a light appearing in my room, which continued to increase until the room was lighter than at noonday, when immediately *a personage appeared at my bedside, standing in the air, for his feet did not touch the floor.*
>
> *He had on a loose robe of most exquisite whiteness.* It was a whiteness beyond anything earthly I had ever seen; nor do I believe that any earthly thing could be made to appear so exceedingly white and brilliant. *His hands were naked, and his arms also, a little above the wrist; so, also were his feet naked, as were his legs, a little above the ankles. His head and neck were also bare.* I could discover that he had *no other clothing*

---

4. D & C 27:1.
5. D & C 97:1.
6. Rev. 22:8-13.
7. Lk. 2:8-14.

on but this robe, as it was open, so that I could see into his bosom.

Not only was his robe exceedingly white, but his *whole person was glorious beyond description, and his countenance truly like lightning.* The room was exceedingly light, but not so very bright as immediately around his person. When I first looked upon him, I was afraid; but the fear soon left me.[8]

Angels may come to a worthy recipient often. A case in point is Nephi, of whom the scripture says that "so great was his faith on the Lord Jesus Christ that angels did minister unto him daily."[9]

4. *Unidentified Voices.* At times men receive revelation by hearing a voice speak. No being appears, and no identification is made, yet an important message is communicated. The following record left by the prophet Joseph serves to illustrate this form of revelation:

I prophesy, in the name of the Lord God, that the commencement of the difficulties which will cause much bloodshed previous to the coming of the Son of Man will be in South Carolina.

It may probably arise through the slave question. *This a voice declared to me, while I was praying earnestly on the subject, December 25th, 1832.*

I was once praying very earnestly to know the time of the coming of the Son of Man, *when I heard a voice repeat the following:*

Joseph, my son, if thou livest until thou art eighty-five years old, thou shalt see the face of the Son of Man; therefore *let this suffice, and trouble me no more on this matter.*

I was left thus, without being able to decide whether this coming referred to the beginning of the millennium or to some previous appearing, or whether I should die and thus see his face.[10]

Voices have been a frequent source of warning to members of the Church. Bishop Charles W. Nibley recorded a warning given by this means to President Joseph F. Smith:

While he [Joseph F. Smith] was a hard-headed, successful business man, yet very few in this dispensation have been more gifted

---

8. Joseph Smith 2:30-32.
9. 3 Ne. 7:18.
10. D & C 130:12-16.

with spiritual insight than he. As we were returning from an eastern trip, some years ago on the train, just east of Green River, I saw him go out to the end of the car, on the platform, and immediately return and hesitate a moment, and then sit down in the seat just ahead of me. He had just taken his seat when something went wrong with the train. A broken rail had been the means of ditching the engine and had thrown most of the cars off the track. In the sleeper we were shaken up pretty badly, but our car remained on the track.

The President immediately said to me that he had gone on the platform when he heard a voice saying, 'Go in and sit down.'

He came in, and I noticed him stand a moment, and he seemed to hesitate, but he sat down.

He said further that as he came in and stood in the aisle he thought 'Oh pshaw, perhaps it is only my imagination;' when he heard the voice again, 'Sit down,' and he immediately took his seat, and the result was as I have stated.

He, no doubt, would have been seriously injured had he remained on the platform of that car, as the cars were all jammed up together pretty badly. He said, 'I have heard that voice a good many times in my life, and I have always profited by obeying it.'[11]

Young children have been directed or prepared for future experiences by the voices of unseen beings also. A case in point is that of Thomas A. Shreeve:

One day when Thomas was about twelve years old and was walking alone through one of the pleasant lanes of England, meditating on religious matters, he heard a voice calling him, saying, 'Thomas, if you are a good boy, you shall hear and see prophets.' He looked around, but saw no one; yet the incident never left his mind.[12]

5. Dreams. It appears that God ofttimes chooses to reveal His will to man while the mortal recipient is asleep. Nephi told of the commands his father, Lehi, received through the avenue of a dream:

For behold, it came to pass that the Lord spake unto my father, yea, even in a dream, and said unto him: Blessed art thou Lehi, because of the things which thou hast done;

---

11. Preston Nibley, The Presidents of the Church (Salt Lake City, Utah: Deseret Book Company, 1959), p. 266-67.
12. Jenson, II, p. 708.

and because thou hast been faithful and declared unto this people the things which I commanded thee, behold, they seek to take away thy life.

And it came to pass that *the Lord commanded my father*, even in a dream, that he should take his family and depart into the wilderness.[13]

Dreams have often been the means by which the Holy Spirit has prepared people to receive the message of the restored gospel. Elder C. V. Spencer found that a dream had prepared the way for his missionary labors as he went to preach in Colchester, England:

I came in sight of the place, on the top of a long hill, and noticed a woman crossing the road with two pails. She filled them with water and started back, but as she saw me walking towards her, she dropped both pails and came to me, saying, '*I knew you would come; I saw you in a dream.* Come into my house; I have a room all fixed nice and clean for you.'

Here I baptized my first fruits of the gospel, and accomplished a good work.[14]

A dream served as a warning to Elder Wilford Woodruff during his missionary labors in Arkansas:

I thought an angel came to us, and told us *we were commanded of the Lord to follow a certain straight path*, which was pointed out to us, let it lead us wherever it might. After we had walked in it awhile we came to the door of a house, which was in the line of a high wall running north and south, so that we could not go around. I opened the door and *saw the room was filled with large serpents*, and I shuddered at the sight. My companion said he would not go into the room for fear of the serpents. I told him I should try to go through the room though they killed me, for the Lord had commanded it. As I stepped into the room the serpents coiled themselves up, and raised their heads some two feet from the floor, to spring at me. There was one much larger than the rest in the centre of the room, which raised his head nearly as high as mine and made a spring at me. At that instant I felt as though nothing but the power of God could save me, and I stood still. *Just before the serpent reached me he dropped dead at my feet; all the rest dropped dead, swelled up, turned black, burst open, took*

13. 1 Ne. 2:1-2.
14. *Labors in the Vineyard*, p. 16.

fire and were consumed before my eyes, and we went through the room unharmed and thanked God for our deliverance.

I awoke in the morning and pondered upon the dream. We took breakfast and started on our journey on Sunday morning, to visit Mr. Akeman. I related to my companion my dream, and told him we should see something strange. We had great anticipations of meeting Mr. Akeman, supposing him to be a member of the Church. When we arrived at his house he received us very coldly, and we soon found that he had apostatized. He brought railing accusations against the Book of Mormon, and the authorities of the Church.

Word was sent through all the settlements on the river for twenty miles that two 'Mormon' preachers were in the place. A mob was soon raised, and warning sent to us to leave immediately or we would be tarred and feathered, ridden on a rail and hanged. I soon saw where the serpents were. My companion wanted to leave; I told him no, I would stay and see my dream fulfilled.

There was an old gentleman and lady, named Hubbel, who had read the Book of Mormon and believed. Father Hubbel came to see us, and invited us to make our home with him while we stayed in the place. We did so, and labored for him some three weeks with our axes, clearing land, while we were waiting to see the salvation of God.

I was commanded of the Lord by the Holy Ghost to go and warn Mr. Akeman to repent of his wickedness. I did so, and each time he raged against me, and the last time he ordered me out of his house. When I went out he followed me and was very angry. *When he came up to me, about eight rods from the house, he fell dead at my feet, turned black and swelled up, as I saw the serpents do in my dream.*

His family, as well as ourselves, felt it was the judgment of God upon him. I preached his funeral sermon. *Many of the mob died suddenly.* We stayed about two weeks after Akeman's death and preached, baptized Mr. Hubbel and his wife, and then continued on our journey.[15]

A dream was Elder Henry Eyring's notification of release from his missionary service to the Indians in 1860.

In May, 1860, after having labored in the Indian Territory four and a half years, I started for Utah, where I arrived Aug. 29, 1860. At that time the Cherokee Mission was under the

---

15. *Leaves from My Journal,* pp. 13-15.

direct charge of the Presidency in Utah, but it was very difficult in those days to get any news from there. I had had charge of the mission for over two years, and altogether had been in that field nearly four and a half years; hence I began to think that possibly my mission might come to a close before long. Getting no news of any kind from Utah, *I enquired of the Lord and He answered me in a dream*, as follows: I dreamed that I was in the President's office in Salt Lake City, and that I addressed Pres. Young saying: 'I have come of my own accord, but if I have not stayed long enough, I am willing to return and complete my mission.' The president answered: 'It is all right, you have stayed long enough.' On the strength of this dream I started for Utah; and when I met the President, I said to him: 'Pres. Young, I have come without being sent for; if this was not right, I am willing to go back and finish my mission.' He answered pleasantly: 'It is all right, *we have been looking for you.*'[16]

6. *Visions.* Visions are opportunities in which man is able to see events and activities in dimensions which are not visible to the mortal eye. While his physical being remains immobile, he may have the sight of distant places and people paraded before him, or he may be shown events of the past or the future. Such experiences may involve the conveying of tremendous knowledge. The magnitude of the vision shown unto Moses is noteworthy. This prophet

Cast his eyes and *beheld the earth, yea, even all of it; and there was not a particle of it which he did not behold, discerning it by the spirit of God.*

And he beheld also the inhabitants thereof, and *there was not a soul which he beheld not; and he discerned them by the Spirit of God;* and their numbers were great, even numberless as the sand upon the sea shore.

And he beheld many lands, and each land was called earth, and there were inhabitants on the face thereof.[17]

A similar vision was given to the brother of Jared: "And when the Lord had said these words, he showed unto the brother of Jared all the inhabitants of the earth which had been, and also all that would be; and he withheld them not from his sight, even unto the ends of the earth."[18]

---

16. Jenson, I, pp. 312-13.
17. Moses 1:27-29.
18. Eth. 3:25. This was also the nature of a great vision given to Enoch. See Moses 7:3-9.

At times visions are granted to one individual but not to others with him. It was W. W. Phelps, for instance, who saw the vision of the destroyer upon the waters, even though he was in the company of the Prophet and nine other Elders:

> On the 9th, in company with ten Elders, I left Independence landing for Kirtland. We started down the river in canoes, and went the first day as far as *Fort Osage*, where we had an excellent wild turkey for supper. Nothing very important occurred till the third day, when many of the dangers so common upon the western waters, manifested themselves; and after we had encamped upon the banks of the river, at *McIlwaine's Bend*, Brother Phelps, in open vision by daylight, saw the destroyer in his most horrible power, ride upon the face of the waters; others heard the noise, but saw not the vision.[19]

A vision was used to show Brigham Young the constructional pattern for the then future Salt Lake Temple. On April 6, 1853, as the temple cornerstones were laid, he said,

> 'I scarcely ever say much about revelations or visions, but suffice it to say, five years ago last July, 1847, *I was here and saw in spirit the temple not ten feet from where we have laid the cornerstones.* I have not inquired what kind of temple we shall build. Why? Because *it was represented before me. I have never looked upon the ground but the vision of it was there.* I saw it as plainly as if it was in reality before me. Wait until it is done. I will say, however, that it will have six towers to begin with instead of one.'[20]

7. *Revelatory Instruments.* On several occasions in religious history God has granted man the privilege of possessing particular instruments through which the divine will was made manifest. The Urim and Thummim was granted to the ancient Biblical prophets so that they could seek counsel and revelation.[21] A similar instrument had been in the possession of the brother of Jared.[22] It was with the aid of such an instrument that Joseph Smith translated the Book of Mormon.[23] A passage from that work describes the powers granted to those able to possess and use the Urim and Thummim:

---

19. HC, I, pp. 202-03.
20. Hinckley, *Faith of our Pioneer Fathers*, p. 14.
21. See Num. 27:21; I Sam. 28:6.
22. D & C 17:1.
23. D & C 10:1 For a description of the Urim and Thummim and of a similar instrument, the "Seer Stone," see the author's book, *The Prophecies of Joseph Smith*, pp. 107-08. See also Mos. 28:13-14.

Now Ammon said unto him: I can assuredly tell thee, O king, of a man that can translate the records; for he has wherewith that he can look and translate all records that are of ancient date; and *it is a gift from God. And the things are called interpreters, and no man can look in them except he be commanded,* lest he should look for that he ought not and he should perish. *And whosoever is commanded to look in them, the same is called a seer.* . . .

And Ammon said that *a seer is a revelator and a prophet also; and a gift which is greater can no man have,* except he should possess the power of God, which no man can; yet a man may have great power given him from God.

But a seer can know of things which are past, and also of things which are to come, and by them shall all things be revealed, or, rather, shall secret things be made manifest, and hidden things shall come to light, and things which are not known shall be made known by them, and also things shall be made known by them which otherwise could not be known.

Thus God has provided a means that man, through faith, might work mighty miracles; therefore he becometh a great benefit to his fellow beings.[24]

The Book of Mormon also tells of the Liahona, another instrument through which revelation was received: "He beheld upon the ground a round ball of curious workmanship; and it was of fine brass. And within the ball were two spindles; and the one pointed the way whither we should go into the wilderness."[25] Nephi told how the instrument functioned:

And it came to pass that I, Nephi, beheld the pointers which were in the ball, *that they did work according to the faith and diligence and heed which we did give unto them.*

And there was also written upon them a new writing, which was plain to be read, which did give us understanding concerning the ways of the Lord; and *it was written and changed from time to time, according to the faith and diligence which we gave unto it.* And thus we see that by small means the Lord can bring about great things.[26]

8. *Signs and Manifestations.* There have been instances when signs and manifestations have been used to reveal or assist

24. Mos. 8:13, 16-18.
25. 1 Ne. 16:10.
26. 1 Ne. 16:28-29.

in the revealing of God's will. During the days of the prophet
Daniel, Belshazzar, the king, gave an impious feast in which he
and his guests desecrated the vessels plundered from the temple
in Jerusalem. Their feast was suddenly interrupted by a sign
from heaven, for "in the same hour came forth fingers of a man's
hand, and wrote over against the candlestick upon the plaister
of the wall of the king's palace; and the king saw the part of
the hand that wrote."[27] Daniel was summoned to interpret the
sign — which told that Belshazzar's kingdom would be conquered
by the Medes and Persians.[28]

In the latter days, Elder Thomas A. Shreeve was given a
series of manifestations through the Holy Ghost which directed
him to change the locale of his missionary labors:

> I had a strange dream concerning my labors. I thought
> that I was called to take a mission to the East. The idea was
> very vivid in my mind, though no steps or time seemed to have
> been made clear to me. When I awoke, I thought upon the mat-
> ter, and interpreted it as meaning that after my return to Zion,
> I should have another mission — probably to Europe. With
> this view, I attempted to dismiss the matter from my mind;
> but I found the effort futile. The idea remained persistently
> with me for three or four days; and then one afternoon when I
> took up a book and sought to read, *suddenly the printed lines
> were blurred from me, and these words started out from the page:*
>
> 'You must go to New Zealand.'
>
> I rubbed my eyes, astonished, and looked again. The words
> had disappeared, and for a few moments I was able to read the
> book. *But again these words came upon the page, shutting out
> the printed lines from my sight:*
>
> 'You are wanted in New Zealand.'
>
> *This strange thing was repeated again and again.* But I
> did not permit myself to accept it as a requirement; because I
> remembered the definite understanding which I had made with
> Brother May concerning my labors in New South Wales, and
> the date of our mutual journey to New Zealand in December
> or January following. I dropped the book for a time, and then
> picked it up again. *The strange appearance of this command
> was repeated.* Not only on this day and with this book did I

27. Dan. 5:5.
28. Dan. 5:25-31.

experience this wondrous manifestation; but *day after day with any book or newspaper which I attempted to read, was the appearance repeated.*[29]

It should be noted that while signs and manifestations may serve to communicate God's will, they often are not complete in themselves and require some form of interpretation.

10. *Promptings and Impressions.* Impressions sent by the Spirit are among the most common methods in which revelation is given to man. They are also among the most difficult to perceive and to verify as to divine origin. There is a definite difference between receiving an impression from the Holy Ghost and merely "taking a notion" to do something. A revealed impression carries with it to the recipient a feeling of rightness and correctness. A decision made without the influence of the Holy Ghost does not carry this feeling, but rather leaves its originator with an unconcerned, take-it-or-leave-it attitude. A divine prompting or impression is carried both to the mind and the heart and comprises both a message and a feeling. Decisions made without the Holy Ghost are matters of the mind only, and do not carry the feeling with the thought. Impressions of the Spirit may or may not come with exact wording being formed in the mind, yet their message is usually definite. Very often, although an inspired impression does not convey a complete understanding of a situation it does instruct the recipient as to how to best approach a problem or start down the path which will make the situation unfold in accordance with the will of the Lord. Often the situation becomes clear at a later time and can be fully comprehended without further guidance from the Spirit.

Promptings and revealed impressions often enable individuals to surmount small personal problems which are retarding their progress. Elder Orson F. Whitney wrote of just such a situation. At this time he was a missionary in England serving as editor of the *Millennial Star*:

'I found myself in an overworked, run-down condition, manifesting a decided lack of physical and mental vigor. One morning I was endeavoring to write the usual editorial, but could make no headway, and wore out the whole day in a vain attempt to produce something worth reading. At last I threw down my pen and burst into tears of vexation.

---

29. *Helpful Visions* pp. 49-50.

'*Just then the Good Spirit whispered: "Why don't you pray?"*

As if a voice had addressed me audibly, I answered, 'I do pray.' I was praying five times a day — secret prayers, morning, noon and night; and vocal prayers, with the rest of the household, at breakfast and dinner time. 'I do pray — why can't I get some help' I asked almost petulantly, for I was heartsick and half-discouraged.

'*Pray now,*' said the Spirit, '*and ask for what you want.*'

I saw the point. It was a special, not a general prayer, that was needed. I knelt and sobbed out a few simple words. I did not pray for the return of the Ten Tribes nor for the building of the New Jerusalem. I asked the Lord in the name of Jesus Christ to help me write that article. I then arose, seated myself, and began to write. *My mind was now perfectly clear, and my pen fairly flew over the paper. All I needed came as fast as I could set it down — every thought, every word in place.* In a short time the article was completed to my entire satisfaction.[30]

11. *Inspiration.* This term is often used to mean the same as "prompting" or "impression." To some, however, it carries a different connotation. There are times when the Holy Spirit floods a person's mind with understanding. The person is given new thoughts, new concepts, new viewpoints. This is a different experience from being directed or prompted to do or say something. Inspiration, in this sense, deals with the bestowal of revealed knowledge. This type of inspiration was granted to Joseph Smith and Oliver Cowdery immediately after their ordination by John the Baptist:

> Our minds being now enlightened, *we began to have the Scripture laid open to our understandings, and the true meaning and intention of their more mysterious passages revealed unto us* in a manner which we never could attain to previously, nor ever before had thought of.[31]

Man to Seek Knowledge of the Mysteries

One of the major themes of the scriptures is that God will reveal the mysteries of His kingdom unto those who diligently seek such a blessing. A mystery may be simply defined as a question for which a particular individual does not know the

---

30. Hinckley, *Faith of our Pioneer Fathers,* pp. 216-17.
31. HC 1:43.

answer. Others may know the answer to the problem; to them there is no element of mystery involved. Nowhere in the scripture is commandment given to avoid the seeking of answers to the mysteries. Rather, man is continually admonished to capture knowledge from the realm of the unknown through revelation. He may thereby increase his preparation for exaltation.

A revelation given to Oliver Cowdery is typical of the commandments and invitations God has given man to seek out the mysteries of the kingdom. The Lord said to him,

> Behold thou hast a gift, and blessed art thou because of thy gift. Remember it is sacred and cometh from above —
>
> And if thou wilt inquire, thou shalt know mysteries which are great and marvelous; therefore thou shalt exercise thy gift, *that thou mayest find out mysteries*, that thou mayest bring many to the knowledge of the truth, yea, convince them of the error of their ways.
>
> Make not thy gift known unto any save it be those who are of thy faith. Trifle not with sacred things.[32]

Another example of a person's seeking a knowledge of the mysteries and obtaining the knowledge he desired is the story of Nephi. While yet a youth he obtained a visitation from the Lord and gained knowledge of a land of promise and the fate of his loved ones. "And it came to pass that I, Nephi, being exceeding young, nevertheless being large in stature, and *also having great desires to know of the mysteries of God, wherefore, I did cry unto the Lord;* and behold he did visit me, and did soften my heart."[33]

Alma taught that the privilege of receiving knowledge of the mysteries of God is given to many; all who will not harden their hearts against the revelations may receive them and continue to do so until they know the things of God in full:

> And now Alma began to expound these things unto him, saying: *It is given unto many to know the mysteries of God; nevertheless they are laid under a strict command that they shall not impart only according to the portion of his word which he doth grant unto the children of men, according to the heed and diligence which they give unto him.*

---

32. D & C 6:10-12.
33. 1 Ne. 2:16. For the Savior's message to Nephi, see 1 Ne. 2:19-24.

And therefore, he that will harden his heart, the same receiveth the lesser portion of the word; and he that will not harden his heart, to him is given the greater portion of the word, *until it is given unto him to know the mysteries of God until he know them in full.*

And they that will harden their hearts, to them is given the lesser portion of the word until they know nothing concerning his mysteries; and then they are taken captive by the devil, and led by his will down to destruction, Now this is what is meant by the chains of hell.[34]

Nephi saw that diligence in seeking was the key to gaining knowledge of the mysteries: *"For he that diligently seeketh shall find; and the mysteries of God shall be unfolded unto them, by the power of the Holy Ghost,* as well in these times as in times of old, and as well in times of old as in times to come; wherefore, the course of the Lord is one eternal round."[35]

Ammon proposed a four-point formula allowing man to gain knowledge of the mysteries and reveal things never before revealed:

Yea, he that repenteth and exerciseth faith, and bringeth forth good works, and prayeth continually without ceasing — *unto such it is given to know the mysteries of God; yea, unto such it shall be given to reveal things which never have been revealed;* yea, and it shall be given unto such to bring thousands of souls to repentance, even as it has been given unto us to bring these our brethren to repentance.[36]

The Lord has promised that those who fear Him and serve Him in righteousness may be shown the mysteries of the past, the future, and of the eternities:

For thus saith the Lord — I the Lord, am merciful and gracious unto those who fear me, and delight to honor those who serve me in righteousness and in truth unto the end.

Great shall be their reward and eternal shall be their glory.

And to them will I reveal all mysteries, yea, all the hidden mysteries of my kingdom from days of old, and for ages to come, will I make known unto them the good pleasure of my will concerning all things pertaining to my kingdom.

34. Al. 12:9-11.
35. 1 Ne. 10:19.
36. Al. 26:22.

Yea, *even the wonders of eternity shall they know, and things to come will I show them,* even the things of many generations.

And their wisdom shall be great, and their understanding reach to heaven; and before them the wisdom of the wise shall perish, and the understanding of the prudent shall come to naught.

For by my Spirit will I enlighten them, and by my power will I make known unto them the secrets of my will — yea, even those things which eye has not seen, nor ear heard, nor yet entered into the heart of man.[37]

Another revelation contains the Savior's promise that the keeping of His commandments is the key to gaining knowledge of the mysteries: *"Unto him that keepeth my commandments I will give the mysteries of my kingdom,* and the same shall be in him a well of living water, springing up unto everlasting life."[38]

This pattern of scriptures clearly indicates that the opportunity of knowing the mysteries is open to all who are righteous, and that God encourages man to explore and seek the mysteries of His kingdom.

Scriptures to Reveal Mysteries

Nephi, as he began to inscribe the plates which later became the Book of Mormon, intimated that his purpose was to record his knowledge of the mysteries of God. His witness was that he, "Having been highly favored of the Lord in all my days; yea, *having a great knowledge of the goodness and the mysteries of God,* therefore I make a record of my proceedings in my days."[39] Alma also indicated a similar purpose for the Book of Mormon when he told his son, Helaman,

Behold, it has been prophesied by our fathers, that they should be kept and handed down from one generation to another, and be kept and preserved by the hand of the Lord until they should go forth unto every nation, kindred, tongue, and people, *that they shall know of the mysteries contained thereon.*[40]

Paul explained that his writings in the Bible were recordings of revelations explaining the mysteries:

37. D & C 76:5-10.
38. D & C 63:23.
39. 1 Ne. 1:1.
40. Al. 37:4.

How that *by revelation he made known unto me the mystery:* (as I wrote afore in few words,

Whereby, when ye read, ye may understand my knowledge in the mystery of Christ.)[41]

Some Knowledge Withheld by God

God, in His wisdom, withholds some knowledge from His children until they are prepared to receive it. Man can learn the ways and will of God only through revelation from the Divine and is dependent upon this avenue for further growth. As Jacob taught,

Behold, great and marvelous are the works of the Lord. How unsearchable are the depths of the mysteries of him; and *it is impossible that man should find out all his ways. And no man knoweth of his ways save it be revealed unto him;* wherefore, brethren, despise not the revelations of God.[42]

An example of how God may choose to withhold knowledge is found in the Pearl of Great Price. Moses was informed by God that "worlds without number" had been created but he was also told, "Only an account of this earth, and the inhabitants thereof, give I unto you."[43]

It must be recognized that God may choose to reveal things to one individual which He withholds from another. Words intended for one individual or group may be held back from others. Such is the case with the marvelous prayer Jesus offered while visiting among the Nephites:

And when he had said these words, he himself also knelt upon the earth; and behold he prayed unto the Father, and *the things which he prayed cannot be written,* and the multitude did bear record who heard him.

And after this manner do they bear record: The eye hath never seen, neither hath the ear heard, before, so great and marvelous things as we saw and heard Jesus speak unto the Father;

And *no tongue can speak, neither can there be written by any man, neither can the hearts of men conceive so great and marvelous things as we both saw and heard Jesus speak;* and

---

41. Eph. 3:3-4.
42. Jac. 4:8.
43. Moses 1:35.

no one can conceive of the joy which filled our souls at the time we heard him pray for us unto the Father.[44]

In a similar instance, the brother of Jared was shown all things, but was commanded to seal them up, and the rest of mankind have not yet received this knowledge:

> For he had said unto him in times before, that if he would believe in him that he could show unto him all things — it should be shown unto him; Therefore the Lord could not withhold anything from him, for he knew that the Lord could show him all things.

> And the Lord said unto him: *Write these things and seal them up: and I will show them in mine own due time unto the children of men.*[45]

Man is promised that when he becomes sanctified this information will be granted him:

> And in that day that they shall exercise faith in me, saith the Lord, even as the brother of Jared did, *that they may become sanctified in me, then will I manifest unto them the things which the brother of Jared saw,* even to the unfolding unto them all my revelations, saith Jesus Christ, the Son of God, the Father of the heavens and of the earth, and all things that in them are.[46]

In a similar manner, righteousness may someday enable man to receive other knowledge which has been withheld, such as an unfolding of the revelations of John:

> Behold, when ye shall rend that veil of unbelief which doth cause you to remain in your awful state of wickedness, and hardness of heart, and blindness of mind, then shall the great and marvelous things which have been hid up from the foundation of the world from you — yea, when ye shall call upon the father in my name, with a broken heart and a contrite spirit, then shall ye know that the Father hath remembered the covenant which he made unto your fathers, O house of Israel.

> *And then shall my revelations which I have caused to be written by my servant John be unfolded in the eyes of all the people.* Remember, when ye see these things, ye shall know

---

44. 3 Ne. 17:15-17.
45. Eth. 3:26-27.
46. Eth. 4:7.

that the time is at hand that they shall be made manifest in very deed.[47]

Even Nephi wrote that those who fail to accept the Book of Mormon in the last days will lose the opportunity for further knowledge, for that book will be used to try their faith:

> And when they shall have received this, which is expedient that they should have first, to try their faith, and *if it shall so be that they shall believe these things then shall the greater things be made manifest unto them.*
>
> *And if it so be that they will not believe these things, then shall the greater things be withheld from them, unto their condemnation.*
>
> Behold, I was about to write them, all which were engraven upon the plates of Nephi, but the Lord forbade it, saying: I will try the faith of my people.[48]

Man should never make the assumption that an avenue of revelation is not available to him without seeking an answer. If God chooses to refuse to grant the requested information, then it would seem that the reply may be similar to His words to Joseph Smith on one occasion: "Let this suffice, and trouble me no more on this matter."[49] If a man receives such a reply, then he would do well to heed the counsel granted to Joseph's wife, Emma, in a similar situation: "Murmur not because of the things which thou hast not seen, for they are withheld from thee and from the world, which is wisdom in me in a time to come."[50] But if he receives no reply at all, then let him not assume that his question is one God will not answer, but rather that he has not yet prepared and humbled himself sufficiently to receive communication from God.

In the absence of complete understanding of such a matter, man would do well to limit his comment to others on the question and follow the example of Alma, who said, "now these mysteries are not yet fully made known unto me; therefore I shall forbear."[51]

---

47. Eth. 4:15-16.
48. 3 Ne. 26:9-11.
49. D & C 130:15.
50. D & C 25:4.
51. Al. 37:11.

Revelation to Guide the Church

Important instruction concerning the form that revelation should take within the Church was given in a revelation to the elders in 1831. They were told,

O hearken, ye elders of my church, and give ear to the words which I shall speak unto you.

For behold, verily, verily, I say unto you, *that ye have received a commandment for a law unto my church, through him whom I have appointed unto you to receive commandments and revelations from my hand.*

And this ye shall know assuredly — that there is none other appointed unto you to receive commandments and revelations until he be taken, if he abide in me.

But verily, verily, I say unto you, that none else shall be appointed unto this gift except it be through him; for if it be taken from him he shall not have power except to appoint another in his stead.

And *this shall be a law unto you, that ye receive not the teachings of any that shall come before you as revelations or commandments;*

And this I give unto you that you may not be deceived, that you may know they are not of me.

For verily I say unto you, that he that is ordained of me shall come in at the gate and be ordained as I have told you before, to teach those revelations which you have received and shall receive through him whom I have appointed.

And now, behold, I give unto you a commandment, that when ye are assembled together ye shall instruct and edify each other, that ye may know how to act and direct my church, how to act upon the points of my law and commandments, which I have given.

And thus ye shall become instructed in the law of my church, and be sanctified by that which ye have received, and ye shall bind yourselves to act in all holiness before me —

That inasmuch as ye do this, glory shall be added to the kingdom which ye have received. Inasmuch as ye do it not, it shall be taken, even that which ye have received. . . .

Again I say, hearken ye elders of my church, whom I have appointed: *Ye are not sent forth to be taught, but to teach the children of men the things which I have put into your hands by the power of my Spirit;*

And ye are to be taught from on high. Sanctify yourselves and ye shall be endowed with power, that ye may give even as I have spoken.[52]

This message is instructive because it sets the following pattern:

1. One man in the church (the Prophet and President, in this case Joseph Smith) is appointed by the Lord to receive commandments and revelations for the Church.

2. The teachings of others shall be rejected as commandments and/or revelations if they are asserted to be guidance for the entire Church.

3. Individual members will still be given revelation to enlighten their own understanding and to aid them in teaching others.

To the President, then, is granted the responsibility of being God's spokesman to the entire church:

And again, the duty of the President of the office of the High Priesthood is to preside over the whole church, and *to be like unto Moses* —

Behold, here is wisdom; yea, *to be a seer, a revelator, a translator, and a prophet, having all the gifts of God* which he bestows upon the head of the church.[53]

He, and he alone, holds this privilege and responsibility. Although his counselors, the Quorum of the Twelve, and the Church Patriarch are also acknowledged and sustained as prophets, seers, and revelators, theirs is not the privilege of setting forth God's will for the entire church. They constantly affirm that such responsibility is the President's, and they continually assert their loyalty to him. Their relationship to the Prophet seems to be the same as that enjoyed by Oliver Cowdery, the second elder of the church, who became an Assistant President to the First Presidency. To him the Lord said,

Behold, I say unto thee, Oliver, that it shall be given unto thee that *thou shalt be heard by the church in all things whatsoever thou shalt teach them by the Comforter,* concerning the revelations and commandments which I have given.

---

52. D & C 43:1-10, 15-16.
53. D & C 107:91-92. See also D & C 46:29.

But, behold, verily, verily, I say unto thee, *no one shall be appointed to receive commandments and revelations in this church excepting my servant Joseph Smith, Jun., for he receiveth them even as Moses.*

And *thou shalt be obedient unto the things which I shall give unto him,* even as Aaron, to declare faithfully the commandments and the revelations, with power and authority unto the church.

And if *thou art led at any time by the Comforter to speak or teach, or at all times by the way of commandment unto the church, thou mayest do it.*

But *thou shalt not write by way of commandment, but by wisdom;*

And *thou shalt not command him who is at thy head,* and at the head of the church;

For *I have given him the keys of the mysteries,* and the revelations which are sealed, until I shall appoint unto them another in his stead.

And now, behold, I say unto you that you shall go unto the Lamanites and preach my gospel unto them; and inasmuch as they receive thy teachings thou shalt cause my church to be established among them; and *thou shalt have revelations, but write them not by way of commandment.*[54]

As seen throughout this chapter, individual members of the church may expect and will continually receive revelation to aid them in their personal growth. They should not attempt, however, to impose their additional light on others by representing it to be God's commandment to the entire church. If a revelation is meant for everyone, it will come through the President of the Church. Personal revelation should be treated with the discretion indicated in chapter V.

Summary

1. Revelation is communication from God to man.

2. All knowledge of eternal truth which mankind now possesses has been revealed by the Divine. The only avenue for obtaining further information of the things of God is revelation for "man can receive nothing except it be given him from heaven."

---

54. D & C 28:1-8.

3. Revelation has been given in many ways, such as

    A. personal appearances of Deity,

    B. the voice of God speaking to man,

    C. the ministering of angels,

    D. the speaking of unidentified voices,

    E. dreams,

    F. visions,

    G. revelatory instruments,

    H. signs and manifestations,

    I. promptings and impressions, and

    J. inspiration.

4. A mystery is a question for which a particular individual does not know the answer. That which constitutes a mystery for one individual is not necessarily a mystery for another.

5. The scriptures emphasize that man is to seek diligently an understanding of the mysteries. Seeking and receiving answers to one's questions or mysteries is a process of drawing nearer to God.

6. To gain continual revelation man must keep the commandments, enjoy the companionship of the Holy Ghost, and seek further guidance.

7. A major purpose of the scriptures of the Church is to explain the mysteries of God. Many of the doctrines now known and accepted by the Church were considered mysteries in other eras.

8. God decides what knowledge man is ready to receive and apportions his revelations accordingly. Some knowledge is withheld by God.

9. Some choice revelations granted to individuals in other dispensations have not been preserved for man to use today. God has promised to make these revelations known when people are finally prepared to receive them.

10. Revelation for the entire Church, which is given to the President and Prophet of the Church, is considered the commandment and will of God and is binding upon all Latter-day Saints.

11. Revelation given to others should not be considered binding upon the Church unless it is verified and approved by the Prophet. Such revelations may be of great value to the members but are not binding as doctrine.

12. Individual members will still be given revelation to enlighten their own understanding and to aid them in teaching others. They should not impose their increased understanding on others by representing it to be God's commandment to the entire Church.

CHAPTER XIII
Prophecy

Prophecy a Gift for Many

Prophecy[1] is one of the most valuable gifts of the Spirit. Paul admonished the Saints to "follow after charity, and desire spiritual gifts, *but rather that ye may prophesy*."[2] He knew the gift had much value for the Church and explained its benefits to the believers:

He that prophesieth speaketh unto men to *edification, and exhortation, and comfort.*

He that speaketh in an unknown tongue edifieth himself; but *he that prophesieth edifieth the church.*[3]

Unlike some of the other gifts of the Spirit, which may serve as a sign to convert others to the Church, this gift bears its greatest fruit among the members: "Wherefore tongues are for a sign, not to them that believe, but to them that believe not: but *prophesying serveth not for them that believe not, but for them which believe.*"[4]

The gift of prophecy is one which is often manifested among the lay membership of the Church. It is manifested in two ways: the ability to fortell events and the ability to understand and interpret the prophecies made by others. A prophecy certainly does not have to be uttered by a General Authority or other Church official to be true and valid. Paul taught that "*ye may all prophesy one by one, that all may learn, and all may be comforted.*"[5] Neither is priesthood a prerequisite for possessing the gift of prophecy, for the scriptures in several instances mention women as possessing the gift. The Book of Acts tells of four young girls, "four daughters, virgins, which did prophesy."[6] The

---

1. I Cor. 12:10; D & C 46:22; Moro. 10:13.
2. I Cor. 14:1.
3. I Cor. 14:3-4.
4. I Cor. 14:22.
5. I Cor. 14:31.
6. Acts 21:9.

New Testament also speaks of Anna, the prophetess, who testified of the divinity of the baby Jesus in the temple.[7]

Like other gifts of the Spirit, the gift of prophecy is influenced by the spiritual condition of the individual who possesses it. Paul taught that prophecy depended on faith.[8] But more than faith, one must encourage the constant companionship of the Holy Ghost. He must be content to be only the spokesman for the Divine, and base his prophecies only on the guidance of the Spirit, without interjecting his own views. Lehi recognized this principle as he said that he would "*prophesy according to the workings of the Spirit which is in me.*"[9] In a modern commandment God tells man that "as ye shall lift up your voices *by the Comforter*, ye shall speak and prophesy *as seemeth me good.*"[10] Jacob also knew that to prophesy correctly one must allow the Holy Ghost to speak through him and then the words of the prophecy would be true:

> Behold, my brethren, he that prophesieth, *let him prophesy to the understanding of men; for the Spirit speaketh the truth and lieth not.* Wherefore, it speaketh of things as they really are, and of things as they really will be; wherefore, *these things are manifested unto us plainly, for the salvation of our souls.* But behold, we are not witnesses alone in these things; for God also spake them unto prophets of old.[11]

Purposes of Prophecy

Prophecies have been spoken to accomplish many purposes. They are varied and profound, yet they seem to fall into particular categories which can be readily classified. One type of prophecy deals with the growth of God's work. Such a prophecy was made by Heber C. Kimball to Parley P. Pratt in 1836. The latter recorded,

> It was now April. I had retired to rest one evening at an early hour and was pondering my future course when there came a knock at the door. I arose and opened it when Elder Heber C. Kimball and others entered my house and being filled with the spirit of prophecy, they blessed me and my wife and he prophesied as follows: 'Brother Parley, thy wife shall be healed from

---

7. Lk. 2:36.
8. Ro. 12:6.
9. 2 Ne. 1:6.
10. D & C 42:16.
11. Jac. 4:13.

this hour and shall bear a son and his name shall be Parley and he shall be a chosen instrument in the hands of the Lord to inherit the Priesthood and to walk in the steps of his father. He shall do a great work in the earth, ministering the word and teachings to the children of men. Arise, therefore, go forth in the ministry, nothing doubting, take no thought for your debts nor the necessaries of life for the Lord will supply you with abundant means for all things. *Thou shalt go to Upper Canada, even to the city of Toronto, the capital, and there thou shalt find a people prepared for the fullness of the Gospel and they shall receive thee; and thou shalt organize a Church among them* and it shall spread into the regions round about and many shall be brought to a knowledge of the truth and shall be filled with joy, and *from the things growing out of this mission, shall the fullness of the Gospel be spread to England* and cause a great work to be done in that land.'[12]

Another purpose of prophecy has been to indicate the future of kingdoms, nations, cities and communities.[13] Especially numerous are examples of prophecies given in the last days showing the future of small communities. Brigham Young, the great colonizer, made numerous prophecies of this type. One such utterance was made to Marriner W. Merrill at his home in Richmond, Utah.

Brigham Young was in Brother Merrill's home, and he pointed over to where Lewiston is now located and said, '*Brother Merrill, this will be the granary of the Cache Valley!*' He told Brother Merrill to call a man to go over to that place to preside as bishop. So Brother Merrill called William H. Lewis to go there

---

12. Hinckley, *Faith of Our Pioneer Fathers,* pp. 125-6. The fulfillment of this prophecy has been summarized in this manner:

    All of these prophecies, the one relating to the birth of his son, and the other to his Canadian Mission, were literally and marvelously fulfilled. Parley had a son born to him. He went to Toronto and he converted John Taylor, his wife, and many others, and they carried this Gospel to Great Britain. They baptized the George Cannon family, who came to America and who have made a contribution to the Church which can never be measured. The far-reaching consequences of this prophecy are amazing. This declaration of Heber C. Kimball in Parley P. Pratt's house that April night alone would have written Elder Kimball's name among the modern prophets. John Taylor became an Apostle and President of the Church, and a powerful champion of Mormonism in France, in the British Isles, and in New York City. (*Faith of Our Pioneer Fathers,* p. 126)

13. Other works by the author have cited numerous examples dealing with the fate of nations and kingdoms. See *Prophecy — Key To The Future* and *The Prophecies of Joseph Smith.*

and act as bishop. Brother Lewis went over, but the wind blew
and the sand piled up against the fences and he came back and
said that he would not give his small farm in Richmond for all
of Lewiston, and wanted to be released. Brother Merrill told
him that the Prophet of the Lord had said that that would be
the granary of Cache Valley, and suggested that he go back
there and stay with it. Brother Lewis did so and later became
one of the wealthiest farmers of Cache Valley, and the Lewiston
Sugar Factory has been one of the best and most successful that
was built.[14]

Another prophecy of this type was made in a prayer offered by
Alexander Barron as he dedicated a community site in Millard
County, Utah:

> Brother Barron offered the dedicatory prayer, in which he
> prophesied, that *the desert in Pahvant Valley would truly blos-*
> *som as a rose,* and that *a highway would be 'thrown up' through*
> *the valley, which would connect the Atlantic and the Pacific*
> *oceans.* Streams of living water would flow out of the ground,
> and the valley would be settled from the mountains East toward
> the West, North and South, and in time become a great agri-
> cultural center.[15]

A third type of prophecy outlines the future course of particular individuals. Patriarchal blessings, for instance, fall into
this category. Other such prophecies made by Latter-day Saints
in various callings have also been concerned with this area. For
instance, Daniel Tyler recounted a prophecy made a year before
his entry into the Swiss mission at a prayer meeting in Salt Lake
City. It was given at a time when he had suffered with a broken
leg for seven months and had despaired of being able to use his
leg without crutches again.

> After the meeting was opened, *Sister More arose and be-*
> *gan to speak in tongues.* She addressed her remarks to me, and
> I understood her as well as though she had spoken the English

---

14. Hinckley, *Faith of Our Pioneer Fathers,* pp. 184-5.
15. Jenson, IV, p. 730. The highway referred to is probably U.S. 6, a major
    east-west artery, or possibly U.S. 91 which, though running north and
    south, connects other major east-west highways. Concerning the agricul-
    tural growth of the area, the following can be cited as typical evidence:
    In 1922 President Alonzo A. Hinckley, while acting as Commis-
    sioner of Agriculture in Utah, stated that Millard County had pro-
    duced more hay and grain and alfalfa seed in 1922 than any other
    locality in Utah, thus verifying the prophecy of Brother Barron.
    (Jenson, IV, p. 730)

language. She said: 'Your leg will be healed, and you will go
on a foreign mission and preach the gospel in foreign lands. No
harm shall befall you, and you shall return in safety, having
great joy in your labors.'

This was the substance of the prophecy. It was so different from my own belief and the fears of many others that I
was tempted not to give the interpretation, lest it should fail
to come to pass. *The Spirit, however, impressed me and I arose,
leaning upon my crutches, and gave the interpretation.*

Not long afterwards *I was told in a dream what to do to
strengthen my fractured limb,* and it began to receive strength
immediately, and in the short space of about one week I dis-
pensed with my crutches and walked with a cane.[16]

One should also consider the strange administration and
prophecy bestowed on Lorenzo Dow Young as another example
of this type of prophecy.

My disease was ponouned [sic] to be the quick consump-
tion. I sank rapidly for six or seven weeks. For two weeks I
was unable to talk. Dr. Williams, one of the brethren, came to
see me, and, considering my case a bad one, came the next day
and brought with him Dr. Seely, an old practicing physician,
and another doctor whose name I have forgotten. They passed
me through an examination. Dr. Seely asserted that I had
not as much lungs left as would fill a tea saucer. He appeared
a somewhat rough, irreligious man. Probably, with what he
considered a good-natured fling at our belief in miracles, he said
to my father, as he left the house:

'Mr. Young, unless the Lord makes your son a new pair of
lungs, there is no hope for him!'

At this time I was so low and nervous that I could scarcely
bear any noise in the room. The next morning after the visit
of the doctors, my father came to the door of the room to see
how I was. I recollect his gazing earnestly at me with tears
in his eyes. As I afterwards learned, he went from there to the
Prophet Joseph, and said to him: 'My son Lorenzo is dying;
can there not be something done for him?'

The Prophet studied a little while and replied, 'Yes! Of
necessity, I must go away to fill an appointment, which I cannot put off. But you go and get my brother Hyrum, and with
him, get together twelve or fifteen good faithful brethren; go to
the house of Brother Lorenzo, and all join in prayer. One be

16. *Scraps of Biography,* pp. 41-2.

mouth and the others repeat after him in unison. After prayer,
divide into quorums of three. Let the first quorum who administer, anoint Brother Young with oil; then lay hands on him,
one being mouth and the other two repeating in unison after
him. When all the quorums have, in succession, laid their hands
on Brother Young and prayed for him, begin again with the
first quorum, by anointing with oil as before, continuing the
administration in this way until you receive a testimony that
he will be restored.'

My father came with the brethren, and these instructions
were strictly followed. The administrations were continued until
it came the turn of the first quorum the third time. Brother
Hyrum Smith led. *The Spirit rested mightily upon him. He
was full of blessing and prophecy.* Among other things, *he said
that I should live to go with the Saints into the bosom of the
Rocky Mountains, to build up a place there, and that my cellar
should overflow with wine and fatness.*

At that time, I had not heard about the Saints going to the
Rocky Mountains: possibly Brother Smith had. After he had
finished *he seemed surprised at some things he had said, and
wondered at the manifestations of the Spirit.* I coughed no
more after that administration, and rapidly recovered.[17]

A fourth type of prophecy consists of prophetic warnings of
impending danger. This type of prophecy was voiced by a companion of Jacob Hamblin, who recorded the warning and its
outcome.

We commenced to descend the difficult cliff to the crossing of
the river. While doing so, Brother Nathan Terry said he had
a dream the night before, and that it had been on his mind all
day, and he believed it meant something. *In the dream he saw
the company riding along the trail, when he heard the report
of a gun. He looked around, and saw one of the company fall
to the ground, and he thought he went and put the person on
his horse, and they continued their journey.*

After descending the cliff, I was some distance in the rear
of the company, when suddenly, what appeared like a flash of
lightning came over me. It was with great difficulty that I could
breathe. Not being able to help myself, I partly fell to the
ground.

I lay there some time, when one of the Kanab Indians who
was with us came along, saw my situation, and hurried on to
camp.

---

17. *Fragments of Experience.* pp. 43-5.

Brother Terry came back to me after dark. He administered to me in the name of the Lord, when the death-like grip that seemed to have fastened on my lungs let go its hold, and I could again breathe naturally.[18]

One of the most common forms of prophecy is a revelation of an approaching death. Such prophecies are occasions for sorrow and yet cannot be withheld and constrained. Joseph Smith uttered such a prophecy as he blessed a missionary, Elder Andrew Lamoreaux, during his tour to Washington in 1839. He

Laid his hands on Elder Lamoreaux and blessed him, and prophesied upon his head, that *he would go on a mission to France, learn another tongue and do much good, but that he would not live to return to his family, as he would fall by the way as a martyr.* The Prophet wept, as he blessed him and told him these things, adding that *it was pressed upon him and he could not refrain from giving utterance to it.* Elder Lamoreaux talked with his family about it when he left them in 1852, and endeavored to persuade them that this was not the time and the mission upon which he should fall, but to believe that he would at this time be permitted to return again. When the 'Luminary' brought the tidings of his death, they exclaimed, 'Surely, Brother Joseph was a Prophet, for all his words have come to pass.'[19]

Thus it can be seen that the gift of prophecy has been granted to many people and for many different purposes. As the Lord proclaimed through the prophet Joel,

And it shall come to pass afterward, that *I will pour out my spirit upon all flesh; and your sons and your daughters shall prophesy,* your old men shall dream dreams, your young men shall see visions:

And also upon the servants and upon the handmaids in those days will I pour out my spirit.[20]

Tests of Prophetic Veracity

The scriptures set forth two methods which can be used to discover whether prophecies are true or false. One test is found in the Doctrine and Covenants which says, "Behold, it shall be given unto him to prophesy; and thou shalt preach my gospel and

18. *Jacob Hamblin,* pp. 104-5.
19. Jenson, III, 667.
20. Joel 2:28-9.

call on the holy prophets to prove his words, as they shall be given him."[21] If a prophecy deals with a subject about which other prophecies have been made, the new prophecy should harmonize with the voice of previous revelation. This test can only be applied, of course, if others have prophesied about the same thing. It is thus a limited test, for many prophecies tell of coming events which are as yet unknown to others.

A second and more encompassing test of prophecy is that which was proposed by the prophet Jeremiah, who said that *"when the word of the prophet shall come to pass, then shall the prophet be known,* that the Lord hath truly sent him."[22] The complete fulfillment of a prophecy is the safest indication that a prophecy is true. This test is also of limited value for it requires the passage of time so that the prophecy in question can be accomplished.

The above tests of prophecy, as outlined in the scriptures, are primarily tests of the mind rather than of the Spirit. Prophecies are revelations, and can be tested with the same tests which apply to any revelation. These are outlined in chapter II of this book.

The Gift to Interpret Prophecy

The apostle Peter taught,

We have also a more sure word of prophecy; whereunto ye do well that ye take heed, as unto a light that shineth in a dark place, until the day dawn, and the day star arise in your hearts:

Knowing this first, that *no prophecy of the scripture is of any private interpretation.*

For the prophecy came not in old time by the will of man: but holy men of God spake as they were moved by the Holy Ghost.[23]

No prophecy is to be given "private" interpretation. Man must have the Spirit to understand the workings of the Spirit. Without the guidance of the Holy Ghost man cannot hope to understand and comprehend fully the words of prophecy or inspir-

21. D & C 35:23.
22. Jer. 28:9.
23. II Pet. 1:20-21.

ation. Man must have the spirit and gift of prophecy to understand prophecy. Nephi taught this necessity when he told how his people had responded to the prophecies of Isaiah:

> Behold, Isaiah spake many things which were hard for many of my people to understand; for they know not concerning the manner of prophesying among the Jews.
>
> Wherefore, hearken, O my people, which are of the house of Israel, and give ear unto my words; for because the words of Isaiah are not plain unto you, nevertheless *they are plain unto all those that are filled with the spirit of prophecy.*[24]

Possession of the spirit of prophecy was also stressed by Paul, as being necessary for understanding and accepting his words. The apostle wrote, "If a man think himself to be a prophet, or spiritual, let him acknowledge that the things that I write unto you are the commandments of the Lord."[25]

Concerning the spirit of prophecy in connection with the events of the last days, Elder Orson Pratt once said,

> The Latter-day Saints are not in darkness; they are the children of light, although many of us will actually be asleep. We shall have to wake up and trim up our lamps or we shall not be prepared to enter in; for we shall all slumber and sleep in that day, and some will have gone to sleep from which they will not awake until they awake up in darkness without any oil in their lamps. But, as a general thing, the Saints will understand the signs of the times, if they do [not] lie down and get to sleep. Others have their eyes closed upon the prophecies of the ancient Prophets; and not only that, but they are void of the spirit of prophecy themselves. *When a man has this, though he may appeal to ancient Prophets to get understanding on some subjects he does not clearly understand, yet, as he has the spirit of prophecy in himself, he will not be in darkness; he will have a knowledge of the signs of the times; . . . and he will have his eye fixed on the signs of the times, and that day will not overtake him unawares.*[26]

---

24. 2 Ne. 25:1, 4.
25. 1 Cor. 14:37.
26. *Journal of Discourses* (2nd photo lithographic reprint, 1961, Los Angeles, California: General Printing & Lithograph Co., 1860), VII, p. 189.

Prophecy Not Predestination

Prophecy is, of course, conditional in its nature. One should not assume that fate has predestined the future to take place in a certain manner which is fixed and sealed through the utterance of a prophecy. Changed situations can affect the fulfillment of prophecy. Jonah, for instance, proclaimed to the inhabitants of Nineveh that "yet forty days, and Nineveh shall be overthrown."[27] Yet the inhabitants of that city repented in sackcloth and ashes and thus escaped the threatened destruction. An excerpt from the Book of Isaiah also shows that God will change the course of the future from that which has been prophesied if circumstances so warrant:

> In those days was Hezekiah sick unto death. And Isaiah the prophet the son of Amoz came unto him, and said unto him, Thus saith the Lord, Set thine house in order: for *thou shalt die, and not live.*
>
> Then Hezekiah turned his face toward the wall, and prayed unto the Lord,
>
> And said, Remember now, O Lord, I beseech thee, how I have walked before thee in truth and with a perfect heart, and have done that which is good in thy sight. And Hezekiah wept sore.
>
> Then came the word of the Lord to Isaiah, saying,
>
> Go, and say to Hezekiah, Thus saith the Lord, the God of David thy father, *I have heard thy prayer, I have seen thy tears: behold, I will add unto thy days fifteen years.*[28]

Thus the course of prophecy can be altered if circumstances and attitudes change. In this sense, prophecy must be regarded as conditional. But, when circumstances remain constant and nothing happens to change the will of God, then prophecy is like King Nebuchadnezzar's dream of which the prophet Daniel said, *"The dream is certain, and the interpretation thereof sure."*[29]

Summary

1. Prophecy is one of the most valuable gifts of the Spirit.

2. Prophecy is designed primarily to edify the members of the Church.

---

27. Jonah 3:4.
28. Is. 38:1-5.
29. Dan. 2:45.

3. Prophecies are spoken by men and women, adults and children. It is one of the most commonly manifested of the spiritual gifts.

4. To prophesy is to function as a spokesman for God.

5. Prophecy serves numerous purposes, such as

    A. to indicate the course and growth of God's work;

    B. to indicate the future and potential of kingdoms, nations, cities and other political and geographical entities;

    C. to outline the future actions of individuals;

    D. to give warnings of impending danger; and

    E. to prepare for approaching death.

6. If prophecy is inspired of God it will not be in conflict with the scriptures. It may, however, deal with events not even mentioned by other prophecies.

7. The most accurate proof of the validity of a prophecy is its fulfillment.

8. No prophecy is to be interpreted "privately." Prophecy is to be interpreted only through the spirit of prophecy, which is given as a gift of the Spirit.

9. The course of prophecy may be altered, but only if circumstances change so as to alter the will of God. In this way, prophecy must be considered conditional. Without a change of the situation, however, true prophecy will come to pass with completeness and accuracy.

CHAPTER XIV

Speaking in Tongues

Purpose of the Gift of Tongues

One of the most easily recognized gifts of the Spirit is that of the gift of tongues.[1] This gift has been granted to the Saints on many occasions in the New Testament times as well as in the latter-days. The apostle Paul apparently enjoyed the gift of tongues to a great degree, for he wrote to the Corinthian Saints that "I thank my God, I speak with tongues more than ye all."[2] It is clear that Paul had insight into the purposes of the various spiritual gifts. He dwelt particularly on the gift of tongues and emphasized the various purposes of the gift. First, he saw the importance of the gift of tongues as a special method of communicating with God, "For he that speaketh in an unknown tongue *speaketh not unto men, but unto God:* for no man understandeth him; howbeit in the spirit he speaketh mysteries."[3] Second, he saw that the gift was one that turned inward. He observed that it served to strengthen the individual who possessed the gift rather than others:

> *He that speaketh in an unknown tongue edifieth himself;* but he that prophesieth edifieth the church.
>
> *I would that ye all spake with tongues,* but rather that ye prophesied: for greater is he that prophesieth than he that speaketh with tongues, except he interpret, that the church may receive edifying.
>
> Now, brethren, if I come unto you speaking with tongues, what shall I profit you, except I shall speak to you either by revelation, or by knowledge, or by prophesying, or by doctrine?[4]

Third, he saw that this gift is primarily a tool to aid in the conversion of those who are outside the church: *"Wherefore tongues are for a sign, not to them that believe, but to them that believe not:* but prophesying serveth not for them that believe not, but

---

1. I Cor. 12:10, 28, 30; D & C 46:24; Moro. 10:15.
2. I Cor. 14:18.
3. I Cor. 14:2.
4. I Cor. 14:4-6.

for them which believe."[5] But in asserting this objective, he warned, "If therefore the whole church be come together into one place, and all speak with tongues, and there come in those that are unlearned, or unbelievers, will they not say that ye are mad?"[6]

Counsel on the Use of the Gift

It is necessary that the counsel offered in the scriptures concerning the gift of tongues be considered. It should be recognized that this is a gift to be experienced after one's entering into a full commitment for service to Christ and after his fulfilling the ordinances involved therewith:

> Wherefore, my beloved brethren, I know that if ye shall *follow the Son*, with full purpose of heart, acting *no hypocrisy* and no deception before God, but with real intent, *repenting* of your sins, *witnessing unto the Father* that ye are willing to take upon you the name of Christ by baptism — yea, by *following your Lord and your Savior down into the water*, according to his word, behold, then shall ye receive the Holy Ghost; yea, then cometh the baptism of fire and of the Holy Ghost; and *then can ye speak with the tongue of angels*, and shout praises unto the Holy One of Israel.

> But, behold, my beloved brethren, thus came the voice of the Son unto me, saying: After ye have repented of your sins, and witnessed unto the Father that ye are willing to keep my commandments, by the baptism of water, and have received the baptism of fire and of the Holy Ghost, *and can speak with a new tongue*, yea, even with the tongue of angels, and *after this should deny me, it would have been better for you that ye had not known me.*[7]

Paul admonished the followers of Christ to be sure that the gift be used for the edification of the church, "Forasmuch as ye are zealous of spiritual gifts, *seek that ye may excel to the edifying of the church.*"[8] He saw also that the hearers of words spoken in a foreign tongue must be able to understand them to gain from them, so he gave the instruction to *"let him that speaketh in an unknown tongue pray that he may interpret."*[9] His counsel was

---

5. I Cor. 14:22.
6. I Cor. 14:23.
7. 2 Ne. 31:13-14.
8. I Cor. 14:12.
9. I Cor. 14:13.

that "if there be no interpreter, let him keep silence in the church; and *let him speak to himself, and to God.*"[10] And finally, he recognized that when this gift is manifested it may be poured out upon more than one individual at the same time, so he cautioned the individuals to take turns: "If any man speak in an unknown tongue, let it be by two, or at the most by three, *and that by course; and let one interpret.*"[11]

Gift of Tongues to be Manifested in the Last Days

Prophecy specifically denotes this gift as characteristic of Christ's church in the last days. While addressing Himself to those of the last days, Moroni warned,

> And again I speak unto you who deny the revelations of God, and say that they are done away, that there are no revelations, nor prophecies, nor gifts, nor healing, *nor speaking with tongues, and the interpretation of tongues;*
> Behold I say unto you, *he that denieth these things knoweth not the gospel of Christ;* yea, he has not read the scriptures; if so, he does not understand them.[12]

Moroni also reminded them of the words of the Master: "*And these signs shall follow them that believe* — in my name shall they cast out devils; *they shall speak with new tongues;* they shall take up serpents; and if they drink any deadly thing it shall not hurt them; they shall lay hands on the sick and they shall recover."[13]

Gift of Tongues Manifested in Three Forms

The gift of tongues may be manifested in three ways: an individual either speaks fluently in a foreign or unknown language with little or no academic or environmental preparation; or he is enabled to learn a foreign tongue in an abnormally rapid manner; or small children who do not yet have a vocabulary are given the ability to speak.

Two notable Biblical events are prime examples of the first type of manifestation of this gift. One occurred on the Day of Pentecost when the Savior's disciples experienced the coming of the Holy Ghost like the rushing of a mighty wind and as cloven

10. I Cor. 14:28.
11. I Cor. 14:27.
12. Morm. 9:7-8.
13. Morm. 9:24.

tongues of fire. At this time "they were all filled with the Holy Ghost, and began to speak with other tongues, as the Spirit gave them utterance."[14]

The second instance in which this type of manifestation is recorded in the Bible is in the history of the centurion, Cornelius, who called Peter to preach to him and his household. Though both he and his household were as yet unbaptized and were not of the house of Israel, the Holy Ghost fell upon them. They were granted the gift of tongues as a manifestation that they had received the Holy Ghost:

> While Peter yet spake these words, the Holy Ghost fell on all them which heard the word.
>
> And they of the circumcision which believed were astonished, as many as came with Peter, because that on the Gentiles also was poured out the gift of the Holy Ghost.
>
> For they heard them speak with tongues, and magnify God.[15]

There are no other examples of this gift recorded in the Bible or other scriptures of the church. However, references are made to it in the Book of Mormon, particularly, and it is clear that the gift was well known and understood even before the time of Christ. Omni wrote that he would deliver up the Book of Mormon plates to King Benjamin, "Exhorting all men to come unto God, the Holy One of Israel, and believe in prophesying, and in revelations, and in the ministering of angels and *in the gift of speaking with tongues*, and in the gift of interpreting languages, and in all things which are good."[16] Alma, while calling the people of Ammonihah to repentance, spoke of the gifts they had experienced in the past, reminding them of their

> Having been visited by the Spirit of God; having conversed with angels, and having been spoken unto by the voice of the Lord; and having the spirit of prophecy, and the spirit of revelation, and also many gifts, *the gift of speaking with tongues*, and the gift of preaching, and the gift of the Holy Ghost, and the gift of translation."[17]

---

14. Acts 2:4.
15. Acts 10:44-46.
16. Om. 25.
17. Al. 9:21.

Perhaps Nephi was referring to another aspect of the gift of tongues when he said:

> Do ye not remember that I said unto you that after ye had received the Holy Ghost ye could speak with the tongue of angels? And now, *how could ye speak with the tongue of angels save it were by the Holy Ghost?*
>
> Angels speak by the power of the Holy Ghost; wherefore, they speak the words of Christ.[18]

The gift of tongues has played a prominent part in the restored Church. This gift sometimes exhibits itself in unlikely circumstances. One such circumstance arose during a testimony meeting held in the home of Sarah Williams in Wales in 1847.

> At one time an East Indian called at the house as a testimony meeting was about to begin. She spoke inquiringly to Captain Dan Jones, who presided, about the strange caller, and was told to invite him in. During the meeting, the spiritual gifts were exercised and *one man, by the gift of tongues, spoke in the native language of the East Indian, telling him he ought to be baptized.* The stranger asked to have the ordinance performed at once, but was persuaded to wait till the close of the meeting, when it was attended to.[19]

The journal kept by Jane Grover records another strange circumstance in which the gift of tongues was made available. This incident took place in 1847 while crossing the plains.

> One morning we thought we would go and gather goose-berries. Father Tanner (as we familiarly called the good, patriarchal John Tanner) harnessed a span of horses to a light wagon, and, with two sisters by the name of Lyman, his little grand-daughter and I, started out. When we reached the woods we told the old gentleman to go to a house which was in sight, and rest, while we picked the berries.
>
> It was not long before the little girl and I strayed some distance from the others, when, suddenly, we heard shouts. The little girl thought it was her grandfather, and she was going to answer, but I prevented her thinking it might be Indians. We walked forward until within sight of Father Tanner, when we saw he was running his team around. We thought it nothing strange at first, but as we approached, we saw Indians gathering around the wagon, whooping and yelling as others came and joined them. We got into the wagon to start, when

---

18. 2 Ne. 32:2-3.
19. Jenson, II, p. 535.

four of the Indians took hold of the wagon, and two others
held the horses by the bits, and another came to take me out
of the wagon. I then began to be afraid as well as vexed, and
asked Father Tanner to let me get out of the wagon and run
for assistance. He said, 'No, poor child, it is too late!' I told
him they should not take me alive.

Father Tanner's face was as white as a sheet! The Indians
had commenced to strip him. They had taken his watch and
handkerchief, and while stripping him, were trying to pull me
out of the wagon. I began silently to appeal to my Heavenly
Father. While praying and struggling, *the Spirit of the Almighty fell upon me, and I arose with great power, and no
tongue can describe my feelings. I was as happy as I could be.*
A few moments before, I saw worse than death staring me in
the face, and now my hand was raised by the power of God,
and *I talked to those Indians in their own language.* They let
go the horses and wagon, and stood in front of me while I
talked to them by the power of God. They bowed their heads
and answered 'yes' in a way that made me know what they
meant. Father Tanner and the little girl looked on in speechless amazement. I realized our situation. Their calculation
was to kill Father Tanner, burn the wagon, and take us women
prisoners. This was plainly shown to me. When I stopped talking, they shook hands with all of us and returned all they had
taken from Father Tanner, who gave them the handkerchief,
and I gave them berries and crackers. By this time the other
two women came up and we hastened home.

*The Lord gave me a portion of the interpretation of what
I had said,* which is as follows: 'I suppose you Indian warriors
think you are going to kill us. Don't you know the Great Spirit
is watching you, and knows everything in your hearts? We have
come out here to gather some of our Father's fruit. We have
not come to injure you; and if you harm us, or injure one hair
of our heads, the Great Spirit will smite you to the earth, and
you shall not have power to breathe another breath. We have
been driven from our homes and so have you. We have come
out here to do you good and not to injure you. We are the
Lord's people, and so are you; but you must cease your murders and wickedness. The Lord is displeased with it and will
not prosper you if you continue in it. You think you own all
this land, this timber, this water and all these horses. You
do not own one thing on earth, not even the air you breathe.
It all belongs to the Great Spirit.'[20]

20. *Scraps of Biography* pp. 17-19.

Benjamin Brown made fun of the gift of tongues while attending an L.D.S. meeting as an investigator. He was able to duplicate the gift by the power of the Devil.

> I had experienced the Spirit of the Lord in a similar way elsewhere, so that when the Elders of the Church, at this meeting, urged upon me to yield obedience to the gospel they preached, which possessed such evidences as the manifestations of the ancient gifts, I treated the Elders very lightly, and replied, that as for the gift of tongues, I could speak in tongues as well as any of them. So I could, for directly one of them manifested this gift, *the gift of tongues rested upon me, and gave me the same power.*
>
> *Thus did the devil seek to blind me,* and turn that testimony which the Lord had given me, for the truth, almost into an evidence against it.[21]

He told how that influence of the Devil made him turn away from his investigation of the gospel until he was rebuked by two of the three Nephites. Then he cast off that evil spirit and began to study the Book of Mormon.

> Here my mind half yielded to the belief which arose within me, that perhaps it might be true, whereupon I took the book and laid it before the Lord, and pleaded with Him in prayer for a testimony whether it was true or false, and, as I found it stated that the three Nephites had power to show themselves to any person they might wish to, Jew or Gentile, *I asked the Lord to allow me to see them for a witness and testimony of the truth of the Book of Mormon* and I covenanted with Him, if He complied with my request, that I would preach it, even at the expense of my life, should it be necessary.
>
> The Lord heard my prayer, and, about five days afterwards, *two of the three visited me in my bedroom.* I did not see them come, but I found them there.
>
> One spoke to me for some time, and reproved me sharply on account of my behavior at the time when I first attended the meeting of the Saints, and treated so lightly the gift of tongues. *He told me never, as long as I lived, to do so again, for I had grieved the Spirit of the Lord, by whose power that gift had been given.*
>
> *This personage spoke in the Nephite language, but I understood, by the Spirit which accompanied him, every word as*

21. *Gems for the Young Folks* p. 59.

plainly as if he had spoken in English. I recognized the language to be the same as that in which I heard Father Fisher speak at the meeting.

Such a rebuke, with such power, I never had in my life, before nor since, and never wish to have again. I was dumb before my rebuker, for I knew what he said was right and I felt deserving of it.

How these men went, I do not know, but directly they were gone, *the Spirit of the Lord said to me, 'Now, you know for yourself! You have seen and heard! If you now fall away, there is no forgiveness for you.'*[22]

Some individuals are given the gift of tongues in a particular manner, time after time, such as Elizabeth Ann Whitney, who continually enjoyed the gift while singing.

She was among the first members of the Church to receive the gift of tongues, which she always exercised in singing. The Prophet said that the language was the pure Adamic tongue, the same that was used in the garden of Eden, and he promised that if she kept the faith, the gift would never leave her. It never did, and many who heard her sing never forgot the sweet and holy influence that accompanied her exercise of this heavenly gift. The last time she sang in tongues was on the day she was 81 years old. It was at the home of Sister Emmeline B. Wells, the latter having arranged a party, in honor of Mother Whitney's birthday. At a meeting held in the Kirtland Temple, Sister Whitney sang in tongues and Parley P. Pratt interpreted, the result being a beautiful hymn descriptive of the different dispensations from Adam to the present age.[23]

The second form in which the gift of tongues is manifested is in the aiding of individuals to learn a new language in an abnormally rapid manner. Surprisingly enough, this type of manifestation is often given to humble missionaries who seem to be having an especially difficult time learning a new tongue by their own efforts. A good example is found in the experience of Alonzo A. Hinckley as he entered the Dutch mission in 1897:

When I first arrived in Holland to fill a mission in 1897, I was unable to learn the language. I wrote home to my father and asked him to call upon the Bishop of the Ward, the Patriarch of the Stake, and other men in whom he had confidence, and

---

22. *Ibid.* pp. 60-61.
23. Jenson, III, pp. 563-64.

invite them to join him in praying to the Lord in my behalf
that I might acquire the language and be able to deliver my
message to the people.

I had never sought for a sign because I was fearful of
them, but I did seek the Spirit of the Lord to help me touch
the hearts of men. *I not only prayed to the Lord to assist me
to learn the Dutch language, but I also studied it as faithfully
as I could.* I succeeded in learning two or three sentences which
enabled me to deliver my literature from door to door.

One day, when I was alone, visiting among the people at
Rotterdam, it was my duty to go back to the homes in which
I had left tracts and take up the literature. As I went to gather
the booklets, *some power, that I cannot understand, possessed
me until I quaked and trembled.* I stood and looked at the house
at which I was to call and felt as if I could not go to the door.
But I knew my duty and so, with fortitude and determination
I went to the house, raised the knocker and dropped it. Almost instantly, the door opened and an irate woman stepped
out and closed it behind her. She talked in a very loud, shrill
voice, berating me most severely.

I did not realize for a moment, that *I was understanding
Dutch as clearly as though she had been speaking English.*
I felt no supernatural power, or influence, or feeling. I just
knew every word she was saying. She spoke so loudly that a
carpenter, who was working across the street, building a porch
on a little store, heard her, and I suppose, thought I was
abusing the woman, for he came over to where we stood and
brought his son with him and greatly to my alarm, he carried
a broadax. The man took his position near me and listened to
the woman, who continued her tirade against me in a shouting
voice.

I did not grow angry because of the woman's abuse, but
to the contrary, *my soul was filled with a burning desire to speak
her language and to testify of the divinity of the Gospel and of
the Lord Jesus Christ.* I thought if I could only explain to her
the importance of my message and the good it would do her,
she would not berate me as she does now.

In a few moments she ceased her abuse and I began speaking. And *I spoke the Dutch language. I defended the Truth
and bore testimony of the restoration of the Gospel.*

I had forgotten the large man who stood near me with his
ax, and, as I looked at the woman and delivered my message
of truth, he put his arms across my shoulders and, looking the

woman in the face said, 'The Mormon Church may have its black sheep, but this is a man of God.'

Her bitterness now gone, the woman replied, 'I know it.'

After the conversation, I went back home, hardly touching the ground. It dawned upon me that the prayers I had offered — and perhaps as a result in part, of the hard study I had made — and the prayers of those at home, had been answered in a moment, for I had spoken the Dutch language intelligently for the first time in my life.[24]

An experience similar to Elder Hinckley's took place during the mission of Gearsen S. Bastian, who was called to the Danish mission in 1888.

He had much difficulty in acquiring the language, and after a few weeks he became discouraged, and thought it impossible for him to learn the language. But the Lord gave him a marvelous manifestation of his power. His missionary companion was released to return home, and Elder Bastian was left in charge of the Randers branch. Only once had he attempted to speak before the public and he was not able to say but a few words. Sunday came, and at the appointed time for worship the meeting hall was well filled. After the opening exercises he called upon one of the native Elders to speak, but he had

---

24. Hinckley, *Faith of Our Pioneer Fathers* pp. 231-33. This gift left and then returned to Brother Hinckley. He continued his narrative with this statement:

In ecstasy, I rushed home to tell Brother Thatcher in the office, and to tell the President of the mission; but when I attempted to speak to my great dismay, I was the same as before, I could not understand nor speak the language.

President Farrell asked me if I would go to meeting that night.

'Yes, President Farrell,' I answered, 'after a man has been blessed of the Lord as I have been, I will gladly go. But I beg of you not to call upon me to speak even if you call upon someone to interpret what I say.'

'Very well,' he agreed, 'I promise you, Brother Hinckley, that if you go you will not be asked to speak.'

I went to meeting, and everything progressed nicely, as I thought, until Brother DeBry, the Branch President arose and, contrary to Brother Farrell's promise, announced 'We shall now hear from Elder Hinckley.'

President Farrell stepped forward, greatly embarrassed, and, addressing me, asked, 'Brother Hinckley, shall I interpret for you?'

I felt a power I can not describe. 'Wait, President Farrell,' I said as I stood upon my feet. And then I began to speak, not in my native tongue, but in the Dutch language. And, then and there, I delivered the first discourse in my life in the tongue of that mission. (p. 233).

only occupied a few minutes, when *a burning desire to speak filled the soul of Elder Bastian. He arose, and under the influence and power of God he preached the gospel with much plainness in the Danish language for an hour and twenty minutes.* At the close of the meeting the native brethren and sisters all flocked around him to congratulate him; and they claimed that he had spoken the language with as much plainness as they could have spoken; and they rejoiced greatly. *But as yet he could not converse with them;* nevertheless the Lord had given to him a testimony that he should henceforth have freedom and power in preaching the gospel.[25]

The rapid acquiring of a new tongue with the assistance of the Spirit is done through a mixture of diligent study and special aid from the Lord. This was the method by which President Joseph F. Smith, learned a new language as a fifteen-year-old missionary to the Sandwich Islands:

Brother Pratt, who was spokesman in setting him apart, declared that he should receive the knowledge of the Hawaiian language, '*by the gift of God as well as by study.*' This prophecy was literally fulfilled, for in less than four months from his arrival he was able to make a tour of the island of Maui, to preach, baptize and administer the Sacrament, etc., all in the native language.[26]

The gift of interpretation of tongues is often received by missionaries as a prelude to receiving the gift of tongues in this manner. This was the finding of Elder George Q. Cannon, who, as a young man, also filled a mission to Hawaii.

My desire to learn to speak was very strong; it was present with me night and day, and I never permitted an opportunity of talking with the natives to pass without improving it. I also tried to exercise faith before the Lord to obtain the gift of talking and understanding the language. One evening, while sitting on the mats conversing with some neighbors who had dropped in, I felt an uncommonly great desire to understand what they said. *All at once, I felt a perculiar sensation in my ears; I jumped to my feet, with my hands at the sides of my head, and exclaimed to Elders Bigler and Keeler who sat at the table, that I believed I had received the gift of interpretation! And it was so.*

25. Jenson, I, p. 345.
26. Jenson, I, p. 69.

From that time forward I had but little, if any difficulty in understanding what the people said. I might not be able at once to separate every word which they spoke from every other word in the sentence; but I could tell the general meaning of the whole. This was a great aid to me in learning to speak the language, and I felt very thankful for this gift from the Lord.

I mention this that my readers may know how willing God is to bestow gifts upon his children. If they should be called to go as missionaries to a foreign nation, whose language they do not understand, *it is their privilege to exercise faith for the gifts of speaking and interpreting that language, and also for every other gift which they may need.*[27]

But after receiving this gift of interpretation Elder Cannon still applied himself to diligent study to learn the language fully and fluently. Of his condition after several months in the mission field he wrote,

I had become so accustomed to talking in the Sandwich Island language that it was hard for me to speak in my mother tongue. I well remember how difficult it was for me to pray in English, when called upon to do so, in the family circle, the evening after I got to Lahaina.

I had been so anxious to learn the language that I would not read any book in English excepting the Book of Mormon and the Doctrine and Covenants, and had even trained myself to think in that language. I did this so that I might be thoroughly familiar with it for I was anxious to preach the gospel in exceeding plainness unto the people.

Of course it required an effort on my part to thus train myself; but I was paid for it all, in the fluency with which I used the language. *I was able to speak and write it with greater ease and correctness than my mother tongue.*[28]

The third type of manifestation of the gift of tongues is the giving of the ability to speak to children too young to have learned to speak or to comprehend what they are saying. In the Book of Mormon, one reads of small children being given this gift by the Savior as he ministered to the Nephites: "And it came to pass that he did teach and minister unto the children of the multitude of whom hath been spoken, and he did loose their tongues, and they did speak unto their fathers great and

27. *My First Mission,* pp. 23-24.
28. *Ibid.* p. 47.

marvelous things, even greater than he had revealed unto the people; and he loosed their tongues that they could utter."[29]

Summary

1. The gift of tongues serves three major purposes:
    A. to provide a special method for direct communication with God;
    B. to strengthen the individual who possesses it; and
    C. to serve as a tool in converting those who have not yet accepted the gospel.

2. This gift is obtained after making a full commitment to Christ and is to be used for the edifying of the Church.

3. The gift of tongues is to be employed in an orderly fashion and to be used only when one is present to interpret.

4. The gift of tongues is to be manifested in the last days and to serve as a characteristic of Christ's true Church.

5. The gift of tongues is manifested in three forms:
    A. an individual is able to speak in an unknown tongue without special preparation;
    B. an individual is able to learn a new language in an unusually rapid manner; and
    C. small children are given the ability to speak beyond their vocabulary and comprehension.

6. Few examples of the gift of tongues are given in the scriptures. Frequent references to the gift, however, make it clear that Saints of other eras were well acquainted with it.

7. The gift sometimes exhibits itself in unusual circumstances, such as chance meetings with people of other languages, etc.

8. Some people have the gift but are able to use it only in special means of expression such as singing or poetry.

9. The gift of tongues is often accompanied by the gift of interpretation of tongues.

10. Many people are given special facility with a language they are trying to learn in connection with their own prayerful and diligent study.

---

29. 3 Ne. 26:14.

CHAPTER XV

Interpretation of Tongues

Nature of the Gift

· The gift of interpretation of tongues[1] is often linked with the gift of tongues and is just as impressive in its manifestation. Through this gift the Holy Ghost grants the ability to understand and interpret the words of a language unknown to the hearer. The foreign language may be the words of an individual speaking through the gift of tongues or it may be the speaker's native language.

Perhaps the greatest use of this gift is to complement the gift of tongues so that that gift will edify those who are listening. Paul emphasized the need for this gift when he wrote, "Wherefore *let him that speaketh in an unknown tongue pray that he may interpret.*"[2]

The scriptures contain no unequivocal example of the use of this gift, although it may have been manifest together with the gift of tongues on the Day of Pentecost.[3]

One of the best known instances of the gift of interpretation of tongues in the restored Church is that which took place during President David O. McKay's visit to New Zealand in 1921. He said of this experience,

> One of the most important events on my world tour of the missions of the Church was the gift of interpretations of the English tongue to the Saints of New Zealand at a session of their conference, held on the 23rd day of April, 1921, at Puke Tapu Branch, Waikato District, Huntly, New Zealand.
>
> The service was held in a large tent, beneath the shade of which hundreds of earnest men and women gathered in anxious anticipation of seeing and hearing an Apostle of the Church, the first one to visit that land.

---

1. I Cor. 12:10; D & C 46:25; Moro. 10:16.
2. I Cor. 14:13.
3. Acts 2:5-12.

When I looked over that vast assemblage and contemplated the great expectations that filled the hearts of all who had met together, I realized how inadequately I might satisfy the ardent desires of their souls, and I yearned, most earnestly, for the gift of tongues that I might be able to speak to them in their native language.

Until that moment I had not given much serious thought to the gift of tongues, but on that occasion, I wished with all my heart, that I might be worthy of that divine power.

In other missions I had spoken through an interpreter, but, able as all interpreters are, I nevertheless felt hampered, in fact, somewhat inhibited, in presenting my message.

Now, I faced an audience that had assembled with unusual expectations, and I then realized, as never before, the great responsibility of my office. From the depth of my soul, I prayed for divine assistance.

When I arose to give my address, I said to Brother Stuart Meha, our interpreter, that I would speak without his translating, sentence by sentence, what I said, and then to the audience I continued:

I wish, oh, how I wish I had the power to speak to you in your own tongue, that I might tell you what is in my heart; but since I have not the gift, *I pray, and I ask you to pray, that you might have the spirit of interpretation, of discernment, that you may understand at least the spirit while I am speaking,* and then you will get the words and the thought when Brother Meha interprets.

My sermon lasted forty minutes, and I never addressed a more attentive, a more respectful audience. My listeners were in perfect rapport — this I knew when I saw tears in their eyes. *Some of them at least, perhaps most of them, who did not understand English, had the gift of interpretation.*

Brother Sidney Christy, a native New Zealander, who had been a student at Brigham Young University, at the close of my address, whispered to me, 'Brother McKay, they got your message!'

'Yes,' I replied, 'I think so, but for the benefit of some who may not have understood, we shall have Brother Meha give a synopsis of it in Maori.'

During the translation, some of the Maoris corrected him on some points, showing that they had a clear conception of what had been said in English.[4]

---

4. Middlemiss, *op. cit.*, pp. 73-75.

The gift of interpretation of tongues can serve to relate incidents happening at the same moment hundreds of miles away. Benjamin Brown told of such an incident which occurred in the Portland Branch, when the divine communication came in the form of poetry:

One Sunday morning, while opening the meeting with prayer, the gift of tongues came upon me, but thinking of Paul's words, that it is sometimes wisdom not to speak in tongues unless one is present who can interpret, and forgetting that a sister possessing the gift of interpretation was present, *I quenched the Spirit, and it left me.*

Immediately after, another brother spoke in tongues, the interpretation of which was, that *'The Lord knew we were anxious to learn of the affairs of our brethren in Missouri, and that if we would humble ourselves before Him, and ask, He would reveal unto us the desires of our hearts.'*

Missouri was some thousand miles from Portland, We accordingly bowed again in supplication before the Lord, and, after rising from our knees and re-seating ourselves, *the same brother broke out singing in tongues in a low, mournful strain.*

But judge our feelings when *the interpretation was given, and was found to be some thirteen or fourteen verses of poetry, descriptive of affairs in Missouri, and the murder of our brethren there,* telling us that just at that time —

'Our brethren lay bleeding on the ground.

With their wives and children weeping around.'

We had so often proved the truth of similar communications, that we felt as assured of the truth of this shocking news as though our eyes actually beheld the horrid sight. Our hearts were filled with sorrow.

In a fortnight afterwards we received a letter from John P. Greene, a faithful Elder of the Church in Missouri, who was, at the time he managed to write, secreted in the woods. The letter detailed and confirmed all the events previously revealed in tongues, proving that on the very day we had been informed of the transactions occurring a thousand miles off, the bleeding corpses of our brethren lay stretched on the ground after the slaughter. It was either at or about this time, that the massacre at Haun's Mill took place.[5]

---

5. *Gems for the Young Folks*, pp. 67-68.

On some occasions several may be blessed with the gift of interpretation when the gift of tongues is manifested. Josephine D. Booth, while visiting a Church service at Cardston, Alberta, Canada, witnessed just such an occasion.

> At one meeting, which particularly impressed me, five people spoke in tongues, and there were at least four in the congregation who had the interpretation each time, and who rose up in power and testified that it came from Almighty God.[6]

On other occasions individuals speak with the gift of tongues and then are given the gift of interpretation so that they and others can know exactly what was said. Lorenzo Dow Young received this multiple blessing in 1832 while laboring as a missionary in New York.

> I visited the town of Hector, where, by my preaching, as before stated, a Campbellite church had been organized. I preached in the same house that I had occupied on the previous occasion. Soon after I commenced to talk, such a spirit of darkness and opposition prevailed in the house, that for the first and only time in my life, I was entirely bound. I stood speechless. The congregation looked at me as if wondering what could be the matter. A sensation such as I had never felt before came over me. My tongue seemed numb or paralyzed. In a short time *I commenced to speak in an unknown tongue.* I probably spoke about fifteen minutes. *Soon after ceasing to talk, the interpretation came clear and distinct to my mind. I at once gave it to the congregation.*
>
> I had no further difficulty, I talked about an hour. My old friend, Squire Chase arose and testified that what he had heard was the truth, and that the power of God had been made manifest. He and several others shed tears. Their hearts were softened by the influence of the good Spirit.[7]

Sometimes the gift of tongues and interpretation of tongues are given together, the process being all for the benefit of one individual and all taking place in his own mind. Brother George Halliday, while laboring in the British mission, experienced this type of blessing:

> Wednesday morning came and with it a drenching rain storm, through which the Elders tramped the whole six miles,

---

6. Jenson, I, p. 504.
7. *Fragments of Experience,* pp. 39-40.

hungry and penniless. Shortly before arriving at St. Just, and while they were crossing a plowed field with the mud clinging to their boots so they could scarcely walk, the Lord deigned to comfort them *by giving Elder Halliday the gift of tongues and the interpretation of the same,* in which it was made known to him that the lady whom they were going to visit had been favored with a vision, in which she had seen himself and Elder Chislett; also that she was the owner of several houses, one of which she was going to allow them to use to hold meetings in, and that he was going to baptize her that very night.

As *soon as this had passed through his mind, for he had not spoken aloud, but to himself,* he joyfully slapped his companion on the shoulder and exclaimed, 'Cheer up, John! I have had a revelation!! He then proceeded to relate all that had been revealed to him.[8]

Summary

1. The gift of interpretation of tongues consists in a person being inspired to understand someone speaking in a language unknown to the hearer.

2. Probably the most important use of this gift is to complement the gift of tongues so that that gift will be of edification to those listening.

3. The gift of interpretation sometimes enables the recipient of the gift to translate in poetry.

4. The gift of interpretation may be granted to several people at the same time. At times a person speaking in tongues may not have the gift of interpretation and may not know what he has said. In other instances the person who speaks in tongues may also have the gift to interpret his words for those around him.

---

8. *Early Scenes in Church History,* pp. 33-34.

CHAPTER XVI

Six Gifts of Self-Expression

Gifts of Communication Often Manifested

Paul's enumeration of spiritual gifts refers to those of wisdom and knowledge.[1] (The *receiving* of these gifts are discussed in Part II.) The corresponding latter-day revelation says:

> And again, verily, I say unto you, to some is given by the Spirit of God, the word of wisdom;
>
> To another is given the word of knowledge, *that all may be taught to be wise and to have knowledge.*[2]

This hint as a facility for *communicating* as well as for *receiving* wisdom or knowledge is confirmed by Moroni's rendering:

> For behold, to one is given by the Spirit of God, that he may *teach the word of wisdom;*
>
> And to another, that he may *teach the word of knowledge* by the same Spirit.[3]

Clearly the facilities to receive and to communicate are often granted to the same person.

Thus most of the categorizations discussed in this chapter are embraced in the major scriptural listings. The remainder are so clearly endowments of spiritual power that they can only be classed as gifts of the Spirit. In this general area particularly, tendencies to overlap and merge render rigid classification difficult, but those used here have been made with care and serve well the purposes of our consideration.

Most of these six gifts, the gifts of speaking, of writing, of translating, of teaching, of expounding the scriptures, and of bearing testimony, are probably the most often witnessed in the Church today. It would seem, however, that they are among the least often recognized as being actual gifts of the Spirit.

1. I Cor. 12:8.
2. D & C 46:17-18.
3. Moro. 10:9-10.

True, people often speak of "talented" or "gifted" speakers and of people with "strong testimonies" of the gospel, but most Latter-day Saints fail to recognize that these are special abilities which are granted by the Holy Ghost.

These gifts of self expression are similar in nature and the oral ones in particular are often granted by the Spirit to the same individual.

The Gift of Speaking

A promise to bestow the gift of speaking is found in the Doctrine and Covenants, Section 100, and is addressed to Joseph Smith and Sidney Rigdon:

> Therefore, verily I say unto you, lift up your voices unto this people; *speak the thoughts that I shall put into your hearts,* and you shall not be confounded before men;
> *For it shall be given you in the very hour, yea, in the very moment, what ye shall say.*[4]

But the Lord continued by qualifying the nature of His gift. In doing so He explained the manner in which the Holy Ghost makes a man's word's effective and forceful:

> But a commandment I give unto you, that *ye shall declare whatsoever thing ye declare in my name, in solemnity of heart, in the spirit of meekness, in all things.*
> And I give unto you this promise, that inasmuch as ye do this the Holy Ghost shall be shed forth in bearing record unto all things whatsoever ye shall say.[5]

Since the early days of the Church the Saints have been commanded to follow the path that will best allow them to enjoy this gift of the Spirit. The Lord has said,

> Neither take ye thought beforehand what ye shall say; but *treasure up in your minds continually the words of life, and it shall be given you in the very hour* that portion that shall be meted unto every man.[6]

Heber J. Grant enjoyed the gift of speaking through the Spirit, and told in General Conference[7] how this gift was instrumental in the conversion of his half-brother.

---

4. D & C 100:5-6.
5. D & C 100:7-8.
6. D & C 84:85. See Mt. 10:18-20.
7. October, 1922.

I remember what to me was the greatest of all the great incidents in my life, in this Tabernacle. I saw for the first time, in the audience, my brother who had been careless, indifferent, and wayward; who had evinced no interest in the gospel of Jesus Christ.

As I saw him for the first time in this building, and as I realized that he was seeking God for light and knowledge regarding the divinity of this work, I bowed my head, and *I prayed God that if I were requested to address the audience that the Lord would inspire me by the revelations of his Spirit, by that Holy Spirit in whom every true Latter-day Saint believes, that my brother would have to acknowledge to me that I had spoken beyond my natural ability, that I had been inspired of the Lord.*

I realize that if he made that confession, then I should be able to point out to him that God has given him a testimony of the divinity of this work. . . .

I took out of my pocket a book that I always carried, called a *Ready Reference*, and I laid it down on the stand in front of me when I stood up to speak. It was opened at the passages that tell of the vicarious work for the dead, of the announcement that Jesus Christ went and preached to the spirits in prison, and proclaimed the gospel of Jesus Christ to them. . . .

I remember standing there feeling that this was perhaps the greatest of all the great themes that we as Latter-day Saints had to proclaim to the world. I laid the book down, opened at that page. *I prayed for the inspiration of the Lord and the faith of the Latter-day Saints, and I never thought of the book from that minute until I sat down at the end of a thirty-minute address.* I closed my remarks at twelve minutes after three o'clock, expecting that President George Q. Cannon would follow me. Brother Angus came to the upper stand and said, 'George, please occupy the balance of the time.'

He said, 'No, I do not wish to speak.' Brother Angus refused to take 'No' for an answer.

Brother Cannon said, finally: 'All right, go take your seat, and I will say something.' and he arose and said in substance:

'There are times when the Lord Almighty inspires some speakers by the revelations of his Spirit, and he is so abundantly blessed by the inspiration of the Living God that it is a mistake for anybody else to speak following him, and one of those

occasions has been today, and I desire that this meeting be dismissed without further remarks.' And he sat down.

I devoted the thirty minutes of my speech almost exclusively to a testimony of my knowledge that God lives, that Jesus is the Christ, and to the wonderful and marvelous labors of the Prophet Joseph Smith, bearing witness to the knowledge God had given me that Joseph was in very deed a prophet of the true and Living God.

The next morning my brother came into my office and said, 'Heber, I was at a meeting yesterday and heard you preach.'

I said, 'The first time you ever heard your brother preach, I guess?'

'Oh, no,' he said, 'I have heard you many times.'

He said, 'I generally come in late and go into the gallery. I often go out before the meeting is over. *But you have never spoken as you did yesterday. You spoke beyond your natural ability. You were inspired of the Lord.'* The identical words I had uttered the day before, in my prayer to the Lord! . . .

The next day, when he came and repeated my words, I said to him, 'Are you still praying for a testimony of the gospel?'

He said, 'Yes, and I am going nearly wild.'

I asked, 'What did I preach about yesterday?'

He replied, 'You know what you preached about.'

I said, 'Well, you tell me.'

'You preached upon the divine mission of the prophet Joseph Smith.'

I answered, 'And I was inspired beyond my natural ability; and I never spoke before — at any time you have heard me, as I spoke yesterday. Do you expect the Lord to get a club and knock you down? *What more testimony do you want of the gospel of Jesus Christ than that a man speaks beyond his natural ability and under the inspiration of God, when he testifies of the divine mission of the Prophet Joseph Smith?'*

The next Sabbath he applied to me for baptism.

When one speaks by the power of the Spirit the audience is often able to detect that the speaker is receiving supernatural guidance. This was clear to Daniel Tyler, who enjoyed the promptings of the Holy Ghost in an extemporaneous discourse he delivered at the age of sixteen.

8. Hinckley, *Heber J. Grant: Highlights in the Life of a Great Leader,* pp. 183-6.

The gift of prophecy was poured out upon me. I also received the gift and interpretation of tongues. But what then and ever since has seemed to me the greatest gift I received was to speak easily and fluently in my own language. This was the first gift I received. It came upon me in great power. A few months after my baptism several leading Elders from Kirtland, Ohio, were about to be dragged from our school house by a mob who had assembled to tar and feather them. When the Elders and others failed to stop them from disturbing the meeting, I stepped upon a form or bench and began to talk to the people. Five minutes had not elapsed when, aside from my voice, a pin dropping upon the floor might have been easily heard. After I had spoken about ten or fifteen minutes the mob left the house, and, after consulting outside a few moments, retired, and we had a good meeting.

This circumstance had gone out of my mind until about 1849, while stopping over night at the house of a brother named Brim. Alfred O. Brim, who was one of the mob, called my attention to it, and asked me if I knew that they had a keg of tar and a feather bed in the carriage in which they came to the meeting.

I replied that I did not think I even heard of it. He said they brought the tar and the feathers with the full intent to use them on the Elders, but *they were so surprized at the power with which I spoke that they knew I was helped by some invisible spirit. They had known me since I was seven years old, and were satisfied that I had not made up the speech, and that I was not capable of doing so. They decided that it must be of the Lord, or of the devil. Of this they could not be the judges,* not, as they said, having the discerning of spirits. Hence one of them suggested that lest they be fighting against God, they had better retire. All agreed to it and they left.[9]

The same gift of speech through the power of the Spirit was granted to David W. Patten in 1835. This power undoubtedly saved the lives of Elder Patten and Warren Parish on the occasion of their false arrest and trial.

The mob gathered to the number of one hundred, all fully armed. They took from Elder Patten his walking stick and a penknife, and went through with a mock trial; but would not let the defendants produce any witnesses; and without suffering them to say a word in defense, the judge pronounced them guilty of the charge preferred. *Brother Patten, being filled with*

9. *Scraps of Biography,* pp. 28-9.

the Holy Ghost, arose to his feet, and by the power of God bound them fast to their seats while he addressed them. He rebuked them sharply for their wicked and unjust proceedings. Bro. Parrish afterwards said, 'My hair stood up straight on my head, for I expected to be killed.' When Patten closed, the Judge addressed him, saying, 'You must be armed with concealed weapons, or you would not treat an armed court as you have this.' Patten replied, '*I am armed with weapons you know not of, and my weapons are the Holy Priesthood and the power of God.* God is my friend, and he permits you to exercise all the power you have, and he bestows on me all the power I have.[10]

Amasa Potter found that he was granted special aid from the Holy Ghost as he spoke on one occasion. This aid came in the form of lines of writing which appeared to him on the walls of the courthouse in which he was preaching.

I was introduced to the congregation as Elder Potter, with the remark that I would continue the subject of the gospel. I arose with fear and trembling; for it was the first time in my life that I had stood in a pulpit. Before me was a large Bible and prayer book. I must say that my mind was confused; but I took a text from the Bible that lay open before me. It was from the Prophet Amos:

'Surely the Lord God will do nothing, but he revealeth His secret unto His servants the prophets.'

After reading it I spoke a few more words and became dumb that I could not speak. I stood there without speaking about two minutes, when the words of President Heber C. Kimball came to me: He said that the time would come when I should be at a loss to know what to say to the people 'and, at that time,' he said, '*if you will commence to declare the divine mission of Joseph Smith in this our day, and the divine authenticity of the Book of Mormon, the Lord will loosen your tongue and you shall say the very things that are needful to be said to the people.*' When this came to my mind I commenced declaring these things to the congregation. I had spoken but a few minutes when *I thought I saw several lines of large letters printed on the walls of the house, and I commenced to read them and spoke about one hour. When the letters faded from my sight I then stopped speaking.* I could not tell all that I had said; but my companion told me it was an excellent discourse.[11]

---

10. Jenson, I, p. 78.
11. *Labors In The Vineyard,* p. 79.

At times God reveals things unknown to the speaker as he talks by the power of the Holy Ghost. This happened to Wilford Woodruff as he preached in Memphis, Tennessee. He had arrived in a dirty and tired condition after walking through a muddy swamp. The innkeeper said he would put Elder Woodruff up for the night if he would preach, and then assembled a large congregation intent on finding amusement by discomforting the Elder.

> There were present some five hundred persons who had come together, not to hear a gospel sermon but to have some fun.
>
> Now, boys, how would you like this position? On your first mission, without a companion or friend, and to be called upon to preach to such a congregation! With me it was one of the most pleasing hours of my life, although I felt as though I should like company.
>
> I read a hymn and asked them to sing. Not a soul would sing a word.
>
> I told them I had not the gift of singing; but with the help of the Lord, I would both pray and preach. I knelt down to pray, and the men around me dropped on their knees. *I prayed to the Lord to give me His Spirit and to show me the hearts of the people.* I promised the Lord in my prayer I would deliver to that congregation whatever He would give to me. I arose and spoke one hour and a half and it was one of the best sermons of my life.
>
> *The lives of the congregation were opened to the vision, of my mind, and I told them of their wicked deeds and the reward they would obtain.* The men who surrounded me dropped their heads. Three minutes after I closed I was the only person in the room.[12]

Not only insight into people's lives, but knowledge of the scriptures and of doctrine are brought forth when a man speaks by the power and gift of the Holy Ghost. David Jeffs, as a young missionary in North Carolina, found that this was true:

> My experience in public preaching was very limited; yet I resolved in my heart that I would not refuse to take my turn in any part of the missionary work. My companion and I had appointed a meeting at a friend's house, in Chearokee [sic] County, North Carolina. Some of our enemies, hearing of the

---

12. *Leaves From My Journal*, pp. 17-8.

meeting, sent for one of the leading preachers of the State of
Georgia to defeat the 'Mormons.' I had heard of this preacher,
whose name was Manuel Henry. However, I did not learn of
his coming to our meeting until we were arriving at the house
and heard some one say, 'There comes Manuel Henry; my heart
seemed to stop beating for a minute, my mind was a perfect
blank and I trembled like a leaf. We called the meeting to
order and I had to take hold of a chair in front of me in order
to arise to my feet. Just as we commenced singing all fear left
me, and as I arose to my feet to speak I was as cool and
collected as if I had been in the work for years; *the spirit of
God rested upon me in mighty power and by the help of my
Father in Heaven, I spoke for one hour and twenty-five minutes,
and quoted Scripture that I could not remember ever having
read, and my mind was filled with knowledge.* This was a testimony and a strength to me all through my mission.[13]

Sometimes the Spirit speaks with such power that the person through whom the Holy Ghost is being manifested doesn't
even know what he is saying. Philo Dibble found this to be
true in connection with a discourse he delivered on an impromptu
basis:

Brother Stewart arose, opened the Bible and tried to read,
but had to spell his words, and broke down and said that some
of the brethren would take up the subject and go on with it.
He then called on me. I arose to speak. *The Holy Ghost
came down and enveloped me, and I spoke for over two hours.
When I found the Spirit leaving me I thought it time to close,*
and told my hearers it was the first time I had spoken to a
public congregation.

A Brother Mills who was present, felt so well that he went
home with me and declared that I had delivered the greatest
discourse he had ever heard. Said I: '*Brother Mills, I don't know
what I have said. It was not me; it was the Lord!*'[14]

A revelation given to the Elders of the Church also emphasized that those who speak with the gift of God must do so with
humility and contrition:

Wherefore he that prayeth, whose spirit is contrite, the
same is accepted of me if he obey mine ordinances.

---

13. Jenson, II, p. 52.
14. *Early Scenes In Church History*, p. 92.

He that speaketh, whose spirit is contrite, whose language is meek and edified, the same is of God if he obey mine ordinances.

And again, he that trembleth under my power shall be made strong and shall bring forth fruits of praise and wisdom, according to the revelations and truth which I have given you.[15]

Summary of the Gift of Speaking

1. Gifts of communication are among the most common of the gifts manifested in the Church today. Some do not even realize that they are spiritual gifts.

2. The gift of speaking by the Holy Ghost consists of having the Spirit put into the speaker's mind and heart the words he is to say. It can be manifested to such a degree that the person through whom the Spirit is speaking does not even know what he is saying.

3. Man is commanded to study the things of God continually and then to rely on the Spirit to organize his talk when he is called upon to speak.

4. Those who would receive this gift must seek it with humility and meekness.

The Gift of Writing

Just as the Holy Ghost directs one as he speaks, He can also guide man in writing. One is blessed with the reception of the thoughts he should write in a spontaneous manner, just as if he were speaking them. A revelation given to Joseph Smith and Oliver Cowdery made this evident:

And thou shalt continue in calling upon God in my name, and writing the things which shall be given thee by the Comforter, and expounding all scriptures unto the church.

And it shall be given thee in the very moment what thou shalt speak and write, and they shall hear it, or I will send unto them a cursing instead of a blessing.[16]

A person may enjoy the gift of writing and also have the gift of speaking, yet may find that one gift is more effective than the other for him. Nephi, for instance, knew of the manner in

---

15. D & C 52:15-17.
16. D & C 24:5-6.

which the Spirit worked to accomplish His purposes and to make His gifts manifest. He was called on both to write and to speak for the Lord, and his writings clearly indicate a gift, but he felt that his spoken words were more effective:

> And now I, Nephi, cannot write all the things which were taught among my people; *neither am I mighty in writing, like unto speaking;* for when a man speaketh by the power of the Holy Ghost the power of the Holy Ghost carrieth it unto the hearts of the children of men.[17]

Even Moroni's inspired writing seemed weak to him:

> And I said unto him: *Lord, the Gentiles will mock at these things, because of our weakness in writing;* for Lord thou hast made us mighty in word by faith, but thou hast not made us mighty in writing; for thou hast made all this people that they could speak much, because of the Holy Ghost which thou hast given them;
>
> *And thou hast made us that we could write but little, because of the awkwardness of our hands.* Behold, thou hast not made us mighty in writing like unto the brother of Jared, *for thou madest him that the things which he wrote were mighty even as thou art, unto the overpowering of man to read them.*
>
> Thou has also made our words powerful and great, even that we cannot write them; wherefore, *when we write we behold our weakness, and stumble because of the placing of our words; and I fear lest the Gentiles shall mock at our words.*
>
> And when I had said this, the Lord spake unto me, saying: Fools mock, but they shall mourn; and my grace is sufficient for the meek, that they shall take no advantage of your weakness.[18]

Writing which is inspired by the Holy Ghost has the same power to reach the hearts of men as do sermons spoken through that influence. When read by people who themselves enjoy the influence of the Spirit, inspired writing carries the power of testimony and conversion. As one example, the writing of Joseph Smith often carried this influence:

> In the winter of 1828, Father John Smith received a letter from his nephew Joseph, who then lived in western New York, in which a very striking prediction occurred, fortelling awful judgments upon the present generation because of wickedness and

---

17. 2 Ne. 33:1.
18. Eth. 12:23-6.

unbelief. The letter made a deep impression upon the mind of George A., who, but a boy of eleven years, was capable of appreciating the statements it contained, which he treasured in his memory. His father observed on reading them, *'Joseph writes like a Prophet!'*[19]

The Book of Mormon also carries this power of conversion, and that power has often been commented upon when investigators have first read it.

George Cannon, the father of George Q., read the Book of Mormon through carefully twice before his baptism, and on laying it down after finishing it the second time, he remarked, *'No wicked man could write such a book as this; and no good man would write it, unless it were true and he were commanded of God to do so.'*[20]

Willard Richards was another who recognized the inspired writing of the Book of Mormon when he first perused its pages.

He opened the book without regard to place, and totally ignorant of its design or contents, and before reading half a page, declared that *'God or the devil has had a hand in that book, for man never wrote it.'* He read it twice through in about ten days; and so firm was his conviction of the truth, that he immediately commenced settling his accounts, selling his medicine, and freeing himself from every incumbrance, that he might go to Kirtland, Ohio, seven hundred miles west, the nearest point he could hear of a Saint, and give the work a thorough investigation; firmly believing, that if the doctrine was true, God had some greater work for him to do then peddle pills.[21]

Summary of the Gift of Writing

1. To be able to write under the influence of the Holy Ghost is another of the gifts of the Spirit.

2. When people write under inspiration from God they are shown what they should write in a spontaneous manner.

3. Those who enjoy the gift of writing may also be blessed with the ability to speak under inspiration. Sometimes such individuals find that they are blessed more with one gift than the other.

---

19. Jenson, I, p. 38.
20. Jenson, I, p. 44.
21. Jenson, I, p. 54.

4. Inspired writing carries with it the power of truth and conversion. Those who read inspired writing with the guidance of the Holy Spirit are able to recognize that the writing is inspired.

The Gift of Translation

The gift to translate is a lesser-known manifestation of the workings of the Holy Ghost. This may be because it is not listed in the best known scriptural enumerations of the various spiritual gifts. Nonetheless, it has played a significant part in religious history. This gift apparently exists in two forms, the ability to decipher the words of one language and record them in one's own language when the first language is unknown to the translator, and extra facility in translating when both languages are known.

The first scriptural recording of the use of this gift is the history of King Mosiah, who led a group of Nephites into the land of Zarahemla. The record states that "it came to pass in the days of Mosiah, there was a large stone brought unto him with engravings on it; and *he did interpret the engravings by the gift and power of God.*"[22] Later Ammon, a man from Zarahemla, came in contact with a Nephite king who had found other ancient records and wanted to know their contents. He told the king of the gift of translation which his prophet and leader possessed.

Now Ammon said unto him: I can assuredly tell thee, O king, of a man that can translate the records; for he has wherewith that he can look, and translate all records that are of ancient date; and *it is a gift from God.* And the things are called interpreters, and no man can look in them except he be commanded, lest he should look for that he ought not and he should perish. And *whosoever is commanded to look in them, the same is called seer.*

And behold, the king of the people who are in the land of Zarahemla is the man that is commanded to do these things, and who has this high gift from God.

And the king said that a seer is greater than a prophet.

And Ammon said *that a seer is a revelator and a prophet also; and a gift which is greater can no man have, except he should possess the power of God, which no man can; yet a man may have great power given him from God.*

---

22. Om. 20.

But a seer can know of things which are past, and also of things which are to come, and by them shall all things be revealed, or, rather, shall secret things be made manifest, and hidden things shall come to light, and things which are not known shall be made known by them, and also things shall be made known by them which otherwise could not be known.

Thus God has provided a means that man, through faith, might work mighty miracles; therefore he becometh a great benefit to his fellow beings.[23]

The same gift of translation was granted to Joseph Smith, to whom the Lord said in March, 1829:

And *you have a gift to translate the plates;* and this is the first gift that I bestowed upon you; and I have commanded that you should pretend to no other gift until my purpose is fulfilled in this; for I will grant unto you no other gift until it is finished.[24]

The use of this gift was carefully regulated from above. The same revelation told the prophet, "I say unto thee Joseph, when thou hast translated a few more pages thou shalt stop for a season, even until I command thee again; then thou mayest translate again."[25] Previously, Joseph Smith had committed a serious error by entrusting a portion of the Book of Mormon manuscript he had translated to Martin Harris, who subsequently lost it. The Lord reprimanded him by warning,

But remember, God is merciful; therefore, repent of that which thou has done which is contrary to the commandment which I gave you, and thou art still chosen, and art again called to the work;

Except thou do this, thou shalt be delivered up and become as other men, and have no more gift.

And when thou deliveredst up that which God had given thee sight and power to translate, thou deliveredst up that which was sacred into the hands of a wicked man.[26]

Nine months later Joseph Smith and Oliver Cowdery were granted the keys of the gift of translation:

---

23. Mos. 8:13-18.
24. D & C 5:4.
25. D & C 5:30.
26. D & C 3:10-12. At this time Joseph Smith actually lost the gift of translation. See D & C 3:14; 10: 1-3, 7.

And, behold, *I grant unto you a gift, if you desire of me, to translate,* even as my servant Joseph. . . .

And now, behold, I give unto you, and also unto my servant Joseph, the keys of this gift, which shall bring to light this ministry; and in the mouth of two or three witnesses shall every word be established.[27]

Oliver soon thereafter lost the privilege. This is the final mention made in the scriptures of the gift of translation.

Summary of the Gift of Translation

1. The gift of translation consists of (1) the ability to decipher the words of one language and record them in another when the first language is unknown to the translator, and (2) extra facility in translating when the translator knows both the languages.

2. Some individuals have been privileged to possess a translating instrument (interpreters or Urim and Thummim) which enabled them to make use of this gift of the Spirit. Whoever is commanded of God to use such an instrument is called a seer.

3. A seer is a revelator and a prophet as well as a translator.

4. The ability to translate the Book of Mormon was given to Joseph Smith (and for a short time, to Oliver Cowdery) by God as a gift.

The Gift of Teaching

The ability to teach the gospel in a truly effective manner is also gained through the ministrations of the Holy Ghost. A commandment given early in this dispensation says, "teach ye diligently and my grace shall attend you."[28] An important revelation given in 1831 tells of what should be taught and of the functions performed by the Spirit in the teaching process:

And again, the elders, priests and teachers of this church shall *teach the principles of my gospel, which are in the Bible and the Book of Mormon, in the which is the fulness of the gospel.*

And they shall *observe the covenants and church articles to do them, and these shall be their teachings, as they shall be directed by the Spirit.*

27. D & C 6:25, 28.
28. D & C 88:78.

And the Spirit shall be given unto you by the prayer of faith; and *if ye receive not the spirit ye shall not teach.*

And all this ye shall observe to do as I have commanded concerning your teaching, until the fulness of my scriptures is given.

And as ye shall lift up your voices by the Comforter, ye shall speak and prophesy as seemeth me good;

For, behold, the Comforter knoweth all things, and beareth record of the Father and of the Son.[29]

A revelation to Oliver Cowdery also emphasized the subject matter which is to be taught through the gift of the Spirit. "Behold, I say unto thee, Oliver, that it shall be given unto thee that thou shalt be heard by the church in all things whatsoever *thou shalt teach them by the Comforter, concerning the revelations and commandments which I have given.*"[30]

One of the most important characteristics of a good teacher is that he himself must be teachable. All those who desire to be able to teach by the Spirit would do well to seek the tutoring of that same Being:

Let him that is ignorant learn wisdom by humbling himself and calling upon the Lord his God, that his eyes may be opened that he may see, and his ears opened that he may hear;

For my Spirit is sent forth into the world to enlighten the humble and contrite, and to the condemnation of the ungodly.[31]

Those who enjoy the gift of teaching have a constant desire to teach and preach the gospel to those to whom they are called.

As Elder George Q. Cannon wrote,

When an Elder has the spirit of his mission, he cannot rest contented unless he is proclaiming to the people the message with which he is entrusted. Surround him with every comfort his heart can desire, and *if he has that spirit, he will still be anxious to go forth among the people,* even if he knows he will meet with privations and persecution. This was my feeling before the visit of the president of the mission, and after he left, my anxiety increased, and I told the brethren that I must

---

29. D & C 42:12-17.
30. D & C 28:1. See also D & C 42:56-9.
31. D & C 136:32-3.

push out among the natives, and commence preaching to them as well as I could.[32]

Summary of the Gift of Teaching

1. In a modern commandment the Lord promised His grace to those who teach with diligence.

2. Teachers of the Church should teach the principles of the gospel, the covenants and Church articles, the revelations and commandments, and that which is revealed by the Holy Ghost.

3. He who would teach must first seek to be taught by the Lord.

The Gift of Expounding the Scriptures

The ability to expound the scriptures consists of being able to explain scriptural passages clearly, to draw the full meaning from the text. This is a choice gift and one for which there is a great need in the Church.

A Counselor in the First Presidency in the early days of the Church was one who was especially blessed with this gift. While instructing Sidney Rigdon what his relationship to the prophet Joseph should be, the Lord told him,

> I will give unto thee power to be mighty in expounding all scriptures, that thou mayest be a spokesman unto him, and he shall be a revelator unto thee, that thou mayest know the certainty of all things pertaining to the things of my kingdom on the earth.[33]

The Prophet Joseph was also given the ability and responsibility to expound the scriptures:

> And in temporal labors thou shalt not have strength, for this is not thy calling. Attend to thy calling and thou shalt have wherewith to magnify thine office, and to expound all scriptures, and continue in laying on of the hands and confirming the churches.[34]

Emma Smith, the prophet's wife, was another who was promised the gift of the Spirit which would allow her to expound the scriptures. To her the Lord commanded that

---

32. *My First Mission*, p. 31.
33. D & C 100:11.
34. D & C 24:9.

Thou shalt be ordained under his hand *to expound scriptures, and to exhort the church, according as it shall be given thee by my Spirit.*

For he shall lay his hands upon thee, and thou shalt receive the Holy Ghost, and *thy time shall be given to writing, and to learning much.*[35]

The gift of ability to expound the scriptures is closely related to the gift of speaking. They often overlap and combine. Yet the two are not identical, for a man may speak as prompted by the Holy Ghost and never even quote a scripture, much less explain it.

There are instances in which the Holy Ghost has provided great aid to individuals as they attempted to explain the scriptural basis for the gospel. One elder, H.G.B.,[36] described his receiving of this gift when he made his debut as a speaker in the mission field (Pittsylvania County, Virginia, in 1844). He was suddenly called on to address a large assemblage at the Methodist camp meeting ground when his companion became ill.

Brother Shelton looked wearied and sick, but opened the meeting with singing and prayer, and sang again before he discovered me in the audience. Then he immediately called upon me to come to the stand and preach, as he was too sick and feeble to attempt it.

To say I was scared, would scarcely convey a proper idea of my condition. I was in a tremor from head to feet, and shook like a leaf in a storm, scarcely knowing what I did.

I took up Elder Shelton's Bible which lay upon the front board, and without any premeditation, I opened at the third chapter of John, and read the fifth verse. By the time I had finished reading, all my trembling had left me, and I felt as calm and collected as the quiet that succeeds the storm. *The subjects of the first principles of the gospel were opened to me like print, only plainer and more powerful.*

Faith, repentance, baptism for the remission of sins, and the laying on of hands for the reception of the Holy Ghost, came to me in sucession and in their order. And those priests, doctors, lawyers and people did not appear to me more formidable than so many butterflies.

---

35. D & C 25:7-8.
36. The compiler of the Faith Promoting series chose to use only the initials of some of the individuals whose biographies he published.

No miracle ever performed by the power of God, could have had a more convincing effect upon me, than did the *help that came to me through the power of the Holy Ghost on that occasion.* And I am fully convinced in my own mind that never since have I preached a more effective discourse, nor one accompanied by more of the power of God.[37]

Just as the above Elder saw the scriptural subjects opened out like print, others have actually seen the passages themselves with their spiritual eyes as they talked to their audience. Moses Thatcher experienced this phenomenon during his early days as a missionary.

Wrapt in the spirit he sometimes spoke for an hour, often correctly quoting Scripture he had never read, *the words and sentences, as he declared, appearing before the spiritual eyes, were read, as from an open book.*[38]

Another missionary was shown a vision of a large scroll with a scriptural passage cited on it:

Among those who had come to meeting was a hardened infidel, who was a very cunning reasoner, and who had made it a practice for many yeary [sic] to argue against the divinity of the scriptures. Nothing pleased him more than to draw some minister into a debate, and then to present some of his "unanswerable" arguments against the Bible. He had vanquished every minister in the village, and every itinerant preacher who had held meetings there for years, whom he could succeed in drawing into a debate.

When the young missionary had ceased preaching, some of the audience commenced to ask him questions. Presently the infidel, evidently thinking to easily vanquish so weak an adversary, commenced with his usual routine of questions and at length asked:

'So you believe the flood actually drowned all the animals in the world except those in the ark?'

'Yes, sir,' answered the Elder.

'We know that, not very long after the flood, many kinds of animals were found in various parts of the world at a great distance from where the ark landed, and even upon islands of the sea, far from the mainland, and under such circumstances as would render the theory of transportation by human means

---

37. *A String of Pearls,* p. 57.
38. Jenson, I, p. 129.

an absurdity. Now, how did those animals come to exist in the different and distant islands and continents?'

This question was the infidel's 'trump card.' At the right juncture in his debates he always asked it, and had never yet met with a minister or any other Bible believer, who could satisfactorily answer it.

The young missionary felt his utter inability to answer this question. In trying to frame a reply, he sat gazing abstractly at the ceiling of the room. The audience who remained knew that this was the great argument of the infidel, and did not, for a moment, suppose that the boyish preacher could meet it.

Suddenly there appeared before the young missionary's eyes, as if it were suspended in the air, a scroll. On the scroll appeared, in brilliant golden letters, these words: 'In the days of Peleg the earth was divided.' (Gen. x., 25) Instantly an explanation of the infidel's problem burst upon his mind.

He calmly and deliberately proceeded to explain that, prior to the days of Peleg, this whole earth was one vast continent, inhabited in its various portions, with different kinds of animals; that in the days of Peleg this vast continent was broken up into smaller divisions of land, islands, etc., and that, in this manner, the animals upon its surface accompanied the land in its divisions.

The infidel was confounded, the multitude astonished, and the young, illiterate missionary triumphant. Several remembered the passage of scripture, and none could gainsay the missionary's explanation. The latter, however, had no knowledge of any such passage in the Bible, as he had read but very little of it, and, had the answer not come to him by revelation, he would have been confounded.

The scroll was so plainly visible to him that it seemed as though others could see it, but they did not.[39]

The gift of expounding the scriptures has often taken the form of aiding missionaries to locate scriptural passages to support the teachings and practices of the Church. One elder was given this gift as he was challenged by a protestant deacon, who baited the missionary by saying,

'I have heard say that your preachers are pretty apt with the scriptures, and can produce almost any doctrine you like from the Bible.' I replied that the men were, but that I was but a boy; yet I thought I knew a little of the scriptures.

39. *A String of Pearls,* pp. 75-6.

He remarked 'Your people believe in laying hands on the sick; don't you?'

I answered that we did, and because Christ had said in His remarkable commission to His apostles, that this was one of the signs following, quoting Mark xvi, 15-18. I also quoted James v., 14.

'Yes, yes;' says he, 'that is all very good, but that says only once, and your Elders sometimes lay hands twice in succession on the same person. Whoever heard of Jesus or the apostles doing anything like that?' He then cited an instance where, as he said, Joseph Smith had done this in administering to a sick woman.

The good-natured excitement was intense. The deacon thought I was overwhelmed, and proposed that if I could prove a similar transaction from the scriptures, I might preach in that house that very night.

Eagerness now seized the men, and the deacon chuckled over his presumed victory, and boasted of his acquaintance with the 'Blessed Word.'

I unbuckled my valise, drew forth my little Bible, and opened it intuitively to this passage in Mark viii., 22-25: 'And he cometh to Bethsaida; and they bring a blind man unto him, and besought him to touch him. And he took the blind man by the hand . . . and put his hands upon him, and asked him if he saw aught. And he looked up, and said, I see men as trees, walking. After that he put his hands *again* upon his eyes, and made him look up: and he was restored, and saw every man clearly.'

The reading of this scripture; the sudden finding of it, for I was led to it as clearly as a man leads his horse to the water; its aptness and conclusiveness, accompanied by the jeers of the infidel portion of the crowd, mortified the deacon — he was discomforted.[40]

David Jeffs also told of the aid he was given in locating a scriptural passage on one occasion.

I went into the mission field with very little knowledge of the Bible, and I had to study very hard and depend very greatly upon the inspiration of the Holy Ghost to guide and sustain me in my labors; I had no experience in preaching. The Lord, however, came to my assistance many times. I remember on one occasion, when defending the principles of the Gospel, I quoted

---

40. *Fragments of Experience,* pp. 10-11.

a passage of Scripture that I had heard my companion repeat; the minister with whom I was conversing asked me where such a passage of Scripture was, as he had never read it in the Bible. I told him to let me take his Bible and I opened it, and *there appeared, a certain verse, in very large letters which I read to him.* It was the very passage that I had quoted to him. After reading the passage referred to, it did not appear any larger print than the rest of the chapter, . . .[41]

The subject matter with which this gift deals is, of necessity, those portions of the gospel which are difficult to understand. It is in these areas, of course, that the guidance of the Spirit is most vitally needed. To Joseph Smith and Sidney Rigdon the commandment was given to expound just such areas:

> Behold, thus saith the Lord unto you my servants Joseph Smith, Jun., and Sidney Rigdon, that the time has verily come that it is necessary and expedient in me that you should open your mouths in proclaiming my gospel, the things of the kingdom, *expounding the mysteries thereof out of the scriptures, according to that portion of Spirit and power which shall be given unto you, even as I will.*[42]

A similar responsibility was given to Parley P. Pratt: "I will bless him with a multiplicity of blessings, *in expounding all scriptures and mysteries* to the edification of the school, and of the church in Zion."[43]

It would appear, then, that while some are compelled to limit their efforts and preaching to the simplest principles and teachings of the gospel, others are invited and led by the Spirit to open up the deeper matters of the gospel of Christ. They function under divine supervision in the explaining and clarifying of the doctrines of the Church so that all may understand them.

Summary of the Gift of Expounding the Scriptures

1. The gift to expound the scriptures is the inspired ability to clearly explain the meaning of the scriptures. It has also been manifested in supernatural aid in locating scriptural proofs of the doctrines of the Church.

---

41. Jenson, II, 51-2.
42. D & C 71:1. It is interesting to note some of the difficult areas upon which others with this gift have expounded. They include the coming of Christ, the resurrection of the dead, and the atonement of Christ. (Al. 21:9-10)
43. D & C 97:5.

2. This gift often centers in explanations of the lesser understood portions of the scriptures.

3. The scriptures are to be expounded for the edification of the Church.

4. At times speakers are shown visions while speaking in which they are shown pertinent scriptural quotations.

The Gift of Bearing Testimony

To some a special blessing is granted by the Holy Ghost which enables them to bear their testimonies with added power and effect. Such was the case with Joseph Smith, of whom the Lord said, "I will give unto him power to be mighty in testimony."[44] The testimony borne by Alma to the people of Gideon was a testimony made as a gift of the Spirit. He told them of the covenant of baptism and then added:

> Whosoever doeth this, and keepeth the commandments of God from thenceforth, the same will remember that I say unto him, yea, he will remember that I have said unto him, he shall have eternal life, *according to the testimony of the Holy Spirit, which testifieth in me.* . . .
>
> And now my beloved brethren, *I have spoken these words unto you according to the Spirit which testifieth in me:* and my soul doth exceedingly rejoice, because of the exceeding diligence and heed which ye have given unto my word.[45]

A testimony which is prompted by the Spirit is characterized by boldness. Such were the testimonies of the prophets who labored in the Americas shortly before the crucifixion of the Savior:

> And there began to be men inspired from heaven and sent forth, standing among the people in all the land, *preaching and testifying boldly* of the sins and iniquities of the people, and testifying unto them concerning the redemption which the Lord would make for his people, or in other words, the resurrection of Christ; and *they did testify boldly of his death and sufferings.*[46]

A testimony offered by commandment of God as an utterance of the Spiirt is a message of power and profundity. The testimony

44. D & C 100:10.
45. Al. 7:16, 26.
46. 3 Ne. 6:20.

of the three witnesses to the plates of the Book of Mormon is borne with this power, for they were commanded,

> And after that you have obtained faith, and have seen them with your eyes, *you shall testify of them, by the power of God;*
>
> And ye shall testify that you have seen them, even as my servant Joseph Smith, Jun., has seen them; for it is by my power that he has seen them, and it is because he had faith.
>
> And he has translated the book, even that part which I had commanded him, and as your Lord and your God liveth it is true.
>
> *Wherefore, you have received the same power, and the same faith, and the same gift like unto him.*[47]

Just as strong as the testimony of words is a God-inspired testimony of action, such as the shaking of dust from one's feet in condemnation of a home and it occupants.[48] Such a testimony may be manifested in many actions, as directed by the Holy Ghost, for Christ has commanded that "that which the Spirit testifies unto you even so I would that ye should do. . . ."[49]

Many long for a testimony of the gospel and yet lack the certainty of the truthfulness of their convictions. They may need to learn the basic gospel truths as a foundation for the testimony they seek. Such was the case with Sister Jean Holbrook, who later became one of the first lady missionaries to labor in Great Britain:

> There came a time when doubt entered her mind, and caused her to feel unhappy, but in answer to the humble and sincere prayer of her heart she was told, 'Do not worry about that which you cannot understand. *Try to learn the simple lessons of daily life, and by degrees your mind will expand so that you can grasp the higher gospel truths.*[50]

A testimony and the courage to bear it is sometimes revealed when it becomes necessary to defend the Church. The receiving of a testimony and the desire to proclaim it to others brings a miraculous change to many individuals, and many members of the Church have experienced this mighty change. A typical

47. D & C 17:3, 5-7.
48. See Mt. 10:12-15; D & C 75:19-22; D & C 84:92-5.
49. D & C 46:7.
50. Jenson, I, p. 503.

example is that of Elder J. D. H. McAllister. His missionary companion wrote,

> Elder J. D. H. McAllister traveled with me in Arkansas, and for the first two months of our labors, when called upon to talk, would not occupy above five minutes, and often not half that time. It would then occur to him that the audience would rather hear some one else than him, after which he would not possess courage to try to talk longer, and would take his seat.
>
> He would often say that he could not account for his being called on a mission. '*What can I do? I do not even know that this latter-day work is true. My father has often borne testimony that he knew this work to be true. He is a good man and I believe his testimony; but I do not know it to be true for myself.*'
>
> However, an opportunity occurred that dispelled all these doubts, and planted in the place thereof, facts and certainties.
>
> I had taken a severe cold, and was so hoarse that I could not talk. A meeting was to be held, and at that meeting some one would have to preach.
>
> The only alternative was for him to attend and do the preaching. To do this he had to travel five or six miles across the 'slashes,' face a large congregation composed almost entirely of strangers, and do all the preaching, and that, too, alone.
>
> I never, while in that country, heard the last of the praises heaped upon him by the people for the 'best sermon' they had ever listened to. He had no difficulty in testifying to the divinity of the great latter-day work. *The Holy Spirit rested upon him, and he could not keep back this testimony, which was as new to him as it was to those that heard him.*
>
> That day's work is no doubt remembered by him with the greatest pleasure of any event of his life, and will prove as profitable as any in his future career.[51]

The gift of bearing testimony affects not only the speaker. An important function of the Holy Ghost is to carry a testimony into the hearts of those who are listening. As Nephi taught, "When a man speaketh by the power of the Holy Ghost *the power of the Holy Ghost carrieth it unto the hearts of the children of men.*"[52]

---

51. *Gems For The Young Folks*, pp. 31-2.
52. 2 Ne. 33:1.

This gift may be granted as an aid or reward to those who are seeking to fulfill the will of the Lord, as the father of President David O. McKay discovered when he prayed for relief from the terrible despondency which had overcome him while on a mission to Scotland.

> The discouragement continued for some time after that, when one morning before daylight, following a sleepless night, he decided to retire to a cave, near the ocean, where he knew he would be shut off from the world entirely, and there pour out his soul to God and ask why he was oppressed with this feeling, what he had done, and what he could do to throw it off and continue his work. He started out in the dark towards the cave. He become so eager to get to it that he started to run. As he was leaving the town, he was hailed by an officer who wanted to know what was the matter. He gave some non-committal but satisfying reply and was permitted to go on. Something just seemed to drive him; he had to get relief. He entered the cave or sheltered opening, and said: 'Oh, Father, what can I do to have this feeling removed? I must have it lifted or I cannot continue in this work'; *and he heard a voice, as distinct as the tone I am now uttering, say: 'Testify that Joseph Smith is a Prophet of God.'* Remembering then, what he tacitly had decided six weeks or more before, [to avoid memtioning Joseph Smith because of the prejudice of the people and to preach only the first principles] and becoming overwhelmed with the thought, the whole thing came to him in a realization that he was there for a special mission, and he had not given that special mission the attention which it deserved. Then he cried in his heart, 'Lord, it is enough,' and went out from the cave.[53]

Summary of the Gift of Bearing Testimony

1. The ability to bear one's testimony by the power of the Spirit is another of the spiritual gifts. The Holy Ghost not only aids the speaker, but can also carry his message into the hearts of his listeners.

2. A testimony of the Spirit may be borne with boldness and power.

3. A testimony may also be borne by actions such as shaking the dust from off one's feet.

---

53. Middlemiss, *op. cit.,* pp. 23-4.

272 GIFTS OF THE SPIRIT

4. Those who are seeking a testimony should begin with the simple lessons of life rather than plunge into the more profound aspects of the gospel. A base must be established to support higher principles.

5. When a testimony is revealed, the desire to bear it is also given by the Spirit.

* * *

These six gifts of the Spirit, the gifts of speaking, of writing, of translating, of teaching, of expounding the scriptures, and of bearing testimony are among the most important gifts which God has granted to the Church. Each gift pertains to actions which are often seen performed without the aid of the Spirit, but the most effective performance requires divine aid. They are vital to the growth and internal strength of the Church.

Part V

GIFTS OF
CHURCH
ADMINISTRATION

CHAPTER XVII

Administration

A Gift of Leadership and Organizational Ability

The gift of knowledge of the differences of administration[1] seems to consist of inspired understanding of the agencies and services of the gospel kingdom. One who possesses this gift knows, through the Spirit, the proper functioning of the quorums and auxiliaries of the Church. He understands the relationship between each portion of the Church organization and comprehends the proper jurisdiction of each office, calling and organization. He knows how the various functions of the priesthood should be carried out and receives guidance from the Holy Ghost in performing priesthood and Church leadership functions. He possesses leadership and organizational ability.

This is the gift which aids man to function effectively in directing the activities of the church. It is the gift which enables him to understand the "doctrine of the priesthood" and to function in the priesthood in the manner which will best further the Lord's work. Those who possess this gift enjoy the same blessings as was granted the Prophet Joseph Smith in his receiving of special guidance and direction concerning priesthood functions:

> Let thy bowels also be full of charity towards all men, and to the household of faith, and let virtue garnish thy thoughts unceasingly; then shall thy confidence wax strong in the presence of God; and *the doctrine of the priesthood shall distil upon thy soul as the dews from heaven.*
>
> *The Holy Ghost shall be thy constant companion,* and thy scepter an unchanging scepter of righteousness and truth; and thy dominion shall be an everlasting dominion, and without compulsory means it shall flow unto thee forever and ever.[2]

Priesthood Administration Directed by the Holy Ghost

Those who possess this gift will be blessed with the guidance of the Spirit as they administer and direct affairs in the Church.

1. D & C 46:15.
2. D & C 121:45-46.

Many examples of this direction may be cited. For instance, the choosing of people to be called to preach the gospel is to be done under the direction of the Holy Spirit. Such was the case with Alma, who proclaimed, "*I have been called to preach the word of God among all this people, according to the spirit of revelation and prophecy;* and I was in this land and they would not receive me, but they cast me out and I was about to set my back towards this land forever."[3] This guidance can come to pass in strange ways, as in the calling of Elder German E. Ellsworth to fill a mission to the Northern States:

> Apostle Matthias F. Cowley from Salt Lake City was the visiting authority at a conference in February 1903. At the close of the meeting, German E. was called to the stand and introduced to Elder Cowley who said, 'Brother Ellsworth, all the time I was speaking and looking your way, *I felt like you were wanted in the Northern States Mission.* Will you go if called?'
>
> 'I've only been home from my California mission a little over four years, Brother Cowley,' was the answer.
>
> To this Apostle Cowley said, 'I don't care if you have only been home four weeks, you are wanted in the Northern States Mission.'
>
> This information came as a shock to German E. and his wife, but a great manifestation of tongues in a Sunday Fast Meeting in May settled the question for the interpretation of the tongue by Patriarch Kirkham said, '*My servant German E. Ellsworth has been called by mine authority and acknowledged of me as a missionary to the Northern States.*'
>
> Prior to his departure, when discussing the medical profession with President Joseph F. Smith (head of the Church), German received the admonition: 'You go on this mission. It is far greater to be a doctor of the soul.'[4]

Ordination to priesthood office must be done through the power of the Holy Ghost, as was set forth by Moroni:

> The manner which the disciples, who were called the elders of the church, ordained priests and teachers —
>
> After they had prayed unto the Father in the name of Christ, they laid their hands upon them, and said:

---

3. Al. 8:24. See also D & C 52:1; 68:1.
4. *Our Ellsworth Ancestors,* pp. 54-55. This advice became a prophetic truth as President Ellsworth spent 27 years of his adult life serving as a Mission President. He directed the activities of over 2000 missionaries during his service to the Lord.

In the name of Jesus Christ I ordain you to be a priest, (or, if he be a teacher) I ordain you to be a teacher, to preach repentance and remission of sins through Jesus Christ, by the endurance of faith on his name to the end. Amen.

And after this manner did they ordain priests and teachers, according to the gifts and callings of God unto men; *and they ordained them by the power of the Holy Ghost, which was in them.*[5]

To fulfill a priesthood responsibility to preach, one must be aided by the power of the Holy Ghost, as in the instance of the sons of Alma: "They preached the word, and the truth, *according to the spirit of prophecy and revelation; and they preached after the holy order of God by which they were called."*[6]

To be sealed by the priesthood involves the functioning of the Holy Ghost, for the Lord has revealed that "The more sure word of prophecy means a man's knowing that he is sealed up unto eternal life, *by revelation and the spirit of prophecy through the power of the Holy Priesthood."*[7]

In short, in order that a man be granted God's power, that man must enjoy the gift of the Spirit at the instant the power is used, as well as previously.

When rights to the priesthood are set forth in the scriptures, they are indicated as being dependent on the Holy Ghost or are linked with functions which are known to be carried out by that Being. For instance, "Nevertheless, a high priest, that is, after the order of Melchizedek, may be set apart unto the ministering of temporal things, *having a knowledge of them by the Spirit of truth."*[8] When trials are held before a high council, the decision is to be made based on past revelation or, "In case of difficulty respecting doctrine or principle, if there is not a sufficiency written to make the case clear to the minds of the council, *the president may inquire and obtain the mind of the Lord by revelation."*[9] The very basis of the higher priesthood is to hold the keys of the blessings of the Spirit.

The power and authority of the higher, or Melchizedek Priesthood, is to hold the keys of all the spiritual blessings of the church —

5. Moro. 3:1-4. See also D & C 18:32, 20:60.
6. Al. 43:2. See also D & C 42:6, 13; 50:10-22.
7. D & C 131:5.
8. D & C 107:71.
9. D & C 102:23.

To have the privilege of receiving the mysteries of the kingdom of heaven, to have the heavens opened unto them, to commune with the general assembly and church of the Firstborn, and to enjoy the communion and presence of God the Father, and Jesus the mediator of the new covenant.[10]

It is clear, then, that *"the rights of the priesthood are inseparably connected with the powers of heaven."*[11] Man cannot have the one without the other. In fact, no priesthood function is carried out properly without the assistance of the Holy Ghost.

Priesthood Leaders May Discern All Spiritual Gifts

Priesthood officials are particularly blessed in regard to spiritual gifts, for to them may be granted the ability to discern them all:

All these gifts come from God, for the benefit of the children of God.

And *unto the bishop of the church, and unto such as God shall appoint and ordain to watch over the church* and to be elders unto the church *are to have it given unto them to discern all those gifts lest there shall be any among you professing and yet be not of God.*[12]

To the President of the Church is granted the privilege of having all the spiritual gifts:

And again, the duty of the President of the office of the High Priesthood is to preside over the whole church, and to be like unto Moses —

Behold, here is wisdom; yea, to be a seer, a revelator, a translator, and a prophet, *having all the gifts of God which he bestows upon the head of the church.*[13]

It would appear that other church leaders who seek the privilege may also enjoy the opportunity of possessing the full blessing of the entire series of the gifts of the Spirit. This may come in response to their own seeking and self-preparation:

And it shall come to pass that he that asketh in Spirit shall receive in Spirit;

10. D & C 107:18-19.
11. D & C 121:36.
12. D & C 46:26-27.
13. D & C 107:91-92.

That unto some it may be given to have all those gifts, that there may be a head, in order that every member may be profited thereby.[14]

The Gift of Administration to be Used with Caution

It is sometimes difficult for men blessed with leadership and organizational ability to remain humble and to refrain from asserting improper authority. The Prophet Joseph recognized this tendency in his day and wrote:

We have learned by sad experience that it is the nature and disposition of almost all men, as soon as they get a little authority, as they suppose, they will immediately begin to exercise unrighteous dominion.

Hence, many are called, but few are chosen.[15]

Just as the gifts of the Spirit can function only in righteousness, so also is the priesthood power withheld from those who are not worthy:

That they may be conferred upon us, it is true; but when we undertake to cover our sins, or to gratify our *pride*, our vain *ambition*, or to *exercise control or dominion or compulsion* upon the souls of the children of men, in any degree of unrighteousness, *behold, the heavens withdraw themselves; the Spirit of the Lord is grieved; and when it is withdrawn, Amen to the priesthood or the authority of that man.*

Behold, ere he is aware, he is left unto himself, to kick against the pricks, to persecute the saints, and to fight against God.[16]

Many times individuals speak of people being called and chosen. It seems that men are called and granted priesthood authority, but while they hold the authority they are not chosen to function in a priesthood office of responsibility. Two reasons are offered in the scripture to explain why men are given authority but not opportunity. The first deals with vanity: "And why are they not chosen? Because their hearts are set so much upon the things of this world, and aspire to the honors of men."[17] The second reason seems to be that some fail to seek the enlightenment of the Spirit which will help them function

---

14. D & C 46:28-29.
15. D & C 121:39-40.
16. D & C 121:37-38.
17. D & C 121:34-35.

properly in priesthood office: "But behold, verily I say unto you, that there are many who have been ordained among you, whom I have called but few of them are chosen. They *who are not chosen have sinned a very grevious sin, in that they are walking in darkness at noon-day.*"[18]

Summary

1. This gift of the Spirit is one of leadership and organizational ability. It consists of an inspired understanding of the organization and activities of the Church and of the proper method of their functioning.

2. Those who possess this gift have been granted a knowledge of the doctrine of the Priesthood.

3. The Holy Ghost directs priesthood administration in matters such as the calling of officials, ordinations, sealings, trials, and all other rights and responsibilities of the Priesthood.

4. The President of the Church possesses all the spiritual gifts. Local Priesthood officials enjoy their own gifts but are granted the ability to discern all gifts so order in the Church can be maintained.

5. Men tend to assume more authority than they should have. If this extension of authority is because of pride, vain ambition, or a desire to compel others, the Spirit will be withdrawn.

6. Some men are given the Priesthood but later fail to receive callings within the Church because their hearts are set on the things of the world or because they fail to seek the enlightenment of the Holy Ghost.

---

18. D & C 95:5-6. Two parables of the Master also deal with the matter of being called and chosen. They are found in Mt. 20:1-16 and 22:1-14.

CHAPTER XVIII
Diversities of Operations

Two Manifestations of the Gift

The gift of knowledge of the diversities of operations[1] of the Spirit is manifested in two ways. First, it is manifested as the ability to discern whether the aims and activities of others are inspired of God, of men, or of Satan. It deals with activities, events, causes, and programs both of individuals and groups. (In contrast, the gift of the discerning of spirits deals more with the attitudes and personalities of individuals.) The gift of knowledge of the diversities of operations is the power whereby one may recognize whether a professedly moral or reformatory activity is really for that purpose or is for the satisfaction of greed and selfishness.

The second manner in which this gift is manifested is by enabling them to be aware of various events which take place which would affect their work. It is the gift of being able to keep abreast of the times and being aware of what is going on.

Knowledge of Whether Activities and
Events are Inspired of God

Perhaps the best known example of this gift was given by the Savior when he differentiated between service to worldly and service to godly powers. When the Pharisees and Herodians met Him with the double-edged question, "Is it lawful to give tribute unto Caesar, or not?"[2] the Master wisely replied,

> Shew me the tribute money. And they brought unto him a penny. And he saith unto them, Whose is this image and superscription? They say unto him, Caesar's. Then saith he unto them, *Render therefore unto Caesar the things which are Caesar's; and unto God the things that are God's.*[3]

In this instance Jesus showed his recognition of the two levels of operation — that of worldly activity as contrasted with that of the Spirit.

---

1. D & C 46:16.
2. Mt. 22:17.
3. Mt. 22:19-21.

In another instance, the Christ warned of the oppressive acts
of the Scribes and Pharisees, who burdened others with work,
supposedly of a religious nature, but would not labor themselves.
Through the power to discern the diversities of operations, He
knew that the aim of the Scribes and Pharisees was not to further the work of God, but to enhance their own social status,

> Saying, The Scribes and the Pharisees sit in Moses' seat;
>
> All therefore whatsoever they bid you observe, that observe
> and do; but do not ye after their works: for they say, and do not.
>
> *For they bind heavy burdens and grievous to be borne, and
> lay them on men's shoulders; but they themselves will not move
> them with one of their fingers.*
>
> *But all their works they do for to be seen of men:* they
> make broad their phylacteries, and enlarge the borders of their
> garments,
>
> And love the uppermost rooms at feasts, and the chief seats
> in the synagogues,
>
> And greetings in the markets, and to be called of men,
> Rabbi, Rabbi.[4]

At another time He denounced them, saying,

> Beware of the scribes, which desire to walk in long robes,
> and love greetings in the markets, and the highest seats in the
> synagogues, and the chief rooms at feasts;
>
> Which devour widows' houses, and for a shew make long
> prayers: the same shall receive greater damnation.[5]

Another example of Jesus' knowledge of the diversities of
operations is found in His treatment of a situation which arose
while He was teaching in the synagogue. There He found a
man whose hand was withered. He knew that

> The scribes and Pharisees watched him, whether he would
> heal on the sabbath day; that they might find an accusation
> against him.
>
> But *he knew their thoughts,* and said to the man which had
> the withered hand, Rise up, and stand forth in the midst. And
> he arose and stood forth.
>
> Then said Jesus unto them, *I will ask you one thing; Is it
> lawful on the sabbath days to do good, or to do evil? to save life,
> or to destroy it?*

---

4. Mt. 23:2-7.
5. Lk. 20:46-47.

And looking round about upon them all, he said unto the man, Stretch forth thy hand. And he did so: and his hand was restored whole as the other.[6]

It is obvious that Jesus knew that those who watched Him were seeking to accuse Him. His was the ability to discern and interpret their actions.

The scriptures give examples of others who, it would appear, were blessed by the Holy Ghost with the gift of the knowledge of the diversities of operations. Through divine intervention Joseph was given the knowledge that the pregnancy of Mary, his intended bride, was of God. Without this gift he would have rejected her because of his belief that she had been unfaithful.[7] It was also a manifestation of this gift when Elizabeth was shown by the Holy Ghost that the child Mary carried was to be the Savior.[8] In yet another manifestation of this gift, Joseph was warned to flee to Egypt with Mary and the baby Jesus because Herod intended to slay the newborn children of the country.[9]

Knowledge of Current Happenings

Examples are also found in the scriptures of the second phase of the gift of knowledge of the diversities of operations. This is the ability given to an individual to know of events which are to come to pass or which have already taken place which would affect his work or the welfare of the people under his jurisdiction. Jesus used this power when he discerned the condition of the woman at the well:

Jesus saith unto her, Go, call thy husband, and come hither.

The woman answered and said, I have no husband. Jesus said unto her, Thou hast well said, I have no husband:

For *thou hast had five husbands: and he whom thou now hast is not thy husband:* in that saidst thou truly.

The woman saith unto him, Sir, I perceive that thou art a prophet.[10]

---

6. Lk. 6:7-10.
7. Mt. 1:19-20.
8. Lk. 1:41-45.
9. Mt. 2:13-16.
10. Jn. 4.16-19.

Peter experienced the manifestation of this gift:

> A certain man named Ananias, with Sapphira his wife, sold a possession, And kept back part of the price, his wife also being privy to it, and brought a certain part, and laid it at the apostles' feet.
>
> But Peter said, *Ananias, why hath Satan filled thine heart to lie to the Holy Ghost, and to keep back part of the price of the land?*
>
> Whiles it remained, was it not thine own? and after it was sold, was it not in thine own power? why hast thou conceived this thing in thine heart? thou hast not lied unto men, but unto God.
>
> And *Ananias hearing these words fell down, and gave up the ghost:* and great fear came on all them that heard these things.
>
> And the young men arose, wound him up, and carried him out, and buried him.
>
> And it was about the space of three hours after, when his wife, not knowing what was done, came in.
>
> And Peter answered unto her, Tell me whether ye sold the land for so much? And she said, Yea, for so much.
>
> Then Peter said unto her, *How is it that ye have agreed together to tempt the Spirit of the Lord?* behold, the feet of them which have buried thy husband are at the door, and shall carry thee out.
>
> Then *fell she down straightway at his feet, and yielded up the ghost;* and the young men came in, and found her dead, and carrying her forth, buried her by her husband.
>
> And great fear came upon all the church, and upon as many as heard these things.[11]

Another example of the manifestation of the gift of knowledge of the diversities of operations is found in the Book of Mormon. This record tells of Nephi, who, through the use of this gift, gave a sign to show that he was truly a prophet: "Go ye in unto the judgment-seat, and search; and behold, your judge is murdered, and he lieth in his blood; and *he hath been murdered by his brother*, who seeketh to sit in the judgment-seat."[12] When his unbelieving listeners found the judge murdered as Nephi had said, they acccused the prophet of involve-

---

11. Acts 5:1-11.
12. Hel. 8:27.

ment with the deed and arrested him. Again Nephi used his knowledge of the diversities of operations by telling them:

And now behold, *I will show unto you another sign*, and see if ye will in this thing seek to destroy me.

Behold I say unto you: Go to the house of Seantum, who is the brother of Seezoram, and say unto him —

Has Nephi, the pretended prophet, who doth prophesy so much evil concerning this people, agreed with thee, in the which ye have murdered Seezoram, who is your brother?

And behold, he shall say unto you, Nay.

And ye shall say unto him: *Have ye murdered your brother?*

And he shall stand with fear, and wist not what to say. And behold, he shall deny unto you; and he shall make as if he were astonished; nevertheless, he shall declare unto you that he is innocent.

But behold, ye shall examine him, and ye shall find blood upon the skirts of his cloak.

And when ye have seen this, ye shall say: From whence cometh this blood? Do we not know that it is the blood of your brother?

And then shall he tremble, and shall look pale, even as if death had come upon him.

And then shalt ye say: Because of this fear and this paleness which has come upon your face, behold, we know that thou art guilty.

And then shall greater fear come upon him; and *then shall he confess unto you, and deny no more that he has done this murder.*

And then shall he say unto you, that I Nephi, know nothing concerning the matter save it were given unto me by the power of God. And then shall ye know that I am an honest man, and that I am sent unto you from God.

And it came to pass that they went and did, even according as Nephi had said unto them. And behold, the words which he had said were true; for according to the words he did deny; and also according to the words he did confess.

And he was brought to prove that he himself was the very murderer.[13]

---

13. Hel. 9: 25-38.

It is through this gift of knowledge of the diversities of operations that Heber C. Kimball was able to prophesy of the short stay of the Saints in Nauvoo when others thought their stay would be an extended one:

> When the Saints were about to settle in Commerce, Ill., and though received with open arms by the good people of Illinois, Apostle Kimball looked upon the beautiful site and said sorrowfully, 'This is a beautiful place, *but not a long resting place for the Saints.*' Sidney Rigdon was vexed at the prediction, but its fulfillment is too well known to need repeating here.[14]

By this same gift Elder Kimball was able to encourage the Mormon pioneers in Salt Lake City and promise them that commercial goods would soon be made available to them at reduced prices:

> When hard times pressed the Saints in Salt Lake City, and a thousand miles separated them from commercial points, President Kimball stood up in the Tabernacle and *prophesied that in less than six months clothing and other goods would be sold in the streets of Great Salt Lake City cheaper than they could be bought in New York.* This astonished the people. One of his brethren said to him after meeting that he did not believe it. 'Neither did I,' said Brother Kimball, 'but I said it. It will have to go.' No one saw the possibility of its verification. Six months, however, had not passed away when large companies of emigrants, burning with the gold fever from the East, came into the city, and becoming eager to reach the glittering gold fields of California, they sold their merchandise on the streets for a less price than the New York prices. They sold their large animals for pack animals, and thus more than literally fulfilled the remarkable prophecy of President Heber C. Kimball.[15]

Heber C. Kimball was also able, through this gift, to determine that someone was finding fault with him. Robert Smith, a close friend of Brother Kimball's, wrote,

> In 1857, I was working for Brother Heber and asked him for some goods which he refused to let me have. Feeling bad over it, I went home and laid the matter before the Lord. The next morning when I came to work, Brother Heber called me into his room and said, '*Robert, why have you been complaining to*

---

14. Jenson, I, p. 37.
15. *Ibid.*

the Lord about his servant Heber? Here are the things you asked me for and after this, *don't go to the Lord about every little thing that happens.*[16]

It was through this gift that Willard Richards, Church Historian, was able to leave blanks in the history and indicate that these were to be filled in through personal knowledge by his successor in the Historian's calling, George A. Smith. The latter

Supplied, from memory and otherwise, blanks in the history and records compiled by President Willard Richards, his predecessor in the Historian's Office, who had, *with prophetic pencil, written on the margin, opposite the blanks, 'to be supplied by George A. Smith.'*[17]

Examples of Those Who Lack the Gift

The scriptures also give examples of those who lacked the gift of knowledge of the diversities of operations. Zacharias, unwilling to accept the promise of the angel that he would have a son (John the Baptist) in his old age, was struck dumb because of his reluctance to give heed to the message.[18] He lacked the gift to understand and believe. The case of the Scribes and Pharisees, who commented unfavorably when they saw Jesus and His disciples eating with the publicans and sinners, also shows the lack of this gift. They asked,

How is it that he eateth and drinketh with publicans and sinners?

When Jesus heard it, he saith unto them, They that are whole have no need of a physician, but they that are sick: I came not to call the righteous, but sinners to repentance.[19]

It was the chief priests of the temple who, because they failed to recognize the purpose of Christ's ministry, challenged Him by saying, "By what authority doest thou these things? and who gave thee this authority?"[20]

The Need for This Gift in the Last Days

The scriptures warn of great tribulations in the last days and tell of the need that church members will have for this gift.

16. Hinckley, *Faith of our Pioneer Fathers,* p. 134.
17. Jenson, I, p. 41.
18. Lk. 1:11-20.
19. Mk. 2:16-17.
20. Mt. 21:23.

It is by the gift of knowledge of the diversities of operations that man will be able to detect the evil functioning of Satan and his helpers. Jesus prophesied that "there shall arise false Christs, and false prophets, and shall shew great signs and wonders; insomuch that, if it were possible, they shall deceive the very elect."[21] Again, He warned: "Beware of false prophets, which come to you in sheep's clothing, but inwardly they are ravening wolves."[22] There may even be those within the church who will hold the authority to act in the name of God, but whose unrighteous purposes will have to be discerned by others through this gift. Jesus said,

> Not every one that saith unto me, Lord, Lord, shall enter into the kingdom of heaven; but he that doeth the will of my Father which is in heaven.
>
> Many will say to me in that day, *Lord, Lord, have we not prophesied in thy name? and in thy name have cast out devils? and in thy name done many wonderful works?*
>
> And then will I profess unto them, *I never knew you: depart from me, ye that work iniquity.*[23]

It appears that God, in his wisdom, has seen fit to prepare for such individuals. The discerning gifts — the gifts of knowledge of the diversities of operations and the discerning of spirits — are to be given to the leaders of the church so that they may protect others:

> And unto the bishop of the church, and unto such as God shall appoint and ordain to watch over the church and to be elders unto the church, *are to have it given unto them to discern all those gifts* lest there shall be any among you professing and yet be not of God.[24]

Applying the Gift

There are many times when man must judge as to the good or evil nature of things which go on around him. Though this gift is available to many, its possessors should remember to act with care and good judgment. On some occasions God directs man not to rely on the promptings of His Spirit in a particular matter, but rather to pursue a definite course of action which He

---

21. Mt. 24:24.
22. Mt. 7:15.
23. Mt. 7:21-23. See Lk. 13:24-30, 21:8.
24. D & C 46:27.

indicates. There are times when, as a Latter-day Saint, an individual may want to tell others about the Gospel but does not know whether they will be receptive. He must remember the admonition, "Give not that which is holy unto the dogs, neither cast ye your pearls before swine, lest they trample them under their feet, and turn again and rend you."[25] In such a situation, perhaps most of all, he should remember the rest of the Savior's message on that occasion:

> Ask, and it shall be given you; seek, and ye shall find; knock, and it shall be opened unto you:
>
> For every one that asketh receiveth; and he that seeketh findeth; and to him that knocketh it shall be opened.[26]

The individual should seek the gift, receive the impressions of the Spirit, and then take positive action. Such was the counsel of the Lord when Joseph Smith was translating the Book of Mormon. He was told that he would not always have the gift of discernment during this time; therefore, he was to show the manuscript to none. Only in this way could he be sure there would be no error in his judgment:

> But behold, here is wisdom, and because I show unto you wisdom, and give you commandments concerning these things, what you shall do, show it not unto the world until you have accomplished the work of translation.
>
> Marvel not that I said unto you. Here is wisdom, show it not unto the world — for I said, show it not unto the world, that you may be preserved.
>
> Behold, I do not say that you shall not show it unto the righteous;
>
> *But as you cannot always judge the righteous, or as you cannot always tell the wicked from the righteous, therefore I say unto you, hold your peace until I shall see fit to make all things known unto the world concerning the matter.*[27]

Other advice from the scriptures is available to help man apply the gift of the knowledge of the diversities of operations. As he examines the functions of charities, religious groups, and other organizations, he would do well to heed the instruction that

---

25. Mt. 7:6.
26. Mt. 7:7-8.
27. D & C 10:34-37.

Ye shall know them by their fruits. Do men gather grapes of thorns, or figs or thistles?

Even so every good tree bringeth forth good fruit; but a corrupt tree bringeth forth evil fruit.

A good tree cannot bring forth evil fruit, neither can a *corrupt tree bring forth evil fruit.*

Every tree that bringeth not forth good fruit is hewn down, and cast into the fire.

Wherefore by their fruits ye shall know them.[28]

He should also remember Moroni's explanation that those things which are from God will entice one to do good continually, entice one to love God, entice one to serve God, and persuade one to believe in Christ.

Wherefore, *all things which are good cometh of God; and that which is evil cometh of the devil;* for the devil is an enemy unto God, and fighteth against him continually, and inviteth and enticeth to sin, and to do that which is evil continually.

But behold, *that which is of God inviteth and enticeth to do good continually; wherefore, every thing which inviteth and enticeth to do good, and to love God, and to serve him,* is inspired of God.

Wherefore, take heed, my beloved brethren, that ye do not judge that which is evil to be of God, or that which is good and of God to be of the devil.

For behold, my brethren, it is given unto you to judge, that ye may know good from evil; and the way to judge is as plain, that ye may know with a perfect knowledge, as the daylight is from the dark night.

For behold, the Spirit of Christ is given to every man, that he may know good from evil; wherefore, I show unto you the way to judge; for every thing which inviteth to do good, and to persuade to believe in Christ, is sent forth by the power and gift of Christ; wherefore ye may know with a perfect knowledge it is of God.

But whatsoever thing persuadeth men to do evil, and believe not in Christ, and deny him, and serve not God, then ye may know with a perfect knowledge it is of the devil; for after this manner doth the devil work, for he persuadeth no man to do good, no, not one; neither do his angels, neither do they who subject themselves unto him.

---

28. Mt. 7:16-20.

And now, my brethren, seeing that ye know the light by which ye may judge, which light is the light of Christ, *see that ye do not judge wrongfully; for with that same judgment which ye judge ye shall also be judged.*

Wherefore, I beseech of you, brethren, that ye should search diligently *in the light of Christ that ye may know good from evil; and if ye will lay hold upon every good thing, and condemn it not, ye certainly will be a child of Christ.*[29]

Summary

1. The gift of knowledge of the diversities of operations is manifested in two ways.

    A. It is the inspired ability to discern whether the activities, causes and programs of groups and individuals are inspired of God, men, or Satan.

    B. It is the gift which enables men to be aware of events, both present and future, which will affect them in their callings and will alter the state of well-being of people under their jurisdiction.

2. Numerous examples of those who possessed this gift and those who did not have it are found in the scriptures.

3. This gift is necessary in the last day, for the Lord has promised that men will need to discern between true and false churches and individuals in that time.

4. At times, instead of allowing men to use this gift, God prescribes other courses which are to be followed without deviation.

5. The functions of many charitable organizations, religious groups, social organizations, etc. can be evaluated by the fruits of their labors. That which is from God will

    A. entice to do good continually;

    B. entice to love God;

    C. entice to serve God; and

    D. persuade to believe in Christ.

---

29. Moro. 7:12-19.

CHAPTER XIX

Discerning of Spirits

The Discerning of Spirits

By the gift of the discerning of spirits one may discern the attitudes and personality traits of those with whom he comes in contact as well as recognize the nature and intent of spiritual visitors from beyond the veil.

Discerning Attitudes and Traits

By the power which this gift holds, the Master was able to recognize the nature of Nathanael and to declare before meeting him, "behold an Israelite indeed, in whom is no guile!"[1] Jesus had the power to know the intentions of his betrayer, Judas, while his apostles did not suspect him. He told them, "I speak not of you all: I know whom I have chosen: but that the scripture may be fulfilled, *He that eateth bread with me hath lifted up his heel against me.* Now I tell you before it come, that, when it is come to pass, ye may believe that I am he."[2] When asked who would betray Him, the Master answered,

> *He it is, to whom I shall give a sop, when I have dipped it.* And when he had dipped the sop, *he gave it to Judas Iscariot,* the son of Simon.
>
> And after the sop Satan entered into him. Then said Jesus unto him, That thou doest, do quickly.[3]

It would seem that the gift of discernment was functioning when Peter rebuked Simon the Sorcerer, a baptized but unconfirmed member of the Church. The latter had sought to purchase with money the power to give the gift of the Holy Ghost. To him Peter exclaimed,

> Thy money perish with thee, because thou hast thought that the gift of God may be purchased with money.

---

1. Jn. 1:47.
2. Jn. 13:18-19.
3. Jn. 13:26-27.

Thou hast neither part nor lot in this matter; for *thy heart is not right in the sight of God.*

Repent therefore of this thy wickedness, and pray God, if perhaps the thought of thine heart may be forgiven thee.

For I perceive that thou art in the gall of bitterness, and in the bond of iniquity.[4]

The rebuke Paul gave to another sorcerer, Elymas, leaves no doubt the apostle fully discerned his opponent's spirit:

Then Saul, (who also is called Paul,) *filled with the Holy Ghost,* set his eyes on him.

And said, *O full of all subtilty and all mischief, thou child of the devil, thou enemy of all righteousness,* wilt thou not cease to pervert the right ways of the Lord?

And now, behold, the hand of the Lord is upon thee, and thou shalt be blind, not seeing the sun for a season. And immediately there fell on him a mist and a darkness; and he went about seeking some to lead him by the hand.[5]

Alma, when debating with Korihor, discerned the spirit which motivated that antichrist:

Behold, I know that thou believest, but thou art possessed with a lying spirit, and *ye have put off the Spirit of God that it may have no place in you; but the devil has power over you,* and he doth carry you about, working devices that he may destroy the children of God.[6]

When Amulek opposed the wicked lawyer, Zeezrom, he testified that he discerned the lawyer's thought through the gift of the Spirit: "Now Zeezrom, seeing that thou hast been taken in thy lying and craftiness, for thou hast not lied unto men only, but thou hast lied unto God; for behold, he knows all thy thoughts, and thou seest that thy thoughts are made known unto us by his Spirit."[7]

This gift also has been manifested in the latter days. Through this gift John Taylor was discerned to be a servant of the Lord although he had not yet made mention of his missionary calling:

Elder Taylor accompanied Elder Wilford Woodruff in the autumn of 1839, on a mission to England. He carried with him

---

4. Acts. 8:20-23.
5. Acts 13:9-11.
6. Al. 30:42.
7. Al. 12:3.

a letter of introduction from his wife to her brother and her sister-in-law in Liverpool, and other relatives on the Isle of Man. Soon after his arrival in Liverpool, in January, 1840, Elder Taylor called at the Cannon home and made himself known to the wife and mother, promising to return in the evening when the husband and father would be home from his work. Elder Taylor said nothing about his mission during his short visit nor did he explain the purpose which brought him to England, but there was something about his personality and influence which profoundly impressed the mother, Ann Quayle. As he walked away after his brief visit, she remarked to her eldest son, George: *'There goes a man of God. He has come to bring salvation to our father's house.'*[8]

The wickedness of men is often discerned as they challenge the teachings of the servants of God. Elder John Morgan experienced this as he was interrupted while preaching in Rome, Georgia:

A large well-dressed and apparently influential man arose in the audience and addressing his remarks to Brother Morgan said, 'Mr. Preacher, I have been much interested in your remarks and especially those that infer that signs will follow the believers. Now sir, I live in an adjoining county; have lived there for many years and am what you would call a really influential man among the people, but I want to say to you now that after what you have just said, unless you can give us a sign right here and now I am warning you that it would really be unpleasant for you to ever visit our community. I will see to it that you are handled pretty roughly and driven out.' Thereupon Brother Morgan, in answer to the man's request, quoted the saying of the Savior to the effect that a wicked and adulterous generation seeketh after a sign, and he further said that what applies to a generation applies to a community, what applies to a community applies to an individual and 'Sir, I am amazed that a man of your standing and influence would stand up before this large audience of several hundred people and proclaim yourself an adulterer.' The man, terribly enraged at Brother Morgan's rebuttal, started with an oath toward the pulpit with the intention of doing bodily injury to the Elder. He hadn't gone far when an officer of the law arose. He was dressed in his official uniform and in a stern voice commanded the enraged man to return to his seat. Then turning to Brother Morgan, he said, 'Mr. Preacher, I happen to be the Chief of Police in the city in which

---

8. Hinckley, *Faith of our Pioneer Fathers*, pp. 159-60.

this man lives, and it is very apparent that when you stated that he was a self-confessed adulterer, you hit him in a vulnerable spot. The fact is,' continued the Chief of Police, '*that it was only last month that I arrested this man for that offense in our town and when taken before the court, he pleaded guilty to the charge.*' The man seeking for a sign, according to Brother Morgan, sneaked out a side door and he continued with his sermon."

Elder C. V. Spencer experienced a similar circumstance as he was on the boat, sailing to reach his mission assignment in England. During the trip, a group of men crowded into a cabin and began asking him questions.

When I first sat down I noticed a large, black-eyed, black-haired man, and said to myself, 'When he comes I will have the devil.' After some time he pushed forward and literally covered me with compliments. He then remarked 'You must excuse me, young friend, after your testimony of the goodness of your people, for asking why *such* men as George J. Adams, John C. Bennett, Dr. Foster, Charles Foster and others could not live peaceably in your community?'

My answer followed like lightning: '*It was because they were such gamblers, whore-masters, black-legs and rascals as you are.*'

He made a bound for me; six men caught him, pulled him to the outside of the circle, and slapping him on the back told him with an oath, that if God Almighty had come down out of heaven He could not have told his character any better than the little 'Mormon' had.[10]

The author had an experience with the gift of discernment of spirits while serving in the mission field. It happened in a boarding house in Guatemala City, Guatemala, during the first week of 1957, following an evening of proselyting with my companion, Elder Joseph West.

We were in the dining room and the girls who lived there were eating. We had given them a few lessons, but they hadn't really been interested. But we got to talking. There was a boy friend of one of them there and he started talking too, and asked us what we were preaching. I figured that he was looking for an argument so I sidestepped it by saying that we were called to preach just two things: repentance, and baptism!

---

9. *Ibid.,* pp. 251-52.
10. *Labors in the Vineyard,* p. 14.

That seemed to catch his fancy and he decided to listen to us instead of argue, so we preached repentance and baptism to them on the spot. We had a friend who I had just baptized about two weeks before who was with us, and he started talking to the boy, and before long we were in little groups talking. I started talking to one of the girls, who really needed a little preaching, and she, having already heard an apostasy lesson from us, had quite a few doubts about things in general. She wasn't of a very righteous character, and was in need of some good heavy repenting. As we were talking I suddenly felt the Spirit's influence very strongly and bore my testimony of our calling as servants of the Lord. She asked the question 'how could she, personally, know that we were the Lord's servants.' And then I said just what the Spirit told me to say, and I testified to her that she was living in adultery, and that if she didn't repent she would be punished, and I told her that the fact that I knew it proved that I was an inspired servant of the Lord. Well, she got white as a sheet, and I could read it written all over her face, that what I had told her was true. I left it at that, and didn't push the point farther, but I knew that she had been warned by the Lord, and that if she didn't repent she would be punished. The whole thing left me a little bit shaky when I got to thinking later about what I'd told her — you don't go around calling people adulteresses these days, you know. But it does remind me that the Lord works through his servants, and inspires them, and I was happy to have been His instrument.

A postscript should be added. The next day we returned to the boarding house and found the girl was gone. We made inquiry of our landlady and found that that morning she had packed her bags, paid her rent, and had moved to Mexico.[11]

The spirit of discernment, helped Levi W. Hancock, one of the Seven Presidents of Seventies, to recognize a murderer as he marched with the Mormon Battalion:

A non-Mormon by the consent of the Battalion joined the company and soon after required baptism. Brother Hancock, in company with others of the brethren took him down to the Missouri river and performed the ceremony. On raising him from the water *he said, as if wrought upon by the spirit, 'If I have baptized a murderer, it will do him no good.'* His words had such an effect upon the stranger that he soon afterwards

---

11. *Missionary Journal,* personal file of Duane S. Crowther.

confessed that he was a murderer, having killed his own
brother.[12]

Not all instances of discernment involve the recognizing of
those who are evil or good. The gift may be employed to help
select a suitable mate, as apparently happened to Brigham Young,
who found himself a widower with two small children in 1833.

> It happened that a fast and testimony meeting was held in
> Kirtland, and among those present were Elder Young and
> Sister Mary Ann Angell. The gift of tongues rested down upon
> Elder Young and the interpretation thereof was given by some-
> one present. *The Spirit bore record through that tongue that
> these two faithful souls were designed by God for each other.*
> They were united in marriage, and Sister Mary Ann assumed
> the care of the motherless children.[13]

Guidance in Applying the Gift

The apostle, John, knowing that man needs to be able to recognize the spirits and attitudes which characterize those around
him, gave this admonition:

> Beloved, believe not every spirit, but *try the spirits whether
> they are of God:* because many false prophets are gone out into
> the world.
> *Hereby know ye the Spirit of God: Every Spirit that con-
> fesseth that Jesus Christ is come in the flesh is of God:*
> And every spirit that confesseth not that Jesus Christ is
> come in the flesh is not of God: and this is that spirit of anti-
> christ, whereof ye have heard that it should come; and even now
> already is it in the world.[14]

It was his message also that "we are of God: *he that knoweth
God heareth us; he that is not of God heareth not us.* Hereby
know we the spirit of truth, and the spirit of error."[15]

The power to discern the spirits of others may serve both
as a protection and as a means for accomplishing the Lord's
work. The latter was the case with Joseph Smith, who was told
by the Lord, "Behold, I, the Lord, will give unto my servant
Joseph Smith, Jun., *power that he shall be enabled to discern*

12. Jenson, I. p. 189.
13. Jenson, I, pp. 121-22.
14. I Jn. 4:1-3.
15. I Jn. 4:6.

by the Spirit those who shall go up unto the land of Zion, and those of my disciples who shall tarry."[16] Perhaps the best way to discern the spirits of those who truly love God is by their works, the fruits of their labors; for the Lord in a revelation said,

And again, *I will give unto you a pattern in all things,* that ye may not be deceived; for Satan is abroad in the land, and he goeth forth deceiving the nations —

Wherefore *He that prayeth, whose spirit is contrite, the same is accepted of me* if he obey mine ordinances.

He that speaketh, whose spirit is contrite, whose language is meek and edifieth, the same is of God if he obey mine ordinances.

And again, *he that trembleth under my power shall be made strong,* and shall bring forth fruits of praise and wisdom, according to the revelations and truths which I have given you.

And again, *he that is overcome and bringeth not forth fruits, even according to this pattern, is not of me.*

Wherefore, *by this pattern ye shall know the spirits in all cases under the whole heavens.*[17]

Discerning Spirit Beings

The gift of discernment is also needed by those who receive visitors from the world of spirits and from angels who are resurrected beings. The Evil One has great power to deceive and can even transform himself into an angel of light.[18] Paul suggested that man may receive visitors from beyond the veil and not know it, when he wrote to the Hebrews: "Be not forgetful to entertain strangers: for thereby some have entertained angels unawares."[19]

In the early days of the church many members were experiencing spiritual phenomena which were not coming from God. A warning was given them by the Lord:

Hearken, O ye elders of my church, and give ear to the voice of the living God; and attend to the words of wisdom which shall be given unto you, according as ye have asked and are agreed as touching the church, and the spirits which have gone abroad in the earth.

---

16. D & C 63:41.
17. D & C 52:14-19.
18. II Cor. 11:14.
19. Heb. 13:2.

> Behold, verily I say unto you, that *there are many spirits which are false spirits, which have gone forth in the earth, deceiving the world.*
>
> And *also Satan hath sought to deceive you,* that he might overthrow you.[20]

To those who experienced these visitations by false spirits, instruction was given as to how to reject and repel them:

> Wherefore, it shall come to pass, that *if you behold a spirit manifested that you cannot understand,* and you receive not that spirit, *ye shall ask of the Father in the name of Jesus; and if he give not unto you that spirit, then you may know that it is not of God.*
>
> *And it shall be given unto you, power over that spirit; and you shall proclaim against that spirit with a loud voice that it is not of God —*
>
> Not with railing accusation, that ye be not overcome, neither with boasting nor rejoicing, lest you be seized therewith.[21]

Later, another guide was given to the Saints to help them to discern whether visitors from beyond the veil were of God or of Satan:

> *There are two kinds of beings in heaven,* namely: *Angels,* who are resurrected personages, havings bodies of flesh and bones —
>
> For instance, Jesus said: Handle me and see, for a spirit hath not flesh and bones, as ye see me have.
>
> Secondly: *The spirits of just men made perfect,* they who are not resurrected, but inherit the same glory.
>
> When a messenger comes saying he has a message from God, *offer him your hand and request him to shake hands with you.*
>
> If he be an angel he will do so, and you will feel his hand.
>
> If he be the spirit of a just man made perfect he will come in his glory; for that is the only way he can appear —
>
> Ask him to shake hands with you, but he will not move, because it is contrary to the order of heaven for a just man to deceive; but he will still deliver his message.

---

20. D & C 50: 1-3.
21. D & C 50: 31-33.

If it be the devil as an angel of light, when you ask to shake hands he will offer you his hand and you will not feel anything; you may therefore detect him.

These are three grand keys whereby you may know whether any administration is from God.[22]

Summary

1. The gift of discerning of spirits enables its recipient to determine the attitudes and personality traits of mortal beings and the nature and intent of spiritual beings from beyond the veil.

2. This gift allows one to know whether another individual is acting under the direction of the Spirit of the Lord.

3. Those who possess this gift are able to determine the degree of righteousness of others.

4. This gift can aid people in choosing their mates.

5. Men are commanded to try the spirits of others to see whether they are of God.

6. This gift aids Church authorities in selecting officials for Church callings.

7. Satan can transform himself into an angel of light.

8. A handshake test has been provided to aid man in determining the nature of supernatural visitors.

---

22. D & C 129:1-9.

Part VI

GIFTS OF
SALVATION
AND EXALTATION

CHAPTER XX

Repentance

Godly Sorrow and Worldly Sorrow Contrasted

Repentance is the corrective process by which man turns away from sin and worldliness and seeks to become Godlike in his nature. As Oliver Cowdery defined it, repentance is "forsaking sin and yielding obedience to the gospel!"[1] It is a gift which God bestows upon man, for without promptings and guidance from on high man cannot initiate and carry through this program of self-reform. Concerning the gifts of repentance, Alma told his followers, "*May the Lord grant unto you repentance, that ye may not bring down his wrath upon you, that ye may not be bound down by the chains of hell, that ye may not suffer the second death.*"[2] Paul also saw that repentance was a gift of the Spirit. He taught the Saints in Rome that "the goodness of God leadeth thee to repentance."[3]

True repentance is based on God-inspired sorrow for wrongdoing, which sorrow motivates man to seek to do better. It does not come as a result of earthly sorrowing; there must be the element of inspiration added to make sorrow bring about true repentance. Paul contrasted godly and worldly sorrow when he taught the Corinthians:

> Now I rejoice, *not that ye were made sorry, but that ye sorrowed to repentance: for ye were made sorry after a godly manner*, that ye might receive damage by us in nothing.
>
> *For godly sorrow worketh repentance to salvation not to be repented of: but the sorrow of the world worketh death.*
>
> For behold this selfsame thing, that ye sorrowed after a godly sort, *what carefulness it wrought in you, yea, what clearing of yourselves, yea, what indignation, yea, what fear, yea, what vehement desire, yea, what zeal, yea, what revenge!* In all things ye have approved yourselves to be clear in this matter.[4]

---

1. *Early Scenes in Church History,* p. 76.
2. Al. 13:30.
3. Rom. 2:4.
4. II Cor. 7:9-11.

Mormon saw the need for the gift of the Spirit among his people so that their sorrow would be godly sorrow. His nation was being driven and smitten in continual warfare with the Lamanites, and the suffering and sorrowing of his people were intense. Nevertheless, they did not choose to repent, for the Spirit was not with them.

> And it came to pass that when I, Mormon, saw their lamentation and their mourning and their sorrow before the Lord, my heart did begin to rejoice within me, knowing the mercies and the long-suffering of the Lord, therefore supposing that he would be merciful unto them that they would again become a righteous people.
>
> But behold this my joy was vain, *for their sorrowing was not unto repentance, because of the goodness of God; but it was rather the sorrowing of the damned, because the Lord would not always suffer them to take happiness in sin.*
>
> And they did not come unto Jesus with broken hearts and contrite spirits, but they did curse God, and wish to die. Nevertheless they would struggle with the sword for their lives.[5]

Thus it becomes clear that man must be prompted by the Spirit to repent. If he has shunned the companionship of the Holy Ghost, he will not be able to better his life and return to the ways of God.

Repentance Essential to Exaltation

It is basic to the teachings of God and His Church that man must repent of all his sins to gain entrance to the kingdom of heaven in which God dwells. The words of the Divine unto Adam were to this effect. "Wherefore teach it unto your children, that *all men, everywhere, must repent, or they can in nowise inherit the kingdom of God, for no unclean thing can dwell there,* or dwell in his presence."[6] The same teaching was proclaimed by the Lord as He ministered to the Nephites in the Americas:

> And no unclean thing can enter into his kingdom; therefore nothing entereth into his rest save it be those who have washed their garments in my blood, because of their faith, and *the repentance of all their sins,* and their faithfulness unto the end.

---

5. Morm. 2:12-14.
6. Moses 6:57.

Now this is the commandment: *Repent, all ye ends of the earth*, and come unto me and be baptized in my name, that ye may be sanctified by the reception of the Holy Ghost, that ye may stand spotless before me at the last day.[7]

It appears that those who refuse to repent do so while openly rejecting the enticings of the Spirit, and thereby they forfeit their claim upon the saving powers of Christ. To this type of individual King Benjamin warned, "Wo, wo unto him who knoweth that he rebelleth against God! For salvation cometh to none such except it be through repentance and faith on the Lord Jesus Christ."[8]

Repentance, then, is an essential step along the path to exaltation. Failure to take this step brings grief and suffering. As Jesus taught, *"Surely every man must repent or suffer, for I, God, am endless."*[9]

This Life the Time to Repent

Man's basic business of living — his major objective in mortal life — is to root out his imperfections and to plant in their place the seeds of perfection and holiness. Thus, mortality becomes a period in which man is to prepare for the life to come. It is a period in which the true seeker of eternal joy strives to become Godlike in his own character. The attaining of a God-like character comes through daily introspection and revision of one's thoughts, attitudes, and actions. In short, it comes through continual repentance and self-preparation. Of this process Alma taught,

> Nevertheless, there was a space granted unto man in which he might repent; therefore *this life became a probationary state; a time to prepare to meet God;* a time to prepare for that endless state which has been spoken of by us, which is after the resurrection of the dead.[10]

Repentance cannot be procrastinated, for it is a lengthy and time-consuming process which, to be completely successful, must be continually operative throughout man's mortal life. As Amulek taught,

---

7. 3 Ne. 27:19-20.
8. Mos. 3:12.
9. D & C 19:4.
10. Al. 12:24.

This life is the time for men to prepare to meet God; yea, behold the day of this life is the day for men to perform their labors.

And now, as I said unto you before, as ye have had so many witnesses, therefore, I beseech of you that ye *do not procrastinate the day of your repentance until the end;* for after this day of life, which is given us to prepare for eternity, behold, *if we do not improve our time while in this life, then cometh the night of darkness wherein there can be no labor performed.*[11]

It is vital that one's life be directed toward good continually and that the individual travel this path unswervingly. Just as God will, in His mercy, blot out the sins of the repentant sinner, He will also erase the good deeds of the righteous individual who turns to sin. A revelation of Ezekiel proclaimed this principle with great clarity:

Say unto them, As I live, saith the Lord God, *I have no pleasure in the death of the wicked; but that the wicked turn from his way and live:* turn ye, turn ye from your evil ways; for why will ye die, O house of Israel?

Therefore, thou son of man, say unto the children of thy people, The *righteousness of the righteous shall not deliver him in the day of his transgression: as for the wickedness of the wicked, he shall not fall thereby in the day that he turneth from his wickedness; neither shall the righteous be able to live for his righteousness in the day that he sinneth.*

When I shall say to the righteous, that he shall surely live; if he trust to his own righteousness, and commit iniquity, *all his righteousnesses shall not be remembered; but for his iniquity that he hath committed, he shall die for it.*

Again, when I say unto the wicked, Thou shalt surely die; if he turn from his sin, and do that which is lawful and right;

If the wicked restore the pledge, give again that he had robbed, walk in the statutes of life, without committing iniquity; *he shall surely live, he shall not die.*

None of his sins that he hath committed shall be mentioned unto him: he hath done that which is lawful and right; he shall surely live.

Yet the children of thy people say, The way of the Lord is not equal: but as for them, their way is not equal.

---

11. Al. 34:32-33.

*When the righteous turneth from his righteousness, and
committeth iniquity, he shall even die thereby.*

*But if the wicked turn from his wickedness, and do that
which is lawful and right, he shall live thereby.*

Yet ye say, The way of the Lord is not equal. O ye house
Israel, I will judge you every one after his ways.[12]

It must be recognized that the true process of repentance involves two aspects, the turning away from evil deeds, and the
substituting of righteous thoughts and actions. Man cannot expect to gain exaltation unless both of these functions are fulfilled. Even though a man might turn away from sin and receive
forgiveness for it, if he has not become Godlike in his nature
he cannot expect to dwell in the highest kingdom with Deity.
The gaining of a Godlike nature is that to which Alma referred
when he taught the people of Zarahemla, saying:

And now behold, *I ask of you, my brethren of the church,
have ye spiritually been born of God? Have ye received his
image in your countenances? Have ye experienced this mighty
change in your hearts?*

Do ye exercise faith in the redemption of him who created
you? Do you look forward with an eye of faith, and view this
mortal body raised in immortality, and this corruption raised
in incorruption, to stand before God to be judged according to
the deeds which have been done in the mortal body?

I say unto you, *can you imagine to yourselves that ye
hear the voice of the Lord, saying unto you, in that day: Come
unto me ye blessed, for behold, your works have been the works
of righteousness upon the face of the earth?*[13]

Loss of the Spirit from Failure to Repent

It must be recognized that the gifts of the Spirit are granted
to those who love God and keep all His commandments and to
those who seek so to do.[14] Full observance of the commandments
of God involves a process of complete and continuing repentance
on the part of the individual. The Spirit does not linger with
those who fail to improve their lives and do not attempt to achieve
a continuing progress toward perfection. This was the experience
of the people of Nephi, to whom the Lord warned, "Because of

---

12. Ezk. 33:11-20.
13. Al. 5:14-16.
14. D & C 46:9.

the hardness of the hearts of the people of the Nephites, *except they repent I will take away my word from them, and I will withdraw my Spirit from them,* and I will suffer them no longer, and I will turn the hearts of their brethren against them."[15] Loss of the Spirit brings the beginning of great suffering to the unrepentant. A revelation to Joseph Smith spoke of the intense nature of this suffering and commanded repentance so that it could be avoided.

> *Therefore I command you to repent — repent, lest I smite you by the rod of my mouth, and by my wrath, and by my anger, and your sufferings be sore —* how sore you know not, how exquisite you know not, yea, how hard to bear you know not.
>
> For behold, I, God, have suffered these things for all, that they might not suffer if they would repent;
>
> *But if they would not repent they must suffer even as I;*
>
> *Which suffering caused myself, even God, the greatest of all, to tremble because of pain,* and to bleed at every pore, and suffer both body and spirit — and would that I might not drink the bitter cup, and shrink —
>
> *Nevertheless, glory be to the Father, and I partook and* finished my preparations unto the children of men.
>
> Wherefore, *I command you again to repent, lest I humble you with my almighty power; and that you confess your sins, lest you suffer these punishments of which I have spoken,* of which in the smallest, yea, even in the least degree you have tasted at the time I withdrew my Spirit.[16]

Alma recounted his great suffering as he realized his inadequacy before God and then contrasted it with his feelings as he gained the influence of the Holy Ghost:

> *I was racked with eternal torment, for my soul was harrowed up to the greatest degree and racked with all my sins.*
>
> *Yea, I did remember all my sins and iniquities, for which I was tormented with the pains of hell;* yea, I saw that I had rebelled against my God, and that I had not kept his holy commandments.
>
> Yea, and I had murdered many of his children, or rather led them away unto destruction; yea, and in fine so great had

---

15. Hel. 13:8.
16. D & C 19:15-20.

been my iniquities, that *the very thought of coming into the presence of my God did rack my soul with inexpressible horror.*

Oh, thought I, that I could be banished and become extinct both soul and body, that I might not be brought to stand in the presence of my God, to be judged of my deeds.

And now, for three days and for three nights was I racked, *even with the pains of a damned soul.*

And it came to pass that as I was thus racked with torment, while I was harrowed up by the memory of my sins, behold, I remembered also to have heard my father prophesy unto the people concerning the coming of one Jesus Christ, A Son of God, to atone for the sins of the world.

Now, as my mind caught hold upon this thought, I cried within my heart: O Jesus, thou Son of God, have mercy on me, who am in the gall of bitterness, and am encircled about by the everlasting chains of death.

And now, behold, when I thought this, *I could remember my pains no more; yea, I was harrowed up by the memory of my sins no more.*

And oh, what joy, and what marvelous light I did behold; yea, my soul was filled with joy as exceeding as was my pain!

Yea, I say unto you, my son, that there could be nothing so exquisite and so bitter as were my pains. Yea, and again I say unto you, my son, that on the other hand, *there can be nothing so exquisite and sweet as was my joy.*

Yea, methought I saw, even as our father Lehi saw, God sitting upon his throne, surrounded with numberless concourses of angels, in the attitude of singing and praising their God; yea, and *my soul did long to be there.*

But behold, my limbs did receive their strength again, and I stood upon my feet and did manifest unto the people that I had been born of God.

Yea, and from that time even until now, *I have labored without ceasing, that I might bring souls unto repentance; that I might bring them to taste of the exceeding joy of which I did taste; that they might also be born of God, and be filled with the Holy Ghost.*[17]

Jacob also saw the fate of those who rejected the promptings of the Holy Ghost and issued a call to mankind to avoid this fate. He spoke of the final judgment and the ultimate fate of the unrepentant.

---

17. Al. 36:12-24. See also Al. 38:8.

Wherefore, my beloved brethren, I beseech of you in words of soberness that ye would repent, and come with full purpose of heart, and cleave unto God as he cleaveth unto you. And while his arm of mercy is extended towards you in the light of day, harden not your hearts.

Yea, today, if ye will hear his voice, harden not your hearts; for why will ye die?

For behold, *after ye have been nourished by the good word of God all the day long, will ye bring forth evil fruit, that ye must be hewn down and cast into the fire?*

Behold, will ye reject these words? Will ye reject the words of the prophets; and will ye reject all the words which have been spoken concerning Christ, after so many have spoken concerning him; and deny the good word of Christ, and the power of God, and the gift of the Holy Ghost, and *quench the Holy Spirit*, and make a mock of the great plan of redemption, which hath been laid for you?

Know ye not that if ye will do these things, that the power of the redemption and the resurrection, which is in Christ, will bring you to stand with shame and awful guilt before the bar of God?

And according to the power of justice, for justice cannot be denied, ye must go away into that lake of fire and brimstone, whose flames are unquenchable, and whose smoke ascendeth up forever and ever, which lake of fire and brimstone is endless torment.

O then, my beloved brethren, *repent ye, and enter in at the strait gate, and continue in the way which is narrow, until ye shall obtain eternal life.*[18]

Repentance Prevented by Labors of Satan

The devil continually strives to prevent people from bettering their lives through the repentance process. His efforts are directed towards those who have opened the door to him through sin, and yet who may still attempt to live the gospel and to serve the Lord. An example may be found in this incident which occurred in a Welsh branch of the Church:

In the latter part of the year 1848, the Elders laboring in the Merthyr Tydvil branch had a great deal of trouble with two young women of that branch who very frequently were possessed of evil spirits. They were such a source of annoyance in the

---

18. Jac. 6:5-11.

meetings that, on the day of a general conference which was to be held about the close of the year, they were cautioned by Elder Dan Jones who then presided there, against attending the meeting. To this, however, they paid no attention, and when the meeting was opened, it was only too apparent that they were there. In a short time the meeting was in such an uproar, through the raving and shrieking of those girls, that the speaker could not be heard. Some of the Elders were immediately sent to cast the evil spirits out of them, but they failed to do so, and with difficulty the girls were carried into an adjoining room.

When a presiding Elder has the spirit of his office upon him it is his privilege to know the proper course to take in any emergency. It is his privilege to enjoy communion with the Holy Sprit and have the Lord dictate through him that which will be for the best good of the members over whom he is set to preside. It is also his privilege to discern by what spirit the people with whom he is brought in contact are actuated.

It would seem that Elder Dan Jones had the spirit of discernment on that occasion and was inspired to take the wisest course in dealing with the girls and the stubborn spirits by which they were possessed. *He was satisfied that they were wilfully sinful, or the spirit of God would not be withdrawn from them and the devil suffered to exercise such power over them. He therefore proposed that they be cut off from the Church on account of their transgressions, and the Saints assembled voted unanimously to that effect. No sooner had they done so than the evil spirits left the girls and they became rational. When they were no longer members of the Church, the devil had no further need to try to annoy the Saints through them.* The result was that the girls afterwards saw what their sin had brought them to, repented of it and made public acknowledgement before the Saints, after which they were re-baptized and no more troubled by evil spirits.[19]

Newel Knight also recorded an instance in which an evil spirit attempted to block the course of the repentance process. Once again, sin had opened the way for Satan's followers to enter:

Brother Joseph from time to time sent copies of revelations to me for the benefit of the branch over which I presided in common with all the Saints in Zion. On reading one of these revelations to the branch, my aunt. . . . arose and contradicted

19. *Early Scenes in Church History.* pp. 56-57.

the revelation, saying it must be taken in a spiritual light. She went to such a length that I felt constrained to rebuke her by the authority of the Priesthood. At this time she was angry, and from that time sought to influence all who would listen to her. The result was a division of feeling in the branch, and her husband partook of her spirit until he became so enthusiastic, that he went from branch to branch crying, 'hosanna, glory to God! Zion is redeemed! and blessed is he that bringeth good tidings to the people!' Sister Peck at length began to feel the weight of what she had done, but she could not recall it. She seemed racked with great torment, her mind found no rest, until a burning fever brought her to a sick bed. She sent for several of the Elders to administer to her, but found no relief. At last she sent for P. P. Pratt, Lyman Wight and myself, we laid our hands upon her and administered to her, after which she looked up in despair and said she hoped I would deliver her from the awful state she was in. Her whole frame was racked with intense anguish while her mind seemed almost in despair. Brother Parley said to me; 'Brother Newel, you must do something for her.' My soul was drawn out in pity for her, yet I knew not what to do. *I felt impressed to call the branch together that evening.*

When the meeting had been opened as usual, I arose, not knowing what to do or what to say. After requesting the prayers and united faith of all present, *the Spirit of the Lord came upon me, so that I was able to make plain the cause of Sister Peck's illness — that she had risen up in opposition to the Priesthood which had been placed over that branch of the Church, and contradicted the revelations of God, and that by the sympathies shown her, a division of feeling had gained advantage over them, until Sister Peck had fallen completely under the power of Satan, and could not extricate herself.* I told the brethren and sisters, if they would repent of what they had done, and renew their covenants one with another and with the Lord, and uphold the authorities placed over them, and also the revelations which the Lord had given unto us, it would be all right with Sister Peck, for this would break the bands of Satan and make us free.

I had no sooner closed my remarks than with one united voice, all came forward and agreed to do so. *I then went to Sister Peck, and in the name of Jesus Christ, and by virtue of the Holy Priesthood, commanded the evil powers to depart from her, and blessed her with peace and strength, both of body and mind.* I then dismissed the meeting and told the family to go to bed, and rest as usual, and all would be well. Early the next morning I called to see her, she stretched out her hand as soon as she saw me, and said, O Brother Newel, forgive me! I did not believe one word you said last night, but when I awoke this morning I found I was not in hell. Her rejoicings were very great, and union again prevailed with us, and we all felt we had learned a lesson that would be of lasting benefit to us.[20]

How much better it is for man to heed the promptings of the Holy Spirit than to suffer such torment. Truly to walk in the Spirit and to follow the process of repentance is better than to suffer the loss of all the gifts of the Spirit and to merit only eternal damnation.

Summary

1. Repentance is a gift of God. It is a process in which man turns away from sin and seeks to become Godlike in his nature.

2. Godly sorrow brings repentance unto salvation. Worldly sorrow does not bring repentance but is the sorrowing of the damned.

3. Man must repent of all his sins, for no unclean thing can dwell in the presence of God.

4. Refusal to repent is open rebellion against God.

5. Failure to repent condemns man to suffering.

6. Mortal life is a probationary state. It is the time for man to prepare to meet God.

7. If a wicked man repents, his wicked past will be wiped away. He will not be held accountable for it.

8. If a righteous man turns to sin, his righteous past will be wiped away. He will not be blessed for it.

9. The repentance process not only requires abstaining from evil deeds, it also requires the substituting of righteous thoughts and actions. Those who do this are spiritually born of God and experience a change in their hearts.

10. The Holy Spirit departs from those who refuse to repent.

---

20. *Scraps of Biography,* pp. 73-75.

11. The unrepentant will be forced to suffer the same pain of body and spirit which Jesus suffered.

12. The suffering of the unrepentant is exquisite. By contrast, the joy of the righteous is just as great.

13. Satan and his hosts attempt to molest those who have committed sin and to prevent them from gaining the Spirit unto repentance.

CHAPTER XXI

Charity

Charity the Pure Love of Christ

"Charity is the pure love of Christ, and it endureth forever."[1] It was Mormon who stated this eternal truth and gave man clear insight into the nature of this gift of the Spirit. Charity is manifested in two ways — in Christ's love for mankind and in the love which man has for God and for his fellowman.

Surely the greatest demonstration of the Savior's love for man is found in the sacrifice He made on the cross. Moroni spoke of this love when he prayed, saying,

> Thou hast said that thou hast loved the world, even unto the laying down of thy life for the world, that thou mightest take it again to prepare a place for the children of men.
>
> *And now I know that this love which thou hast had for the children of men is charity.*[2]

Jesus spoke of his sacrifice as a demonstration of His love as He taught His disciples the principle of charity:

> As the Father hath loved me, so have I loved you: continue ye in my love.
>
> If ye keep my commandments, ye shall abide in my love; even as I have kept my Father's commandments, and abide in his love.
>
> These things have I spoken unto you, that my joy might remain in you, and that your joy might be full.
>
> *This is my commandment, That ye love one another, as I have loved you.*
>
> *Greater love hath no man than this, that a man lay down his life for his friends.*[3]

Not only is the atonement a manifestation of Jesus' love, it is also a demonstration of the great love which God the Father

---

1. Moro. 7:47.
2. Eth. 12:33-34.
3. Jn. 15:9-13.

holds for His children, for He allowed His first-born Son to be hung on the cross. The Master taught that *"God so loved the world, that he gave his only begotten Son, that whosoever believeth in him should not perish, but have everlasting life."*[4]

The apostle John also recognized Jesus' suffering as a manifestation of the Father's love:

He that loveth not knoweth not God; for *God is love.*

In this was manifested the love of God toward us, because that God *sent his only begotten Son into the world, that we might live through him.*

Herein is love, not that we loved God, but that he loved us, and *sent his Son to be the propitiation for our sins.*

Beloved, if God so loved us, we ought also to love one another.[5]

Just as the Father and the Son have loved mankind, man is commanded to demonstrate a similar love — both to Deity and to those around them. One may consider the question put forth by the scribe and the answer it elicted from the Savior:

Which is the first commandment of all?

And Jesus answered him, The first of all the commandments is, Hear, O Israel; The Lord our God is one Lord:

And *thou shalt love the Lord thy God with all thy heart, and with all thy soul, and with all thy mind, and with all thy strength: this is the first commandment.*

And the second is like, namely this, *Thou shalt love thy neighbour as thyself. There is none other commandment greater than these.*

And the scribe said unto him, Well, Master, thou hast said the truth: for there is one God; and there is none other but he:

And *to love him with all the heart, and with all the understanding, and with all the soul, and with all the strength, and to love his neighbour as himself, is more than all whole burnt offerings and sacrifices.*

And when Jesus saw that he answered discreetly, he said unto him, Thou art not far from the kingdom of God.[6]

4. Jn. 3:16.
5. I Jn. 4:8-11.
6. Mk. 12:28-34.

Jesus established the spirit of love as a characteristic by which his followers could be identified:

> A new commandment I give unto you, That ye love one another; as I have loved you, that ye also love one another.
>
> *By this shall all men know that ye are my disciples, if ye have love one to another.*[7]

In His teachings He insisted that man must not be content to love only his friends, his love must also extend to his enemies:

> As ye would that men should do to you, do ye also to them likewise.
>
> For if ye love them which love you, what thank have ye? for *sinners also love those that love them.*
>
> And if ye do good to them which do good to you, what thank have ye? for *sinners also do even the same.*
>
> And if ye lend to them of whom ye hope to receive, what thank have ye? for *sinners also lend to sinners,* to receive as much again.
>
> *But love ye your enemies, and do good, and lend, hoping for nothing again; and your reward shall be great, and ye shall be the children of the Highest:* for he is kind unto the unthankful and to the evil.[8]

Charity a Gift of the Spirit

Charity, or love, is bestowed upon man as a gift of the Spirit. Paul taught that *"the love of God is shed abroad in our hearts by the Holy Ghost which is given unto us."*[9] In his epistle to the Colossians he wrote of their *"love in the spirit."*[10] Moroni taught that the *"Comforter filleth with hope and perfect love."*[11] It appears that not only is love given as a gift of the Spirit; but God also functions to help man's love to increase:

> *The Lord make you to increase and abound in love one toward another, and toward all men, even as we do toward you:*

---

7. Jn. 13:34-35.
8. Lk. 6:31-35.
9. Rom. 5:5.
10. Col. 1:8.
11. Moro. 8:26.

To the end he may stablish your hearts unblameable in holiness before God, even our Father, at the coming of our Lord Jesus Christ with all his saints.[12]

The Qualities of Charity

Few gifts of the Spirit have been so carefully described in the scriptures as the gift of charity. One of the most beautiful of these passages is the description made by Paul:

Though I speak with the tongues of men and of angels, and have not charity, I am become as sounding brass, or a tinkling cymbal.

And though I have the gift of prophecy, and understand all mysteries, and all knowledge; and though I have all faith, so that I could remove mountains, and have not charity, I am nothing.

And though I bestow all my goods to feed the poor, and though I give my body to be burned, and have not charity, it profiteth me nothing.

Charity suffereth long, and is kind; charity envieth not; charity vaunteth not itself, is not puffed up,

Doth not behave itself unseemly, seeketh not her own, is not easily provoked, thinketh no evil;

Rejoiceth not in iniquity, but rejoiceth in the truth;

Beareth all things, believeth all things, hopeth all things, endureth all things. . . .

And now abideth faith, hope, charity, these three; but the greatest of these is charity.[13]

Moroni added his description of this gift:

If a man be meek and lowly in heart, and confesses by the power of the Holy Ghost that Jesus is the Christ, he must needs have charity; for *if he have not charity he is nothing;* wherefore he must needs have charity.

And *charity suffereth long, and is kind, and envieth not, and is not puffed up, seeketh not her own, is not easily provoked, thinketh no evil, and rejoiceth not in iniquity but rejoiceth in the truth, beareth all things, believeth all things, hopeth all things, endureth all things.*

Wherefore, my beloved brethren, if ye have not charity, ye are nothing, for *charity never faileth.* Wherefore, cleave unto charity, which is the greatest of all, for all things must fail —

12. I Thess. 3:12-13.
13. I Cor. 13:1-7, 13.

*But charity is the pure love of Christ, and it endureth for-
ever; and whoso is found possessed of it at the last day, it shall
be well with him.*

Wherefore, my beloved brethren, *pray unto the Father with
all the energy of heart, that ye may be filled with this love,*
which he hath bestowed upon all who are true followers of his
Son, Jesus Christ, that ye may become the sons of God.[14]

Mormon also taught the nature of charity as he explained the
sinlessness of little children:

I fear not what man can do; for perfect love casteth out
all fear.

And *I am filled with charity, which is everlasting love;*
wherefore, all children are alike unto me; wherefore, *I love little
children with a perfect love;* and they are all alike and partakers of salvation.[15]

That charity brings freedom from fear was also asserted by John,
who wrote that

Whosoever shall confess that Jesus is the Son of God, God
dwelleth in him, and he is God.

And we have known and believed the love that God hath
to us. *God is love; and he that dwelleth in love dwelleth in
God and God in him.*

Herein is our love made perfect, that we may have boldness
in the day of judgment: because as he is, so are we in this
world.

There is no fear in love; but perfect love casteth out fear:
because fear hath torment. He that feareth is not made perfect
in love.

We love him, because he first loved us.

*If a man say, I love God, and hateth his brother, he is a
liar: for he that loveth not his brother whom he hath seen, how
can he love God whom he hath not seen?*

And this commandment have we from him, That he who
loveth God love his brother also.[16]

Charity is inseparably linked with the gifts of faith and
hope. Together they lead to exaltation:

---

14. Moro. 7:44-48.
15. Moro. 8:16-17.
16. I Jn. 4:15-21.

Wherefore, there must be faith; and if there must be faith there must also be hope; and if there must be hope there must also be charity.

And *except ye have charity ye can in nowise be saved in the kingdom of God;* neither can ye be saved in the kingdom of God if ye have not faith; neither can ye if ye have no hope.[17]

The superiority of charity over knowledge was set forth by Paul in his epistle to the Corinthians:

Knowledge puffeth up, *but charity edifieth.*

And if any man think that he knoweth anything, he knoweth nothing yet as he ought to know.

But if any man love God, the same is known of him.[18]

He saw that charity is the path to perfection and instructed the Colossians that "above all these things put on charity, which is the bond of perfectness."[19]

To lead to perfection, charity must be accompanied by personal purity: "Now *the end of the commandment is charity out of of a pure heart,* and of a good conscience, and of faith unfeigned."[20] This gift is so essential for the attaining of perfection that a modern revelation says it is to be given precedence over all other gifts: "And above all things, *clothe yourselves with the bond of charity, as with a mantle,* which is the bond of perfectness and peace."[21]

The Manifestations of Charity

If a man would truly enjoy the gift of charity, he must act in obedience to the commandments of God. It is through his efforts toward personal righteousness and service to God that man gains true love. John taught that

Hereby we do know that we know him, if we keep his commandments.

He that saith, I know him, and keepeth not his commandments, is a liar, and the truth is not in him.

17. Moro. 10:20-21.
18. I Cor. 8:1-3.
19. Col. 3:14.
20. I Tim. 1:5.
21. D & C 88:125.

But whoso keepeth his word, in him verily is the love of God perfected: hereby know we that we are in him.

He that saith he abideth in him ought himself also so to walk, even as he walked.[22]

In another epistle he wrote that *"this is love, that we walk after his commandments."*[23] Possession of the gifts of the Spirit is manifested not only in accordance to the commandments but in the accomplishment of righteous deeds. Alma admonished his listeners to *"see that ye have faith, hope, and charity, and then ye will always abound in good works."*[24] Charity must be used continually or God will remove the gift and strip the unrighteous of all his talents also: "If the Gentiles have not charity, because of our weakness, that thou [the Lord] wilt prove them, and *take away their talent,* yea, even that which they have received, and give unto them who shall have more abundantly."[25] In contrast, if the gift of charity is manifested fully and completely, it will bring its bearer rich blessings from on High:

Let thy bowels also be full of charity towards all men, and to the household of faith, and let virtue garnish thy thoughts unceasingly, *then shall thy confidence wax strong in the presence of God;* and the doctrine of the priesthood shall distil upon thy soul as the dews of heaven.

The Holy Ghost shall be thy constant companion, and thy scepter an unchanging scepter of righteousness and truth; and *thy dominion shall be an everlasting dominion, and without compulsory means it shall flow unto thee forever and ever.*[26]

Summary

1. Charity is the pure love of Christ. It is the love which He has for mankind, and the love man should have for God and for his fellow man.

2. God has commanded man to love one another as much as He has loved man.

---

22. I Jn. 2:3-6.
23. II Jn. 6.
24. Al. 7:24.
25. Eth. 12:35.
26. D & C 121:45-46.

3. The atoning sacrifice of Jesus shows His great love and the love possessed by God, the Father.

4. Man is commanded to love God fully and completely and to love his fellow man with as much love as he loves himself. This is more basic than the outward ordinances of the Church, though the man who loves God will strive to fulfill the ordinances God has established.

5. The true disciples of Christ are characterized by love for one another.

6. Man must not only love his friends, but also his enemies.

7. Charity is a gift of the Spirit.

8. Numerous qualities of charity are ennumerated. One possessing the gift of charity is
   A. long suffering,
   B. kind,
   C. without envy,
   D. humble,
   E. well behaved,
   F. selfless,
   G. difficult to provoke,
   H. thinks no evil,
   I. sorrows in iniquity,
   J. rejoices in truth,
   K. bears all things,
   L. believes all things,
   M. hopes all things,
   N. endures all things,
   O. never fails,
   P. endures forever.

9. Charity is manifested in the love of little children.

10. God dwells with the possessor of the gift of charity.

11. Charity is inseparably linked with faith and hope.

12. Charity out of a pure heart is the ultimate fulfillment of the commandment.

13. Charity is manifested through obedience to God's commandments.

14. The possessor of charity gains confidence in God and the possession of the Holy Ghost.

CHAPTER XXII

Hope

Man to Hope for Eternal Life

The gift of hope plays a vital role in the life of every true follower of the Master. Man hopes for many things, but the hope inspired as a gift of the Spirit is a hope for exaltation and eternal life. Moroni taught this when he wrote,

> And again, my beloved brethren, I would speak unto you concerning hope. How is it that ye can attain unto faith, save ye shall have hope?
>
> And what is it that ye shall hope for? *Behold I say unto you that ye shall have hope through the atonement of Christ and the power of his resurrection, to be raised unto life eternal,* and this because of your faith in him according to the promise.[1]

Paul also taught hope pertained to life after death. To the Thessalonians he gave the admonition to put on the "breastplate of faith and love; and for an helmet, *the hope of salvation.*"[2] To Titus he wrote that "we should be made heirs *according to the hope of eternal life.*"[3] The Romans received his message that hope leads to salvation and that hope must be based in the unseen, "For we are saved by hope: but *hope that is seen is not hope:* for what a man seeth, why doth he yet hope for? But if we hope for that we see not, then do we with patience wait for it."[4]

The Book of Mormon prophet Jacob also saw that hope must be based in the afterlife. He wrote,

> Wherefore, beloved brethren, be reconciled unto him through the atonement of Christ, his only Begotten Son, and ye may obtain a resurrection, according to the power of the resurrection which is in Christ, and be presented as the first-

---

1. Moro. 7:40-1.
2. I Thess. 5:8.
3. Tit. 3:7.
4. Rom. 8:24-5.

fruits of Christ unto God, having faith, and *obtained a good hope of glory in him.*[5]

Alma told his followers to live, "Having faith on the Lord; *having a hope that ye shall receive eternal life;* having the love of God always in your hearts, that ye may be lifted up at the last day and enter into his rest."[6] He also told of other Nephites who were able to *"retain a hope through faith, unto eternal salvation,* relying upon the spirit of prophecy, which spake of those things to come."[7] The final prophet of the Book of Mormon, Moroni, while praying to God, expressed his knowledge that *"man must hope,* or he cannot receive an inheritance in the place which thou hast prepared."[8] It is clear, then, that hope, as a gift of the Spirit, is directly concerned with exaltation in the celestial kingdom. Man, in spite of his weaknesses and shortcomings, must firmly fix his gaze on the glories of eternity and seek to attain them. They are the motivating force which enables man to bear up the heavy load of service he is called upon to render. As Edward Partridge wrote to his wife,

> I have a strong desire to return to Painesville this fall, but must not; you know I stand in an important station, and as I am occasionally chastened I sometimes feel as though I must fall; not to give up the cause, but to fear my station is above what I can perform to the acceptance of my heavenly Father. *I hope that you and I may so conduct ourselves as to at last land our souls in the haven of eternal rest. Pray for me that I may not fall.*[9]

The gift of hope is granted unto man after he has entered the pathway to exaltation by fulfilling the first principles and ordinances of the gospel. This counsel was set forth by Aaron, to whom a Lamanite ruler had promised he would even give up his kingdom if he could be allowed to experience the joy of hope for eternal life. "If thou desirest this thing, if thou wilt bow down before God, yea, if thou wilt repent of all thy sins, and will bow down before God, and call on his name in faith, believing

---

5. Jac. 4:11.
6. Al. 13:29.
7. Al. 25:16.
8. Eth. 12:32.
9. Jenson, I. p. 220.

that ye shall receive, *then shalt thou receive the hope which thou desirest.*"[10]

Attaining hope must be accompanied by love, study, and the continuing effort for self-improvement which the scriptures refer to as enduring to the end. Nephi taught that following faith, repentance, baptism, and the reception of the Holy Ghost,

> Ye must press forward with a steadfastness in Christ, *having a perfect brightness of hope,* and a love of God and of all men. Wherefore, if ye shall press forward, feasting upon the word of Christ, and endure to the end, behold, thus saith the Father: Ye shall have eternal life.
>
> And now, behold, my beloved brethren, this is the way; and *there is none other way nor name given under heaven whereby man can be saved in the kingdom of God.* And now, behold, this is the doctrine of Christ, and the only and true doctrine of the Father, and of the Son, and of the Holy Ghost.[11]

The gift of hope is inseparably linked with faith and charity, and the reception of all three of these gifts is dependent upon man's meekness and humility:

> Wherefore, *if a man have faith he must needs have hope; for without faith there cannot be any hope.*
>
> And again, behold I say unto you that he cannot have faith and hope, save he shall be meek, and lowly of heart.
>
> If so, his faith and hope is vain, for none is acceptable before God, save the meek and lowly in heart; and if a man be meek and lowly in heart, and confesses by the power of the Holy Ghost that Jesus is the Christ, he must needs have charity; for if he have not charity he is nothing; wherefore he must needs have charity.[12]

Summary

1. Hope must center in an anticipation of the joys of eternal life.

2. Man hopes for unseen things, then waits with patience to achieve them.

---

10. Al. 22:16.
11. 2 Ne. 31:20-1.
12. Moro. 7:42-4.

3. Hope is retained through faith.

4. Hope is attained by obedience to the first principles of the gospel, together with diligent study of the gospel and an effort to endure faithfully to the end.

5. Hope is inseparably linked with faith and charity. The reception of all three of these gifts is dependent upon man's meekness and humility.

CHAPTER XXIII

Eternal Life

Eternal Life the Greatest of the Gifts of God

This book has enumerated many gifts which are sources of great joy to those to whom they are granted. But each of these gifts is only a preparatory blessing which leads the recipient to the greatest of all spiritual gifts, the gift of eternal life. Embodied in this gift is the summation of all of God's labor in His eternal program. It is the culmination of all the rich blessings which God grants to mankind. As He proclaimed, *"This is my work and my glory — to bring to pass the immortality and eternal life of man."*[1] There can be no doubt that this gift is the most glorious of all the blessings granted to man, for the Lord has proclaimed it to be so. A revelation given to Joseph Smith and Oliver Cowdery promised them that "if thou wilt do good, yea, and hold out faithful to the end, *thou shalt be saved in the kingdom of God, which is the greatest of all the gifts of God;* for there is no gift greater than the gift of salvation."[2] In a great vision granted unto the prophet Lehi, God represented eternal life or exaltation in the celestial kingdom as a tree of life. Of this tree Nephi taught, "Wherefore, the wicked are rejected from the righteous, and also from that tree of life, whose fruit is most precious and most desirable above all other fruits; yea, and *it is the greatest of all the gifts of God."*[3]

Like all the other gifts of the Spirit, eternal life is a gift for which man should seek, but which he cannot earn. Man is unable to lay claim to salvation or exaltation and demand it, for he is continually in debt to God. As King Benjamin taught,

> *For behold, are we not all beggars? Do we not all depend upon the same Being, even God, for all the substance which we have,* for both food and raiment, and for gold, and for silver, and for all the riches which we have of every kind?

---

1. Moses 1:39.
2. D & C 6:13.
3. I Ne. 15:36.

And behold, even at this time, ye have been calling on his name, and *begging for a remission of your sins.* And has he suffered that ye have begged in vain? Nay; *he has poured out his Spirit upon you, and has caused that your hearts should be filled with joy, and has caused that your mouths should be stopped that ye could not find utterance, so exceeding great was your joy.*

And now, *if God, who has created you, on whom you are dependent for your lives and for all that ye have and are, doth grant unto you whatsoever ye ask that is right,* in faith, believing that ye shall receive, O then, how ye ought to impart of the substance that ye have one to another.

And if ye judge the man who putteth up his petition to you for your substance that he perish not, and condemn him, how much more just will be *your condemnation for withholding your substance, which doth not belong to you but to God, to whom also your life belongeth;* and yet ye put up no petition, nor repent of the thing which thou hast done.[4]

It is through the atoning sacrifice of Christ, and His grace, that man is saved, not through man's own deeds. Nephi explained this when he wrote that "we labor diligently to write, to persuade our children, and also our brethren, to believe in Christ, and to be reconciled to God; for we know that *it is by grace that we are saved, after all we can do.*"[5] Paul also wrote of the salvation of Christ and saw that it could not be earned, "For by grace are ye saved through faith; and that not of yourselves: it is the gift of God. Not of works, lest any man should boast."[6] Yet this gift is available to all mankind who choose to accept it, and none is turned away who truly desires it.[7]

If God has made this great gift available to all mankind, and if it is a gift which man cannot earn but is, instead, granted by the grace of God, then why does not every man gain exaltation? Why does God choose to grant his grace to some and withhold it from others?

It appears that God desires that man try to mold his life around the teachings of the Savior and strive to live to the best

---

4. Mos. 4:19-22.
5. 2 Ne. 25:23.
6. Eph. 2:8-9.
7. 2 Ne. 26:23-5.

of his ability. While man cannot earn exaltation, he can labor with diligence to serve God and to achieve the qualities of God-hood. To those who manifest such good works and a proper attitude Jesus extends His mercy and the redeeming powers of His atonement. The individuals who would take advantage of this greatest of all gifts must actually choose eternal life through the promptings of the Holy Ghost:

> Wherefore, men are free according to the flesh; and all things are given them which are expedient unto man. And *they are free to choose liberty and eternal life, through the great mediation of all men, or to choose captivity and death,* according to the captivity and power of the devil; for he seeketh that all men might be miserable like unto himself.
>
> And now, my sons, I would that ye should *look to the great Mediator, and hearken unto his great commandments; and be faithful unto his words, and choose eternal life, according to the will of his Holy Spirit.*[8]

Seeking Exaltation

Having made his decision to seek this important gift through the Spirit, the individual must then begin to labor with diligence to further God's work:

> Behold, the field is white already to harvest; therefore, *whoso desireth to reap let him thrust in his sickle with his might, and reap while the day lasts, that he may treasure up for his soul everlasting salvation in the kingdom of God.*[9]

Another prerequisite for the gaining of the gift of eternal life is the faithful fulfillment of the commandments of God. This fulfillment must cover the full range of instruction given by God and encompass "all things."

> Seek to bring forth and establish my Zion. *Keep my commandments in all things.*
> *And, if you keep my commandments and endure to the end you shall have eternal life,* which gift is the greatest of all the gifts of God.[10]

Those who seek this gift must often choose between worldly honor and riches and the blessings of the life to come. As Jesus

---

8. 2 Ne. 2:27-8.
9. D & C 12:3, 14:3.
10. D & C 14:6-7.

taught, "Thou shalt lay aside the things of this world, and *seek for the things of a better*."[11] This series of choices is what might be regarded as the best index of man's desires. As the Master taught, man's heart is where his treasure lies:

> Lay not up for yourselves treasures upon earth, where moth and rust doth corrupt and where thieves break through and steal:
>
> But lay up for yourselves treasures in heaven, where neither moth nor rust doth corrupt, and where thieves do not break through nor steal;
>
> *For where your treasure is, there will your heart be also.*[12]

True belief in the Savior and in the existence of His power is another requirement for exaltation. Jesus taught, "I came unto mine own, and mine own receiveth me not; but unto as many as received me gave I power to do many miracles, and to become the sons of God; and *even unto them that believed on my name gave I power to obtain eternal life.*"[13]

God also insists that those who would partake of this greatest of all gifts must have improved their lives through repentance. They must have sanctified themselves by striving to become holy and Godlike in their nature, for a revelation proclaims that "*unto him that repenteth and sanctifieth himself before the Lord shall be given eternal life.*"[14] This process of repentance and sanctification are the keys to Christ's program for mankind. As He taught to the Nephites,

> And no unclean thing can enter into his kingdom; therefore nothing entereth into his rest save it be those who have washed their garments in my blood, because of their faith, and the repentance of all their sins, and their faithfulness unto the end.
>
> Now this is the commandment: *Repent, all ye ends of the earth, and come unto me and be baptized in my name, that ye may be sanctified by the reception of the Holy Ghost, that ye may stand spotless before me at the last day.*
>
> Verily, verily, I say unto you, this is my gospel; and ye know the things that ye must do in my church; for the works which ye have seen me do that shall ye also do; for that which ye have seen me do even that shall ye do;

---

11. D & C 25:10.
12. Mt. 6:19-21.
13. D & C 45:8.
14. D & C 133:62.

Therefore, if ye do these things blessed are ye, for ye shall be lifted up at the last day.[15]

Another requirement for achieving exaltation is that man must continue to labor in serving God and sanctifying himself throughout his life. Jesus proclaimed, "Behold, I am the law, and the light. Look unto me, and endure to the end, and ye shall live; *for unto him that endureth to the end will I give eternal life.*"[16] How often people serve valiantly in the church until their responsibility is shifted to another, and then fall into inactivity and depart from the ways of the Lord! Such individuals thus forfeit all the results of their previous progress.

One other promise by the Lord should be mentioned. There have been times when people have had to sacrifice their lives for the name of Christ or for His work. To such individuals the blessing of eternal life is granted. Jesus taught,

And *whoso layeth down his life in my cause, for my name's sake, shall find it again, even life eternal.*

Therefore, be not afraid of your enemies, for I have decreed in my heart, saith the Lord, that I will prove you in all things whether you will abide in my covenant, even unto death, that you may be found worthy.

For if ye will not abide in my covenant ye are not worthy of me.[17]

To His disciples He gave the same teaching, but emphasized that man must take up the cross and serve God in life as well as in death:

If any man will come after me, let him deny himself, and *take up his cross, and follow me.*

For whosoever will save his life shall lose it: and *whosoever will lose his life for my sake shall find it.*

For what is a man profited, if he shall gain the whole world, and lose his own soul? or what shall a man give in exchange for his soul?[18]

The true follower of Christ must be ready and able to acknowledge the divinity of Jesus in any and all situations, and may do so knowing that God is watching over him:

---

15. 3 Ne. 27:19-22.
16. 3 Ne. 15:9. See Mt. 10:22.
17. D & C 98:13-15.
18. Mt. 16:24-6.

And fear not them which kill the body, but are not able to kill the soul: but rather fear him which is able to destroy both soul and body in hell.

Are not two sparrows sold for a farthing? and one of them shall not fall on the ground without your Father.

But the very hairs of your head are all numbered.

Fear ye not therefore, ye are of more value than many sparrows. *Whosoever therefore shall confess me before men, him will I confess also before my Father which is in heaven.*

But whosoever shall deny me before men, him will I also deny before my Father which is in heaven.[19]

These, then, are the qualities which man must possess if he is to gain the greatest of all the gifts of the Spirit. Upon fulfilling all these requirements, man may well anticipate the merciful benefits of Christ's atonement in his behalf and may be like those in Alma's day "who died, *firmly believing that their souls were redeemed by the Lord Jesus Christ;* thus they went out of the world rejoicing."[20] He may anticipate the day when his Lord will say unto him, "Well done, good and faithful servant; thou hast been faithful over a few things, I will make thee ruler over many things: *enter thou into the joy of thy Lord.*"[21]

Man Granted the Expectation of Exaltation

The anticipation of exaltation in the Celestial Kingdom can truly be granted to man, if he has diligently endeavored to fulfill all the prerequisites throughout his lifetime. David W. Patten, for instance, was able to bear testimony of the gospel while on his deathbed and then comment, "I feel I have kept the faith, I have finished my course; henceforth there is laid up for me a crown, which the Lord, the righteous Judge, shall give to me."[22]

Some people are granted special assurances of their eventual exaltation. Samuel Smith, brother to the prophet, was one. His father, the first patriarch to the Church, gave him this patriarchal blessing:

Samuel, you have been a faithful and obedient son. By your faithfulness you have brought many into the Church. The Lord

19. Mt. 10:28-33.
20. Al. 46:39.
21. Mt. 25:23.
22. Jenson, I. pp. 79-80.

has seen your diligence, and you are blessed, in that he has never chastised you, but *has called you home to rest; and there is a crown laid up for you which shall grow brighter and brighter unto the perfect day.* When the Lord called you, he said, 'Samuel, I have seen thy sufferings, have heard thy cries, and beheld thy faithfulness; thy skirts are clear from the blood of this generation. Because of these things, I seal upon your head all the blessings which I have heretofore pronounced upon you; and this is my dying blessing I now seal upon you. Even so: Amen.[23]

Some are shown visions which grant them assurance of exaltation. Newel Knight, for instance,

Saw heaven opened, and beheld the Lord Jesus Christ, seated at the right hand of the majesty on high, and had it made plain to his understanding that *the time would come when he would be admitted into His presence to enjoy His society for ever and ever.*[24]

Certainly the prophetic dream of David John should be considered in this context. It was given to him in 1856 while he was investigating the gospel.

"I dreamt," wrote David, "that I saw an angel of the Lord. After he had talked a little with me, he placed his right hand on my left shoulder. His eyes were of a dark brown color, but full of glory. His voice was clear, but full of power and authority. While in his presence I beheld very high mountains. He told me that they were the everlasting hills, over or by which the Latter-day Saints were going to their gathering place. 'Why,' said he, 'are you spending your time in vain here? How is it you will not join the Church of Christ and spend your time there?' I replied 'I hope I am in the Church now, am I not?' 'You know better,' he said. 'Do not ask questions that you know perfectly well, but go on unto perfection. Look towards the firmament.' I looked and beheld the air full with people of every sect and party. *There I saw Christ sitting upon His throne in great glory*, and the people gathered themselves before

---

23. Jenson, I. p. 282. Others are given special assurance by the Prophets of the Lord. Brigham Young told Jacob Hamblin, for instance,
    I know your history. You have always kept the Church and Kingdom of God first and foremost in your mind. That is right. There is no greater gift than that. *If there are any men who have cleared their skirts of the blood of this generation, I believe you are one of them,* and you can have all the blessings there are for any men in the temple. (*Jacob Hamblin,* p. 139)

24. HC, I, p. 85.

Him to be judged. Those that had pleased Him, he commanded
to stand on His right hand, and those that did not, on His left.
He judged them one by one, till they composed two straight
lines, running parallel one against the other for the distance of
about one mile. Those on the left were those of the different
sects and parties of the day; and those on the right were Latter-
day Saints. The Saints seemed lovely, and all smiled, looking
in the face of Jesus as one man looks on another. But the other
line seemed miserable, and full of discontent, sorrow and grief,
turning their faces from Jesus, and could not abide His presence.
'According to this vision,' I said, 'the Saints are right but the
others are not.' 'You see,' he answered, 'who is right and who
is wrong. Look,' said he, 'on thy right hand.' *I looked and there
beheld a large and very extensive valley — the most beautiful
land I ever saw.* We were standing on one side of it, which
was flat. On the side we stood were high and beautiful trees.
Under the shadow of one of them we stood from the heat of the
sun, which was very powerful. On the other side were mountains
or hills, but not very high. Those extended to the extremity of
of the valley. The beauty and glory of the valley, which was
from three to four miles wide, was beyond description. 'Oh,
my God,' I exclaimed, 'I never knew that such a beautiful
scene as this belonged to our earth.' *'This,'* said the angel, *'shall
be thy inheritance and thy seed after thee forever, if thou wilt
obey the commandments of God and do right in the flesh.*
Look, behold thee,' said he. 'I then found myself in a large and
beautiful building. There I saw on the stand one that I knew,
preaching the principles of life.' 'This,' said my guide, 'is the
house of the Lord.' At this I awoke, believing that the spirit
of the Lord and angels filled the room. I arose and bowed
myself before God in prayer, and desired Him, if that messenger
was from Him, to make it known to me once more by the same
messenger; if not, to hide the vision from me. I again retired
to rest, and soon fell into a deep sleep, when suddenly the same
personage appeared, and made known unto me some of the
same things; but he rebuked me this time for spending my time
where I was. He also said; 'Thou wert foreordained before the
foundation of the world to come forth in this age to assist to
build the Kingdom of God upon the earth, and now the time is
up. If thou wilt obey the commandments of God, thy days
shall be long on the earth; if not, thy days shall be short, says
the Lord!' These words pierced my soul, and I again awoke and
spent the remainder of the night in deep reflection, and some-

what grieved in spirit; at other moments I would rejoice exceedingly.[25]

In a series of visions given to Joseph Smith on January 21, 1826, he saw the "celestial kingdom of God, and the glory thereof, . . . I finally saw the Twelve in the celestial kingdom of God. . . . And I saw in my vision all of the Presidency in the celestial kingdom of God, and many others that were present.[26]

On some occasions men have been sealed up to eternal life, or given the authorized promise that they would eventually dwell in the celestial kingdom. If they were to sin, however, they were to have to suffer in Hell until the day of redemption, and then come forth to receive their exalted glory. On January 23, 1833, the prophet Joseph washed the feet of the Elders assembled in conference, and told them,

> As I have done so do ye; wash ye, therefore, one another's feet; and by the power of the Holy Ghost *I pronounced them all clean from the blood of this generation; but if any of them should sin wilfully after they were thus cleansed, and sealed up unto eternal life, they should be given over unto the buffetings of Satan until the day of redemption.*[27]

Summary

1. The gift of eternal life is the greatest of all the gifts of God.

2. The work and glory of God is to bring about the immortality and eternal life of man.

3. Eternal life is a gift which man should seek, but which he cannot earn. It is through the grace of Christ that man is allowed to partake of exaltation through the redeeming power of the atonement.

4. Man may choose eternal life by following Christ, keeping his commandments, being faithful, and being guided by the Spirit.

5. The scriptures outline a program which the earnest seeker of exaltation must follow. He must

---

25. Jenson, I, pp. 489-90.
26. HC, II, pp. 380-82.
27. HC, I, pp. 323-4.

A. thrust in the sickle and reap and endeavor to serve God.

B. fulfill the commandments of God.

C. seek things for the future world rather than for this one.

D. repent and seek sanctification.

E. endure to the end.

F. be willing to live for the Savior or to lay down his life for His cause.

G. acknowledge the divinity of Christ in all situations.

6. Men are granted the expectation of exaltation. They are given the ability to evaluate their own lives and anticipate their future reward.

7. Some men have even been shown the exact location and description of their eternal inheritance in vision.

8. Some have been sealed up unto eternal life. They are promised a place in the celestial kingdom. If they sin after being sealed up, however, they must pay for their sins in the dominion of Satan until the day of redemption.

Author's Testimony

I could not properly end this book without telling of the manner in which this study has increased my testimony of the gospel of Jesus Christ. One does not receive aid from the Spirit in researching and writing a book such as this without knowing that God exists and guides man through His Spirit. Nor does one learn of the numerous instances of Divine guidance which have shaped this Church without knowing that it is God's Church — that it was brought into existence by Him and is functioning under His direction today. One does not test the manifestations of the Spirit of our present Prophet without knowing without doubt that he is a Prophet, a spokesman and a companion of God. One does not study the great gifts promised to man without knowing of God's love for His children and His desire that they might grow and progress. One does not learn of the mighty faith and deeds of the chosen servants of God without being compelled to humbly recognize his own insignificance and lack of faith. And one does not learn of the joys of serving God without having a strong and unyielding desire to serve His Lord and Master. To all these things I bear witness, in the name of Jesus Christ.

Duane S. Crowther

LIST OF QUOTATIONS FROM MAJOR SOURCES

OLD TESTAMENT

BOOK OF MORMON

1 Nephi	
1:1	205
2:1-2	194-95
2:16	203
2:19-24	203
6:4	74
7:17-18	117
10:17	18
10:17	114
10:17	116
10:17	133
10:19	204
15:11	16
15:36	329
16:10	199
16:28-29	117-18
16:28-29	199
17:53-55	35
19:17-18	74

2 Nephi	
1:6	216
2:4	45
2:27-28	331
3:21	118
4:12	24
25:1-4	223
25:23	330
26:23-25	330
27:23	163
28:5-6	164
28:14	173
28:26	174
31:13-14	228
31:20-21	327
32:2-3	231
32:8-9	17
33:1	256
33:1	270
33:1-2	72
33:10-11	74

Jacob	
4:6-7	127
4:8	206
4:11	325-26
4:13	216
6:5-11	312
7:11	75

Enos	
4	18
4-8	116-17
15	115

Jarom	
4	116

Omni	
20	258
25	230

Mosiah	
3:21	117
4:11-12	79-80
4:19-22	329-30
8:13	198-99
8:13-18	258-59
8:16-18	199
8:20	108
15:11	75

Alma	
5:14-16	309
5:45-47	41
7:16	268
7:23	17
7:24	323
7:26	268
8:10	18
8:24	276
9:21	230
12:3	294
12:9-11	203-04
12:24	307
13:27-29	14
13:29	326
13:30	305
21:9-10	267
22:16	326-27
25:16	326
26:12	165
26:22	204
30:42	294
32:21	115
32:27	113
32:28-9, 33	113-14
32:37-40	114
34:14-17	116
34:32-33	308
36:12-24	311
37:4	205
37:11	208
37:15-17	14
37:35	99
38:8	311
39:11	76
40:20	43
43:2	277
46:39	334

Helaman	
8:27	284
9:25-38	285
10:4-5	127

10:6-10	164
10:15-11:18	164
13:8	309-10
14:30-31	81
15:13	79

3 Nephi	
6:20	268
7:18	193
7:19-20	167
8:1	165-66
11:3	24
11:3	69
11:17	68-69
11:28	55
12:1-2	73
12:6	9
14:7-11	15
15:9	333
17:15-17	206-07
18:7	13
18:20	16
18:20	133
19:4	167
26:9-11	208
26:14	238-39
27:19-20	307
27:19-22	332-33

4 Nephi	
5	134

Mormon	
1:15	55
2:12-14	306
9:7-8	229
9:24	2
9:24	229
9:27-28	13
9:25-27	41

Ether	
3:2	16
3:19-20, 25-26	90-91
3:25	197
3:26-27	207
4:7	207
4:15-16	207-08
4:18	2
12:6	115
12:12	173
12:12-21	121-22
12:23-26	256
12:29-30	118
12:32	326
12:33-34	317
12:35	323
12:38-39	55

DOCTRINE AND COVENANTS

75:19-22	269	95:5-6	280	121:37-38	279
				121:39-40	279
76:5-10	204-05	97:1	192	121:45-46	275
76:11-12,		97:5	267	121:45-46	323
19-23	57-58				
76:31-35,		98:13-15	333	124:97-100	3
44-46	73				
		100:5-6	248	128:14	79
84:27	70	100:7-8	248		
84:65-72	2-3	100:10	268	129:1-9	300-01
84:65-73	2	100:11	262		
84:73	4			130:12-16	193
84:85	248	102:23	277	130:15	208
84:92-95	269			130:18-19	91
		107:18-19	278		
88:62	11	107:71	277	131:5	277
88:63	9	107:91-92	210		
88:64-65	17	107:91-92	278	132:27	73
88:78	260				
88:81-82	75	110:1-4	60	133:62	332
88:125	320				
		121:34-35	279		
89:18-19	107	121:36	278	136:32-33	106
		121:37	15	136:32-33	261

PEARL OF GREAT PRICE

Moses		*Moses*—(cont.)		*Joseph Smith*	
1:25-26	165	6:34	165	2:16-17	55-56
1:27-29	197	6:57	306	2:17	69
1:35	206	7:3-9	197	2:30-32	192-93
1:39	329	7:13	165	2:69	30
3:12	307	7:32	81		

ALPHABETICAL INDEX

348 GIFTS OF THE SPIRIT

D

Dalton, Gene, 181.
Daniel, 106-107, 200, 224.
David, 120.
Dead, to be raised, 3, 144-145, 167-171.
Death, unto the Lord, 134, 135, 140.
Devil, devils, evil spirits, Satan, 1, 2, 3, 37-38, 39, 93-94, 101, 105-106, 126, 128, 157-158, 158-159, 160, 173, 233, 251, 281, 284, 288, 290, 293, 294, 299, 300, 301, 312-315, 316.
Dibble, Philo, 38, 38-39, 254.
Discerning of Spirits, 293-301.
Discernment, 288-289, 313.
Disciples, see resurrected Christ, 52-53.
Diversities of Operations, 281-291.
Dreams, 61, 61-62, 83, 88, 89, 89-90, 105-106, 185, 194-195, 195, 195-196, 200, 219, 221.
Dust, shaking from feet as a witness, 269.

E

Early Scenes in Church History, quotations from, 29, 38, 38-39, 126, 136-137, 137-138, 138, 138-139, 148-149, 150-151, 152-153, 244-245, 254, 305.
Elijah, 166, 167, 171.
Elisha, 166, 167, 171.
Ellsworth, German E., 86, 276.
Ellsworth, Mary Smith, 84.
Enos, 18, 115, 166-167.
Enoch, 119, 165.
Esau, 120.
Elizabeth, 283.
Elymas, 294.
Eternal Life, 325-338. See also: Celestial Kingdom.
Evans, Abel, 138-139, 151.
Eventful Narratives, quotations from, 8-9, 23, 26, 29, 31, 101-103.
Evil, knowledge of, 81.
Evil Spirit, See: Devil.
Example, 75-77.
Expounding the Scriptures, gift of, 262-268.
Eyring, Henry, 196-197.
Ezekiel, 308.

F

Faith, 113-130, 322; God works by power of, ii; defined, 115; miracles wrought by, 163-164; no miracles without, 173-174; angels minister because of, 193.
Farrimond, Millie B., 105-106.
Fasting, 133, 134, 141, 142, 181.
Fear, charity brings freedom from, 321.

Feelings and Impressions from the Spirit, 31, 35, 38, 102, 103-104, 143-144, 183-184, 201, 202, 235, 237, 244, 254, 263-264, 270, 297.
Flood, 264-265.
Foolishness of Men, 107-108.
Fordham, Elijah, 149-150.
Forgiveness, 116-117, 155-157.
Fragments of Experience, quotations from, 123-124, 124, 219-220, 244, 265-266.

G

Gardner, Jack, 30-31.
Gedeon, 120.
Gems for the Young Folks, quotations from, 31, 35-36, 39, 90, 135-136, 158-159, 233, 233-234, 243, 270.
Gifts of God, many, ii; deny not, ii; administered in different ways, ii; given by manifestation of the Spirit of God, ii; seek ye earnestly the best, 1, 5; to benefit those who love God, 1; purposes of, 1-2; man may receive more than one, 5, to be used in serving God, 13, to edify the Church, 13.
Giles, Thomas D., 29, 138.
Given, much required where much given, 6.
Glow, characteristic of the Holy Ghost, 36.
God the Father, testifies of Jesus, 67-69.
Good, knowledge of, 81.
Gossip, 105-106.
Governments, gift of, 175-187.
Grant, B. F., 88.
Grant, Heber J., 87-89; revelation concerning apostleship, 177-178; given gift of speaking, 249-250.
Grant, Jedediah M., 178.
Greene, John P., 243.
Grover, Jane, 231-232.

H

Halliday, George, 244-245.
Hamblin, Jacob, 34-35, 84-85, 103-104, 125, 220, 335.
Hancock, Levi W., 297-298.
Harris, Martin, 259; must humble himself, 13-14.
Healing, 2, 3, 33-34, 34, 38-39, 39, 39-40, 104-105, 131-161, 219-220, 266, 282-283.
Haun's Mill Massacre, 104-105, 243.
Helaman, 99, 205.
Helpful Visions, quotations from, 200-201.

Helps and Governments, gift of, 175-187, 261, 263-264, 264, 264-265, 265-266, 266-267.
Henager, ..., 167-168.
Henry, Manuel, 254.
Herod, 283.
Hezekiah, 224.
Hill, G. W., 145.
Hinckley, Alonzo A., 89, 178, 234-236.
History of The Church, quotations from, 25, 42, 56, 58, 59, 60, 72, 73, 92, 94, 159-160, 198, 202.
Hobbs, William, 185-186.
Holbrook, Jean, 269.
Holy Ghost, functions of — manifests truth, ii, 3, 8, 43; witnesses of Christ, ii, 69-73, 261; manifests gifts, ii; testifies, 1; tells what to say, 3; brings to remembrance, 8, 9; with those who remember Christ, 13; beareth record, 25; condemns ungodly, 106, 261; enlightens, 106, 261. Characteristics of — knoweth all things, 261; grieved at sin, 15; searches the deep things of God, 18; reveals to mind and heart, 21-22.
Hope, 115; for eternal life, 14, 135, 319, 320, 322, 325-328.
Humble, humility, 3, 13-14, 80, 106, 254-255, 261.
Huntington, Oliver B., 8-9, 23, 101-103.

I

Indians, 23, 34-35, 145, 196, 211, 231-232, 306; not to be killed, 103-104.
Intelligence, to rise in resurrection, 91.
Interpretation of Tongues, 32, 219, 228, 229, 230, 232, 234, 235, 236-237, 238, 241-245, 251, 276, 298.
Isaac, 119, 120.
Isaiah, 44, 223.

J

Jacob, 119, 120.
Jacob (B. of M.), 127, 206, 216, 311, 325.
Jacob Hamblin, quotations from, 34-35, 84-85, 103-104, 125, 220-221.
James, 68, 132, 155; Savior appears to, 53.
Jarom, 116.
Jeffs, David, 253-254, 266-267.
Jensen, Carl, 152.
Jepthae, 120.
Jeremiah, 222.
Joel, 221.
John the Baptist, 30, 191, 287; had knowledge Jesus was the Son of God, 70.

John the Revelator, 68, 192, 206, 298, 318, 321, 322; sees resurrected Christ, 54.
John, David, 335-337.
Johnson, John, wife of, 148-149.
Jonah, 224.
Jonas, sign of, 4.
Jones, Dan, 231, 312-313.
Joseph (of Egypt), 120.
Joseph (husband of Mary), 283.
Joshua, 171.
Joy, characteristic of the Holy Ghost, 6, 28, 29, 30, 31, 32.
Judas, 293.

K

Kimball, Heber C., 150, 177, 216-217, 252, 286, 286-287.
Kirtland Temple, 25, 58, 234.
Knight, Newel, 28, 37-38, 39, 56-57, 92, 140, 151-152, 313-314, 335.
Knowledge, 292-293; key to the celestial kingdom, 79; true knowledge is knowledge of redeemer, 79; godly knowledge, 79-98, 107; faith not perfect, 114, to be taught, 247.
Korihor, 296.

L

Labors in the Vineyard, quotations from, 32-33, 36-37, 82, 184, 195, 252, 296.
Lambert, Ephraim, 125-126.
Lamoreaux, Andrew, 221.
Latter-day Saint Biographical Encyclopedia, quotations from, 35, 56, 61-62, 71, 82, 83, 85, 92, 95, 105, 122-123, 125-126, 140, 145, 152, 157, 157-158, 175-176, 177, 178, 183, 183-184, 194, 196, 197, 218, 221, 231, 234, 236-237, 237, 244, 251-252, 253-254, 256-257, 257, 257, 264, 266-267, 269, 286, 286, 287, 297-298, 298.
Leaves From My Journal, quotations from, 7-8, 100-101, 144-145, 160, 176-177, 195, 196, 253.
Lehi, 45, 56, 116, 121, 216, 329.
Lewis, William H., 217-218.
Liahona, 117-118, 199.
Limhi, King, 108.
Lindford, Joseph F., 34.
Logan Temple, 85.
Love, 317-324.
Lyman, Amasa M., 71, 157-158.

M

Mary Magdalene, sees resurrected Christ, 52.
McAllister, J. D. H., 270.

McCracken, Alice, testimony of, 24-25; 186.
McKay, David O., saw Christ, 62-63; healed Uruguayan woman with handshake, 154; healed woman in temple, 154-155; to sit in leading councils, 179-180; audience given gift of interpretation, 241-242; experience of father, 271.
McMurrin, James, 179-180.
McMurrin, Joseph W., 183-184.
Merrill, Mariner W., 183, 217-218.
Mighty Prayer, 17-18.
Miracles, 39, 85-86, 122-123, 123-124, 124, 136-137, 137-138, 138, 138-139, 149-150, 153-154, 154-155, 163-174, 184, 185-186.
More Sure Word of Prophecy, 277.
Morgan, John, 167-168, 297-298.
Mormon, 17, 65, 163, 306, 317, 321; sees resurrected Christ, 55.
Moroni, iii, 5, 13, 43, 41, 65, 82, 114, 118, 192-193, 193, 229, 247, 256, 276-277, 290, 317, 319, 320, 325, 326, sees resurrected Christ, 55.
Morris, Hiram, 35.
Moses, 94, 99, 120, 165, 166, 171, 173, 197, 206, 211, 278, 282.
Mosiah, King, 258.
Mountains, faith to remove, 118, 127, 128, 134, 165, 166.
Movements of the Spirit, 37-40.
My First Mission, quotations from, 26, 36, 156-157, 186, 237-238, 261-262.
Mysteries, 108; to be revealed, 106, 202-208, 211, 267.

N

Nathanael, 293.
Nauvoo, 35, 102, 124, 286.
Nebuchadnezzar, King, 224.
Nephi, 24, 72, 117, 121, 163, 165-166, 167, 174, 193, 194, 203, 208, 223, 255-256, 270, 284-285, 329, 330; given complete power, 127, 164.
Nephites, 24, 54, 65, 69, 73, 134, 206, 238, 258, 306, 310, 326, 332; three Nephites, 121-122, 233-234.
Nibley, Charles W., 193.
Noah, 119.

O

Orme, Gilbert C., 29.

P

Page, Hiram, received false revelations, 93-94.
Parables, 6, 15-16.
Parry, John, 126.

Patten, David W., 145, 150-151, 157, 251-252, 334.
Pattern in all things, 299.
Paul, 5, 13, 14, 40, 42, 43, 53, 54, 72, 74, 76, 81, 107, 108, 114, 115, 118, 132, 155, 205, 215, 223, 227-228, 228, 241, 243, 247, 294, 305, 319, 320, 322, 325, 330.
Peace, characteristic of the Holy Ghost, 27, 30.
Pearl of Great Price, 206.
Peck, Martin H., 136-138.
Peleg, 265.
Pentecost, day of, 229-230, 241.
Peter, 22, 52, 53, 68, 80, 129, 132, 136, 180, 222, 284, 293.
Pharisees, 67-68, 281, 282, 287.
Phelps, W. W., 198.
Phillip, 22.
Phillips, Thomas, 185-186.
Physical Sensations, accompany manifestations of the Holy Ghost, 21-40, 45.
Poison, 2, 3, 165.
Potter, Amasa, 36-37, 184, 252.
Pratt, Orson, 150, 223.
Pratt, Parley P., 84, 150, 216-217, 234, 267, 314.
Prayer, See: Ask.
President of the Church, given all spiritual gifts, 280.
Priesthood, 134, 275, 277, 278-280, 288, 314.
Prophecy, 2, 3, 14, 15, 21-22, 24, 43, 75-76, 84-85, 86, 90-91, 94, 113, 177, 178, 179, 179-180, 204-205, 206, 208, 209-210, 215-225, 227, 251, 258, 259-260, 267, 269, 277, 279, 288, 290, 306, 307, 326, 330; more sure word of, 277.
Prophets, testify of Christ, 74-75.

R

Rahab, 120.
Repentance, 116, 117, 305-316.
Required, much, where much given, 6.
Return from dead, 144-145, 167-168, 168-170.
Revelation, 191-213.
Richards, Willard, 257, 287.
Rigdon, Sidney, 84, 85, 150, 286; saw the Father and Son, 57-58; receives gift of speaking, 248; receives gift of expounding the scriptures, 262; to expound mysteries, 267.
Rocky Mountains, 220.
Rogers, Aurelia S., organized Primary, 95-96.

S

Sadduccees, 174.
Salt Lake Temple, 154-155.

Samaritan woman at well, 76-77, 283-284.
Samson, 120.
Samuel, 120.
Samuel the Lamanite, 79, 81.
Sanctify, 210, 307, 332.
Sara, 119.
Satan, See: Devil.
Saul (Paul) of Tarsus, sees resurrected Christ, 54. See: Paul
Scraps of Biography, quotations from, 28, 37-38, 56-57, 151-152, 171-172, 218-219, 231-232, 251.
Scribes, 282, 287, 318.
Scribes and Pharisees, 3-4.
Scripture, opinions expressed in, 42-43; revelations to be in harmony with, 44-45; testify of Christ, 74; reveal mysteries, 205-206.
Second death, 305.
Seer, 198-199, 210.
Seventies, 25, 297; see Savior, 59.
Shock, characteristic of Holy Ghost, 35.
Shreeve, Thomas A., 194, 200-201. 201.
Signs, not to be sought to consume upon lusts, 1; to follow believers, 2, 4, 118; evil generation seeks, 4; signs unto condemnation, 4; signs come by faith, 4; come by the will of God, 4; boast not of, 4; given for profit and salvation, 4; revelation not given to those who seek, 7.
Simeon, recognized divinity of child Jesus, 70.
Simon the Sorcerer, 293-294.
Smith, Amanda, 104-105.
Smith, Emma, 208, 262-263.
Smith, George A., 150, 257, 287.
Smith, George Albert, 86.
Smith, Hyrum, 37, 59, 83, 150, 219-220.
Smith, John, 256-257.
Smith, Joseph, 7, 8, 25, 28, 29, 35, 36, 37, 56, 57, 58, 59, 60, 69, 71, 82, 83, 84-85, 92, 94, 122, 148, 149, 150, 178, 192, 193, 198, 208, 210, 211, 219, 221, 250, 252, 255, 259, 260, 262, 267, 269, 271, 275, 279, 289, 298, 312, 313, 329; saw Father and Son, 7, 55-56, 57-58, 58; saw John the Baptist, 30; said a prophet is not always a prophet, 42; mantel of falls on Brigham Young, 84-85; healed Mrs. Johnson, 148-149; heals Elijah Fordham, 149-150; taught all sickness not caused by sin, 159-160; blesses Lorenzo Snow, 168; sees Moroni, 192-193; prophesies war, 193; used Urim and Thummim, 198; inspiration to, 202; to receive commandments for the Church, 211; gave instructions for special admin-istration, 219-220; prophesied death of missionary, 221; received gift of speaking, 248; received gift of writing, 255; writing of, 256-257; given keys to gift of translating, 260; received gift of expounding scriptures, 262; administered, 266; to expound mysteries, 267; mighty in testimony, 268; to be given doctrine of the priesthood, 275; could not always judge the righteous, 289; given power to discern who should go up to Zion, 298-299; pronounced Elders clean from blood of generation, 337.
Smith, Joseph F., 276; warned on train, 193-194; learned language, 237.
Smith, Joseph Fielding, 86.
Smith, Robert, 286-287.
Smith, Samuel, 332, 333-334.
Smoot, Abraham O., 152-153.
Snow, Eliza R., 170, 177.
Snow, Lorenzo, 170-172; sees Savior, 63-64; received Holy Ghost, 71; received individual revelation of the nature of God, 92; heals child, 141-143; raised woman from the dead, 168-169.
Snow, Zerubbabel, 157-158.
Sorrow, godly and worldly contrasted, 305-306.
Speaking, gift of, 248-255.
Spencer, C. V., 32, 33, 195, 296.
Spirit World, described, 169-170.
Stephen, sees resurrected Christ, 53.
String of Pearls, A, quotations from, 145, 185-186, 263-264, 264-265.
Study, 8, 74.
Suffering for sin, 310-312.

T

Talents, parable of, 6; do not hide, 75-76.
Tanner, John, 171-172; 231-232.
Taylor, John, 8, 85, 217.
Taylor, John W., 178.
Teaching, gift of, 260-262.
Testimony, gift of bearing, 268-272.
Thatcher, Moses, 264.
Thomas, Savior appears to, 53, 129.
Titus, 325.
Tongues, gift of, 177, 218, 227-239, 241, 243, 244, 245, 251.
Trials, by High Councils, 277.
Truth, known through Holy Ghost, ii.
Tyler, Daniel, 218-219, 250-251.

U

Unpardonable Sin, 72, 73, 234.
Unprofitable servant, 6.
Urim and Thummim, 198-199, 260.